THE ALTERNATIVE

AMS PRESS
NEW YORK

THE AUTHOR

Born, November 1896. Served in France First World War; Royal Flying Corps and Trenches. Youngest M.P., November 1918. Minister in Government, 1929. Resigned 1930, on account of Government's refusal either to deal with Unemployment problem or accept his plan for a solution. In 1931, founded New Movement, which spread rapidly throughout Great Britain, despite great opposition from Old Parties, and a special Act of Parliament, which was designed to check it.

Five years in prison and house arrest under Regulation 18B during the Second World War, with many colleagues, on account of political opposition to that war. Defended and justified his position in book *MY ANSWER*. (Published in 1946. Mosley Publications, Ramsbury, Wilts.)

THE ALTERNATIVE

BY

OSWALD MOSLEY

1947

MOSLEY PUBLICATIONS
CROWOOD HOUSE,
RAMSBURY,
WILTS.

Library of Congress Cataloging in Publication Data

Mosley, Sir Oswald, bart., 1896-
    The alternative.

    1. Political science. 2. Economic policy.
3. World politics--1945-   I. Title.
JC258.M62 1972   320.9'04   72-180414
ISBN 0-404-56138-1

Reprinted from the edition of 1947, Ramsbury
First AMS edition published in 1972
Manufactured in the United States of America

AMS PRESS INC.
NEW YORK, N. Y.   10003

CONTENTS

CONTENTS

ERRATUM: Page 91, penultimate line, for page 85 read page 103.

7

PREFACE
July 7, 1947

An explanation of personal position, at the present time, and an analysis of certain events before the war

This book is written by a man without a Party, as an offering to the thought of a new Europe. Deliberately, I refrained from forming again a political movement in Great Britain; in order to serve a new European Idea. At this time, no other is in a position to state any real alternative to the present condition of Europe. The existing rulers of the earth are responsible for this darkness of humanity; they stand on the graves of their opponents to confront the Communist power of their own creation. No alternative can come from the architects of chaos: all others have been silenced. So, I must give myself to this task. My life striving in the politics of Britain made known my name and character: my voice can now reach beyond the confines of one country, because it has been heard before. The past has imposed the duty of the future: I must do this thing because no other can.

The statement of a European alternative could not be undertaken, without limitation of time and circumstance, by the leader of a party in Great Britain. My services are always at the disposal of my country and of Europe, in any capacity, during a period of crisis; which demands the abrogation of every other consideration. This may arise from those deep errors in the whole structure of the present system which evoke economic catastrophe: or, it may come with the further war, which the launching of the last world war made nearly inevitable; if action is not taken in time. But, my life is now dedicated to an Idea which transcends the diurnal politics of normality. Before the war, the deep effort of such politics had carried our new movement within sight of success in face of the initial inertia of English life, and of a subsequent bitterness of

9

THE ALTERNATIVE

opposition without parallel in the annals of the nation. The
inevitable conclusion of our final victory was admitted by some
of our strongest opponents; when they thought that the disaster
of war had, at length, saved them from our challenge. Fact,
figure, quotation and illustration of those events are given in
my other book, *My Answer;* and need not be repeated. Even in
the new circumstances, success in national politics is no less
possible now than it was then. It is true that war was for us a
limitless disaster, and robbed us of the harvest of long striving.
A considerable prejudice was the legacy of the long years of
silence; while we lay in prison, and our enemies found much
courage from the power to lie without reply. But, I have seen
public opinion change too often and too quickly to be depressed,
for a moment, by the thought that any such situation would
endure. To have experienced so many varying periods of
adulation and execration, in the course of one short life, is the
cure for any such illusion. Even within a year of the end of the
war, events had begun to justify us and the feeling of the people
had begun to change. In the end, their profound instinct for
the ultimate truth always pierces that cloud of deception with
which the propaganda of a war inevitably obscures every consideration of fact and of reality. Further, the economic situation
in Britain will no longer retard, but will accelerate, the development of new ideas, to an extent that only the Continent
experienced before the war.

It is, therefore, no doubt concerning the possibility of political
action in Britain which leads me to my present position. It is
certainly not a refusal to serve the British people in their bitter
need; whatever help I can give to them is always at their
disposal. It is rather the conviction that true service to the
British people is now identical with service to the other great
peoples of the West, in the creation of a new European Idea.
The land and the people of Great Britain can now only live in
greatness, and in happiness, by that new union of the Europeans,
through which, alone, all the peoples of the West can win
freedom from present pain, safety from looming menace of
destruction, and the final achievement of a life, greater, richer,

10

higher and more beautiful than they knew before the test, and challenge, of suffering and catastrophe. This union needs a synthesis of the best thought of Europe, and of America, on which we can build an idea that is new. So, this book attempts to synthesise at a higher level the conflict of opposites which has rent the life of our epoch. The Idea, which is born from this synthesis, is beyond both Fascism and Democracy.

It is true that all real things are related to what has gone before. A new Idea should begin by essaying to combine the best in previous thought: one of the greatest minds of European culture praised most the ability to perceive a connection between phenomena that is not easily apparent. To synthesise the thought of a great age into a coherent and purposive whole, would be some service; if it were fully realised. But, the present challenge of Destiny demands a yet higher aspiration. It is necessary, also, to meet facts which are new with thought that is new. May the necessity for a response to that challenge be accepted as an adequate reason both for the combination of thoughts, which were hitherto regarded as antithetical, and for the concept of thought so novel as to appear fantastic to eyes not yet accustomed to the hard light of this new age of Science. This Idea was born of new facts in the long opportunity for intensive reading, reflection and creation; which was afforded, first, by imprisonment and, later, by a complete withdrawal from the world. Such an interlude, in an unusually strenuous life of action, brings a harvest; which may here be judged. The Idea has come: the rest will follow.

It has been objected by many good and greatly valued friends, and it may, also, be the subject of hostile taunt, that an individual without a Party can formulate an Idea, but cannot implement it. To this, I reply, that to state an Idea, which contains the force of truth and of the spirit, is finally to implement it. Nothing, in the end, can resist such an Idea; if it be true. All such Ideas have originally been stated by individuals with nothing to sustain them except the power of the Spirit: and I have very many friends, in many places, who will be ready to listen. The Idea triumphs by moving the souls of men; and all else will be added to it. In the end, the means will be found in the ripeness of time and of occasion; and, in fact, the means are described with some precision in this book. All real things come only in their full time and Season. This Idea could not come before: we had not thought enough, and mankind had not seen enough. It needed a greater experience, and a further vision, to conceive in a comprehensive reality this wider union of the material life and spiritual destiny of great peoples. The force of nature was then against us: the power of God in nature is now with us. This last thought must await the final phase of this book. The previous restriction upon deep new growth was described in an article which I published on January 15, 1947, and now follows in this preface, with a request for the forgiveness of the reader in respect of the very slight extent to which it anticipates the argument of a part of this book.

THE EXTENSION OF PATRIOTISM

We were divided and we are conquered. That is the tragic epitaph of two war generations. Those words alone should adorn the grave of the youth of Europe. That was the fate of my generation in 1914, and that was the doom of a new generation of young soldiers in 1939. The youth of Europe shed the blood of their own family, and the jackals of the world grew fat. Those who fought are in the position of the conquered, whatever their country. Those who did not fight, but merely profited, alone are victorious.

What, then, was the truth concerning the National Socialist or Fascist movements before the war? Our fault was exactly the opposite of that suggested against us. How often in politics is that the fact? How rarely are the people permitted to know anything except the reverse of truth. It was suggested that we might set the interest of other countries before our own: that was an absurd lie. In reality, we were all too National—too narrowly concentrated upon securing the interests of our own nations. That was the true fault of all real National Socialist or Fascist Movements; whether in Britain, Germany, France, Spain, Italy. So far from being willing to serve each other as " Fifth Columns " in the event of a clash between States, our political ideology and propaganda were far too Nationalistic even to mould the minds of men in a new sense of European kinship and solidarity which might have avoided disaster by universal consent. So far from fighting for other countries in a war, we none of us argued with sufficient force in favour of that new sense of European Union which modern fact must now make an integral part of a new creed. Our creed was brought to the dust because the Fascist outlook in each land was too National.

PREFACE

How did it happen? How did that creed, which might have brought the Renaissance of Western Man, confine itself within the limits of a too narrow Nationalism? How did the rush of that mighty river of re-birth lose itself in the dry sands of a past that should have been dead?

There are two reasons; the first practical, the second ideological. For all the fiery idealism of our creed it was ever imbued with the most realistic practical sense. We had, therefore, observed with strong feelings of revulsion the ridiculous structure of that Tower of Babel which the old world erected after the last war. The attempt to solve every problem by bigger and better committees of wider and more diverse nationalities ended in the grotesque failure which our realism foresaw. Their procedure in the face of difficulty was ever to introduce more and more people who were less and less like each other in tradition, thought, feeling and instinct. Consequently and inevitably the difficulties became ever more insuperable until the whole attempt broke down in tragic absurdity. That did not appear to us a practical method. So we tried the opposite approach of each nation building in its own area a system suitable to its own tradition, culture and feeling.

The first stage was, therefore, to divide the world into large self-contained blocks on this realistic basis of natural division. A superstructure of universal friendship and understanding between nations could later have been erected on the solid foundation of these natural and practical areas. In my writing and speeches long before the war, I thus opposed the concept of " Universalism " to that of " Internationalism." It is a practical sense which says, let us begin by cleaning up our own corner when the room is in a mess; afterwards we can discuss the future of the room as a whole. That attitude was, anyhow, a very natural reaction from the performances of Babel which confronted chaos with the confused jabber of a multitude of conflicting tongues and diverse instincts within the old " Internationalism," which began as an ideal and ended as a racket.

But the revulsion from current errors led most protagonists of the new European creed back into what should have been regarded as the obsolete paths of Ultra-Nationalism. On practical grounds it became all too clear that a grotesque medley of races and cultures could never get anywhere; so the realism of the new men reacted too far to the other extreme of a nationalism which, in modern conditions, is unnaturally narrow.

Our ideological opposition to the old Internationalism was naturally even stronger than the practical. The principles of that Internationalism appeared to us an absurdity and an outrage—a complete violation of every self-evident truth of nature which could only bring degeneration and destruction. The argument that every savage was in every way the brother and equal of a European just plainly was not true; every sense and every instinct, all history and knowledge, told us that. Those people were not the same as us; they were obviously and deeply different. So International Brotherhood was founded on an entire negation of the truth. The idea that you could build a world on the premise that all men, or all races, were equal was a dangerous absurdity: yet that was the whole premise of the " democratic "

13

concept which we opposed. In fact, they are obviously not equal in intellect, physique, knowledge, achievement, history or tradition.

Further, the gifts of different races or peoples vary as widely as the gifts of different individuals. To affirm that they are just the same is to state so palpable an untruth that you risk the charge of seeking the destruction of the higher in the interests of the lower. That is, in fact, the charge against Communism. They seek to break down every European value, founded on truths that have endured the test of ages, because the first task in the move to replace the higher by the lower is to tear down the values of the former. Before you put the lower on top you must first prove there is no higher. That argument was, also, very welcome to the International Money Power which knew that the lower could be corrupted for its own purpose, while the higher could not. The higher values of a higher type are the natural barriers to corruption and chaos. The easiest way to remove them is to prove that all men and all peoples are the same; spiritual conquest thus precedes the material triumph.

Such was the ideology and such the teaching from which the National Socialist or Fascist creed reacted so naturally and so vehemently. The tragedy was that the revulsion produced too narrow a Nationalism.

The real idea, which must become the creed of the future, is surely to reject the old Internationalism on the one hand, and, on the other hand, to transcend an exclusive nationalism which divides natural friends and relatives. Man moved from the village to the nation in the natural process of uniting with his nearer kinsmen as his mind and spirit grew. Now the time is come to move from the nation to the continent, or even beyond it, under the same natural impulse and process of next uniting with those nearest to us in blood, tradition, mind and spirit.

The Idea of Kinship is the true Idea; the reaching out of our hands to those who are kindred or of the same kind. The Idea of Kinship can bring the Union of Europe where the old Internationalism failed. As a family of the same stock and kind, Europe should always have been united in Ideal. To-day, the Real as well as the Ideal faces Europe with the alternative of Union or Disaster. So must come a new union of mind and spirit, not only to avoid destruction, but for further purposes of construction. Yet the Idea of Kinship carries us far beyond Europe; there are kindred of our same kind in both Americas. Their spiritual life is also ultimately based on nearly three millenia of European History and Culture. In the deep realities and further ideals of this Age all Nature impels them in their final test to feel and think as we do.

We love our countries, but we must extend that love; the ideal and the practical alike now compel it. The extension of Patriotism; that is the necessity and that is the hope. The New Patriotism will extend to embrace all of like kind, but will not destroy the values of its kind by seeking the unnatural mingling of the old Internationalism which is proved to fail. The Universalism of like kind, within a new union of the spiritual and the material, will protect its members and its values, but will menace no others. Thus shall we of two war generations no longer be divided. Thus shall our ideals, which were so misused and betrayed, at length be realised in ways our eyes could not then see. The anguish of our Age will not have been in vain if now is born the Idea that shall carry men beyond what is called " Democracy," and even beyond Fascism. From the flames which end an epoch rises the Idea of the Future.

Those who are interested to study the author's earlier thoughts on this subject may refer to an essay he published in 1936 under the title *The World Alternative,* in which he wrote " we must return to the fundamental conception of European Union which animated the war generation of 1918 " and later referred to " the union of Europe within the universalism of the Modern Movement." His conception of that time was frustrated by the development of tendencies analysed in the article here reprinted.

PART I

ANALYSIS OF FAILURE

CHAPTER I

THE FAILURE OF BRITAIN AND OF EUROPE

THE worst were ever united; the best were ever divided. That has been the tragedy of Modern Europe which has brought her youth to death; her culture to the dust; her happiness to ruin; her material prosperity to destruction, and her spiritual life to a jeopardy which threatens with eternal night the sunlit heights of the European mind. It is no small moment in the history of man when darkness descends on three millenia of human culture. We stand in front of a potential tragedy without equal in the known annals of time. Small the mind, weak the will and doomed the spirit that cannot rise to such a challenge. The origin of disaster contains a fatal simplicity. It is easy to discern the cause, which is division and war. The family of Europe has been divided and destroyed by internecine conflict exactly as the related communities of Early Greece were rent by the clash of the City States, until even the radiance of Hellas was extinguished. In each case, the communion of blood failed to follow the law of nature to a sacred brotherhood; it served merely to inflame the jealousies and hatreds with which discordant personalities enhanced the fierce collision of rival ideologies. With fatal recurrence History confronts us now with the same classic tragedy on a far larger scale. When the best are divided, no one can benefit except the worst. The division of the classic world could only entail the final triumph of the Barbarian. The division of Europe to-day brings the victory of the two-headed Barbarian of the Modern Age, who can be named—Mob and Money. Communism and Finance are the only beneficiaries from the destruction of Europe. The first now rules nearly half the Continent in public, and the latter rules the other half in private.

The sense, in which the two terms—Mob and Money—are here used, must be defined. Mob is not a term of abuse for the people, as it was on the lips of reaction. In fact, many of those who employed such terms, are clearly included in our definition of Mob, and the great majority of the objects of their contumely are excluded from it. In this definition, Mob is divided from the true mass of the people by a vertical and not by a horizontal separation. Mob may include the occupant of castle or of cottage and may exclude either. It is not a question of wealth or of that artificiality which is now called social class, but of fundamental values. Do the roots still grip and grow in the deep, strong soil of European tradition and culture, so that an ever finer growth of human achievement may evolve to adorn a world which owes nearly all to that inspiration? On the other hand, are they torn from that sure fastness by the febrile winds of envy and hatred for all fine endeavour toward higher forms, until the infection of the Orient can sap their vital life and reduce all to that dull uniformity in which, alone, it can bear the harsh light of comparison. The latter fate may befall alike the occupant of slum or of palace; on that day the victim adheres to the values of Mob.

For, the beginning of Mob is disintegration; only at a later stage does integration occur into the positive evil of Communism. Before that can happen the abiding values of the European must be undermined and destroyed; and a rich man can contribute more to that process by a spiritual adherence to Mob, in a silliness of attitude and frivolity of life, than any poor man will effect by a bitter agitation, which at least contains a dynamism toward better things. The fool, who has mistaken duties for privileges, soon passes: but the seed he has sown remains, and the harvest of destruction is reaped by the ultimate nullity of Communism.

In the beginning, Mob is a question not of class but of values: only in the end, do the scattered fragments of a broken society cohere into an organised disaster. The term must, therefore, in two phases, comprise both the dissolution of decadence and the sinister coherence of Communism. Not until the character of the West is broken can the values of the Orient triumph.

It is sometimes denied that Communism is an Oriental creed, but this objection can scarcely be sustained in face of two indisputable facts; the first that it was invented by a Jew; the second that, after a century of existence, it has flourished in no European country except Russia. In generations of agitation it has not come near to victory in any Western country except in moments of collapse; and, even then, the will to survival of Western Man has so far always exerted itself in time. Communism is the answer of the East, not of the West, to current chaos, and it can only succeed in traversing all values of European life after Mob has done its work by destroying their foundations.

Money, too, as we shall later observe, plays a complementary part in that catastrophe. By Money, however, we do not mean the reward which energy and ability has secured; although this definition approximates closely to the opinion of what is called the " Left." Money, in this modern sense, is neither wage earned by the worker, nor the deserved profit of the productive individual; they both serve the community in the increase of wealth, and a subsequent apportionment of the proceeds, according to effort and merit, would be a relatively easy matter in an Organic State. Money is rather the force which exploits, and, ultimately, destroys them both through the operations of speculative finance. The interests of the producer, whether employer, manager or worker, stand in sharp opposition to the interests of the speculator; it is the vast operations of the latter within the powerful organisation of International Finance which we here designate as " Money." That force stands against the producer, whether by hand or brain, and even against the true interests of every national or continental banking system which serves industry and not speculation. Money and Mob thrive together as the evil twins of chaos. They could not so flourish if any real power of Government existed. They are essentially anarchic forces and can only possess such power in the absence of effective Government.

The key question of the time is why the interest of the people as a whole is subject to these influences, and why the will of the people to better things is never implemented. Why is it that Mob and Money now laugh and dance on all the higher aspirations to which they have sacrificed so much: why is it

21

that their long striving towards a finer civilisation, through many forms, always meets at last the great Negation? For, Mob and Money only prevail when every higher expression of the people's will is denied: they are triumphant only when no real Government exists which can implement that will. In brief, the present situation only arises, because in time of Peace it is impossible to get things done in England. The fact of this frustration is now obvious: our first task is to examine the reasons for it. For this purpose, it is necessary to search beneath the division and frustration of this age for those root historic causes which have inhibited the desire of the British people for a finer life, and have wrecked Europe. We shall find that the basic cause of that dual frustration is the same. It is the spirit of denial which is present in most nations, from various historic causes, but finds strongest expression in the ruling class of Great Britain by reason of circumstances which were particularly favourable to its growth. The great negation, which springs from those conditions, has thwarted the British people and divided Europe. It becomes a menace to world survival in an age which requires the Union of the Europeans; and their persistent progress toward a higher civilisation, as a condition of the continuance of mankind. So, in the first part of this book I ask the British people to examine the deep causes of that bitter frustration which has long oppressed their prosperity and happiness, and now menaces the future existence of humanity.

For this reason, it is necessary to survey the English background and environment which have produced the Eternal Spirit of Denial in the British ruling class. This profound negation is still paramount, despite any appearance of the emergence of new factors in Government. Seldom in history has the will of a great, kindly and dynamic people to better things been so long paralysed and frustrated by the character and power of a dominant minority, or ruling elite, which has imposed its will, outlook and life form on the whole population.

Again, we must define terms: the expression " British Ruling Class " has no reference, whatever, to the divisions of so-called " Social Classes " which have no relation to the realities of power. As in our earlier distinction between " Mob " and " Mass," the division between the ruling class and the rest of the people is vertical—not horizontal. Individual members of that strangely assorted miscellany of politicians, money-men and press-men, which constitutes the present ruling class of Britain, may have started in cottage or castle: that issue soon becomes irrelevant. Once they have attained their position as members of this class they rapidly assume the character, and assimilate the vices, which belong to a society that is well content with the present position, and determined to resist any fundamental change which challenges their comfort. The reason for this attitude will be analysed, and, later, we shall consider some means of preventing that fatal development in men summoned to high service of the State. At this point I desire only to emphasise that the analysis, and the attack, of the present chapter deals with this ruling class alone, and not with the mass of the people whose character, values and latent purpose, are essentially different for reasons which will also be examined. At the end of this survey some appeal will be addressed to the British People, who range from the leaders of industry and the great professions to those who dwell in the back streets of the great cities and provide the workers in peace and soldiers in war; who comprise, also, the squires of the countryside and the farmers and agricultural workers that provide the means of life, whether in war or peace.

THE GREAT NEGATION

It has often been argued that all nations really absorb the colour and texture of national life from a dominant minority, or ruling elite. Seldom has this been so true of any country as the, hitherto, sheltered and naturally favoured island of Britain. It is clear that the conditions of an Island, largely insulated from world stresses, both supported the unchallenged position of such a ruling elite and encouraged the development of their principal characteristics, which were complacency with prevailing circumstances, and resentment of any threat to disturb them. At the same time they were preserved from the rapid decline to a helpless decadence which such favoured surroundings usually promote in an elementary human nature divorced from the necessity of struggle.

The first factor, which saved them from that fate, was the adventure of winning and holding a world-wide Empire, which was largely the work of a small minority constituting a warrior sect drawn mostly from the ruling and yeoman class. The second factor is that strange, but attractive, habit—which is so baffling to foreigners—their great addiction throughout life to hard and dangerous sports. Early in life the young Englishman of the ruling class is assiduously taught to work at play, and to play at work. To the first he can ascribe the preservation of his own qualities, and to the second his failure to preserve in recent times either the Empire or his country's prosperity. Their physical qualities still enable them to fight superbly in a relatively brief effort " when the teams turn out." Their mental and moral qualities then invariably surrender, in the long hard toil and still relatively disciplined effort which peace demands, everything that has been gained, and more, in the short fierce spasm of war. Directly the actual threat to existence is over, the naturally anarchic tendencies emerge which these particular national circumstances have long nurtured. That Oedipus complex, which dominates the latter-day English mind, appears directly the danger is past which postulated great leadership and united effort as the only alternative to doom. The desire becomes overwhelming to destroy the strength to which they so recently looked for protection. So, a national effort is only exerted for destructive ends, and great men are only used for purposes which are foolish.

It was not always so in England. Profoundly different was the Elizabethan spirit; almost Greek in its hard Hellenic gaiety and passionate admiration of the great and vital qualities in nature and in men. What came afterwards to change so deeply the whole character? The answer is broadly, a relaxation of outside pressure—and Puritanism! Let us consider these two events. The English were then a small population facing the immense power of Spain, which was capable, at any time, of landing a large and probably decisive force on these shores. Earlier they confronted the wrath of Catholic Europe under the strong centralised power and commanding personality of Henry VIII. They were living dangerously if ever a nation so lived, and from the depth of their vital spirit surged up, in response to the life challenge, a great outburst not only of life action, but, also, of triumphant music, drama and poetry, which was the genius of the Elizabethan mind and the illumination of Europe. The warrior land was also " a land of singing birds."

But the heroic mood diminished with the relaxation of the outside pressure, and the strange dualism of the English character began to operate. The man of life-enthusiasm and achievement-capacity, of Hellenic charm and cultural expansion, alternates with that cautious, restricted, inhibited prig who conceals his main interest, which is money, behind a mask of smooth piety that is rendered the more effective by the fact that he has deceived himself before deceiving others. These two forces are age-old contenders for the soul of England. They are proved incapable of effective synthesis, despite all attempts and asseverations to the contrary; so the conflict for some time past has been almost completely, if temporarily, resolved by the victory of the latter. But, let no observer of the English scene even now believe that this condition is eternal or unchallengeable. In the glory of the eighteenth century the position was sharply, if temporarily, reversed; the Puritan disappeared from the centre of power, and again the gay, but purposeful, stride of the Elizabethan was felt upon the earth. For a moment, the sun of that frustrated maturity pierced the gloom of inhibition and hypocrisy to radiate an exquisite culture in harmony with all that was elevated and beautiful in Continental life. Was it only coincidence that this period added the Empire to these Islands; was it only chance that the return of Puritanism soon saw a loss of Empire and later the ruin of Europe in two unnecessary wars? Be that as it may, we yet may note that, dormant in the strong stock, are still the great qualities, and the passing of a generation which has been cramped, twisted and deformed in the Procrustean bed of false values can yet permit their resurgence.

Cavalier-Puritan or Hellenic-Elizabethan

The conflict is often crudely summarised in terms of the struggle between the Cavalier and the Puritan. But the Cavalier is merely the man who abandoned the true values of his kind and was defeated; so he is by no means the real representative of that vital way of life which reached apotheosis in Elizabethan times. He was the Elizabethan in decline—the man of action turned soft and silly after relaxation of outside pressure and the life challenge. Like similar specimens to-day, he was just the type who fuddles away what others have won. He is naturally represented by the detractors of the true type as being characteristic, but he is not: he is merely a caricature of the great generation who retained something of their gaiety but little of their underlying seriousness of purpose or capacity for coldly planned and effective action. The Cavalier was the beginning of the " will to comfort " type as opposed to the " will to achievement " which will be examined later in this volume. When the victory of Puritanism superimposed a hypocritical mercantilism on Cavalier silliness, we observe the foundation of the present character of the British ruling class. Then, the only serious thing in life became money; the rest is the triviality of small amusements, But, to be silly and mercenary it is, of course, necessary to assuage your conscience, and placate the opinion of the outside world, by the constant pose that silliness is clean and healthy amusement, and the pursuit of money, in some mystic fashion, is inextricably interwoven with the service of God. Neither the Greek nor the Elizabethan found it necessary so to assure themselves, or the world, concerning a way of life which came freely, spontaneously and beautifully from the great wellspring of nature, and pursued the achievement of ever higher forms in harmony with that Phusis which consciously or unconsciously they both served.

At this point, it will doubtless be objected with small relevance by some modern critic that it is wrong to regard with any favour the Elizabethan spirit, because in that age considerable poverty and suffering among the poor coincided with great achievement. Historians may debate and compare the relative suffering of a

comparative few at that time with the suffering caused to many
by the vast catastrophes of to-day. But, surely it cannot be
denied that the Elizabethans were the first to recognise the
responsibility of the State towards the poor. For the first time
in English history, the man without means of support obtained
legal right to maintenance. Under the " humane " dispensation
of the recent neo-Puritan dominion, this rule has sometimes been
more marked in the breach than the observance. Further, the
Elizabethan had no modern science with which to abolish poverty
—while we have. They could not use a science which they did
not possess; but we can yet use a science which we do possess
to remedy misery rather than to cause it. No more relevant to
this argument is a parade of the innumerable " crudities " and
" barbarities " of the Elizabethan mind. They were the
beginning of a civilisation of genius, not the maturity. They
were the Dawn, the tragedy is the absence of High Noon. What
cut across the further developing of that extraordinary burgeon-
ing of the English genius? What inhibited the full efflorescence?
What cold knife cut clean through the life root of the great
English music, so that it never revived? What confined and
twisted the natural, vital force of Elizabethan drama and poetry
so that it only struggled through again after many years by
means of that explosion of repressed prurience which is called
the Restoration; never again did it achieve even the semblance
of that first free life surge. Why was that continuity of the
Hellenic tradition, which is the soul of Europe, driven from the
place of rebirth, in the soil of England, to live again and to live
for ever in the German genius of Goethe and Schiller—which
was both preluded and followed by all that is finest in the
spirit of France—and was reflected again in the revolt of Byron,
Shelley and Swinburne.

The answer to all these questions is Puritanism—that cold,
dark sickness of the mind and soul. Puritanism bent, twisted
and deformed for generations the gay, vigorous and manly spirit
of the English. Puritanism turned even the Empire, which their
invincible energy and courage won, from what might have been a
Parthenon of human achievement and constructive beauty into

a counting house concealed in a monastery. Puritanism turned a natural friend and early leader of European culture, who might later have participated harmoniously in the building of ever higher forms of civilisation, into the persistent and malignant enemy of all striving and aspiring spirits who served purposes of great construction. In short, Puritanism has been not only the tragedy of England, but the disaster of Europe. A key question not only to the past, but to the present and the future, is—how did Puritanism occur? How could it happen? How, and why, did that superb young man of glorious life potential permit this old witch to settle on his shoulders, rule his life, throttle his vital force and turn his outward and upward surge of creative existence into an inhibited and inverted negation of constructive achievement in himself and others, which gnawed away both life's purpose and joy?

THE SPLIT MIND OF EUROPE—AND OF AMERICA

We must shortly summon to our aid in this diagnosis not only a study of environment in its now observed effect on the development of a civilisation, but, also, some of the lessons of modern psychology in the vast new domain of human knowledge, which begins now to be revealed within the subconscious mind. It is first necessary, however, to record that this division of the mind and spirit exists not only within England but, in various forms, within the Continent of Europe as a whole: while, in America, it has assumed an almost exactly similar form by reason of the export of British Puritanism to that country. In fact, this great discord begins to transcend national boundaries and to assume continental dimensions. Within the Continent of Europe, and within almost every nation, the Doer faces the Denier—and Dynamism confronts the great Negation: on the outcome of this struggle of the mind and spirit depends the supreme question whether the culture and tradition of the West will reach to yet greater heights or succumb, in the lethargy of the final denial, not only to the spiritual values, but, also, to the physical victory of the East.

In the past the division of the Soil has been the strongest thing in all our lives. In the future the division of the Soul will transcend the division of the Soil: in the end the Soul will be stronger than the Soil. This new advance in the mind and spirit of men can only come after the Union of Europe, which is a vital necessity if this Continent, and every nation within it, is to survive. So, we must study the split mind of Europe, which is vividly illustrated by the divergence in outlook between the governing minds of Britain and Germany which has divided two nations whose peoples, in the mass, are more similar than the peoples of any other two nations on the Continent. Europe requires a new synthesis: in all things eternal synthesis. The American and the Frenchman, who, in our thesis, are naturally essential to this new harmony, may feel the examination of these matters has for them little interest or bearing on their problems. Let them not be too sure: in America anyone can observe, for reasons just suggested, the clash between the urge to constructive achievement and an ultimately anarchic spirit of negation, which, in extreme form, will always frustrate the builders of anything great. In fact, it may be postulated that within America, in a potentially acute form, may be discerned the diverse tensions which have divided the governing minds of Germany and of Britain; and for reasons based on differences of hereditary outlook, experience and character, which are not far to seek. It should be added that in the extraordinary achievements of America we, also, see some of the great effects of a union of genius between the English and the German mind. But, for the moment, we are concerned with the division which has brought disaster; and will later regard the immense possibilities of union. Even the exceptional homogeneity of the French has experienced a profound internal tremor from this great convulsion of the European mind, which is manifest, in diverse forms, through the strong resistance to decline evoked by the age-old sense of public duty and faith in the French Army and the related landed classes, from large proprietor to peasant, who stand in eternal but, so far, not always effective opposition to the deeply conflicting operations of the political-Bourse alliance. Their lack of political skill in recent times has often resulted in their acquisition of a fundamentally undeserved reputation of being reactionary, which is belied by the great contributions of their leading minds to advanced thought, notably in the realm of science.

In fact, within the soul of every great nation of European stock is felt this profound division of the European mind; which may assume various forms, but reflects the basic struggle of European values for survival. It can be most clearly observed in the antithesis between the mind which has dominated the comfortable circumstances of England in recent times and the mentality which has prevailed in the more stressful periods of Germany's history: both were the effect of diverse experience on related characters. We have already noted the fact of common observation that the mass of these two peoples, in the outlook and habits of their everyday life, are similar to an extraordinary degree: it is equally true that their cultures are interwoven at every point. Apart from the profound interaction of the philosophical thought of the two nations at all periods, what sentient spirit can recall, without emotion, the immense admiration of Goethe for Shakespeare together, also, with the formative influence of the latter upon Schiller and the whole great generation of German poetry. They, in their turn, moved and influenced profoundly all subsequent English thought of fine and high perception; in fact, they turned all eyes that could hold a vision, whether in Germany or in Britain, towards that radiant Hellenic dawn which witnessed the birth of everything noble and beautiful that Europe holds in common.

DIVERGENCE OF HISTORIC EXPERIENCE

It is only when things have to be done in a rough and practical world that minds or ways diverge. How came this difference? The answer is surely from historic circumstances, particularly in recent times. Let us examine carefully and objectively that difference; for to understand all, it has been said, is to forgive all; and, certainly, on some measure of that comprehension depends the peace and the hope of mankind.

It is evident that the geographical circumstance of the

British was precisely the opposite of that of the Germans. In general, the Channel afforded an almost complete protection. After the passing of the Spanish menace it was over two centuries before a Continental power appeared strong and resolute enough to attempt the effective invasion of these Islands: and the Napoleonic threat, in terms of history, was of short duration. After that it did not seriously occur to the English that a Foreign Power could overcome their Navy and land a force on these shores: except perhaps, for a brief period in 1940, and, even then most people naturally preferred the long mental habit of deriding that possibility to facing the facts which their own neglect had created. This long immunity from the major stresses of History in itself can account for the strong psychological divergence which occurred in the almost identical root stock of the British and German peoples. If you subject initially similar organisms to entirely different conditions and experiences for long enough you are bound to produce a considerable diversity. But, it is naturally much less marked in the mass of the people, whose life in the daily toil and preoccupations of existence must be largely the same in a similar climate and condition. In fact, before the days of large armies the experience was almost identical. The Thirty Years War swept over the mass of the German people as the Civil War swept over the mass of the British people. The former lasted longer and caused more devastation; but, on the Continent, as in England, they were relatively small forces which did the actual fighting. Comparatively few felt personally the stress and clash of arms in addition to the dislocation and discomfort which was merely an accentuation of the ordinary hardships of contemporary existence. It was not, therefore, in the mass of the people that the divergence of experience and, consequently, of character, was so marked. It was in the dominant minority derived from all social strata— the ruling elite—that the difference of experience moulded and delineated so sharply the divergence of character.

The leaders of Germany developed naturally the spirit of the Teutonic Knights; dedicated in discipline and solidarity to devotion for Faith and Cause. These qualities had to permeate

31

the whole governing order of Germany and weld it into a solid monolith of resistance to the outside world. They were impelled to understand the allocation, differentiation and distinction of function in service, rather than social class as the English came to understand it after mercantilism developed. They had so to live, or they would not have survived against the continual threat of Oriental incursion; and the underlying unity of purpose and character was sustained beneath every exhaustion caused by internecine rivalry and struggle.

What was vital in Britain, on the other hand, assumed far more the character of the great Sea Captains, who defied Spain in the sixteenth century and whose spiritual successors founded the Empire in the eighteenth century. It was by reason of circumstance a far more individual and lone-adventurous character than that of the contrasted German. Their success depended on individual initiative in a continual and flexible adaptation to unknown conditions and dangers. They worked, on the whole, without superior command and almost without direction; such conditions develop both self-reliance and a tendency to a certain disregard, if not secret contempt, for a remote authority which can never be present at the moment of decision and is only spasmodically exercised. At its best, that character rises to the heights of initiative and invention; at its worst it tends towards the anarchic and the impossible in great enterprises which require the co-ordination of many minds and qualities. The same cartoonists who love to caricature the Germans as an unreasoning herd would—with impartiality of vilification—define the corresponding character of the English as the perennially impudent and destructive boy, who is adept at breaking windows, but not so good at building houses. But, whether the world loves or hates this character, it has to be recognised as one of the great facts of History; for these men almost casually picked up an Empire on their laughing way.

FIGHTER OR FINANCIER: THE TECHNIQUE OF HUMBUG

It is necessary, however, to our study of the development of the later character of the British ruling class to enquire what proportion of the governing elite of Britain were either laughing or fighting in this period. How much, in fact, did the ruling class, as a whole, contribute to the achievement of Empire, which gave Britain everything, and thus derive from that experience their own character? Is it not true to say that, apart from the already noted exception of the eighteenth century, they ceased both to laugh and to fight after the Cavalier went down, until the two wars of the present age, when, for the surprising reason already observed of a long addiction to hardy sports, they came up in fine fighting trim? But, what were they doing in the long interval? Were they winning the new money or only counting it? Is it true to say that the backers of the Drakes were very numerous but that the Drakes themselves were very few? Can the Historians deny that the Empire was won and held by an incredibly small band of professionals, whose leadership and effective force was drawn almost entirely from the ruling class and the yeoman class, but constituted a small minority even within these classes? (The rank and file, which was tiny in relation to modern armies, was, in large degree fortuitously collected by the press gang.) In the work of Empire-winning and -building the bulk of the ruling classes were not engaged at all. Those picking up the winnings greatly exceeded those who were doing the winning: those, who enjoyed the protection of the Channel for themselves, and the efforts of others overseas to provide them with their wealth and comforts, greatly outnumbered at all periods the small band who struggled and achieved. And, what was the experience of the latter? In the early period they were thanked like Raleigh in the Tower, or Warren Hastings in Westminster Hall, and in the later period in the manner branded by the satirical lines of Kipling, which depict British treatment of their overseas soldiers between wars.

It is necessary to understand that those who won the Empire and established the whole position of Britain in the world were a minority so small as scarcely to affect the character of the whole. This historic fact is necessary to an understanding of the deep effect produced by the protection and insulation from world stresses which was afforded by the Channel to the mass of the British People, and in particular, to the governing elite, who could thereby enjoy, in safety and ever-increasing comfort, the gains of that small band of great adventurers whom they condescended on occasion to back and to support; or at least not too often to execute. Britain, the " cradle of Democracy," in fact owes more than almost any other land to the vigour, initiative and heroism of a very few.

The effect of these conditions and environment on the dominant minority, who enjoyed this exceptional fortune, was, of course, profound. They were largely released from the " sharp glance of necessity," and the inevitable effect of easy conditions on men who have not yet attained a full spiritual development began to operate on the character of this relatively primitive society. The vital surge of the Elizabethan spirit in response to the life challenge began to subside. It was not then so difficult in a subsequent generation for those values to be entirely reversed by the victory of the new Puritan elite who came with the Holy Book in one hand and the Bank Book in the other. Even after their emergence from total eclipse, the Elizabethan aristocracy, which degenerated so swiftly into the Cavalier, bore always, in some degree, the hall-mark of a Financial Mercantilism which was protected and encompassed by a degree of religious humbug seldom witnessed in such full measure, in any other land.

From this period in England dates the wide divergence between what men say and what men do. Nothing is more destructive of moral character in the long run than a public morality which has no relation to private practice. Such damage must be done by religious protestations which have no relation to the urge of nature or the facts of life. A habit of hypocrisy is engendered which is not only nauseating to the outside observer, but finally inhibits in the victim all free and natural participation in constructive achievement, as modern psychology establishes with ever-increasing weight of observed proof. So, the victory of the new elite with new values permeated permanently the outlook of the whole nation to some extent, but, as always happens, affected in far larger degree the character and psychology of the ruling class which became, in an uneasy and never entirely consummated synthesis of externally conflicting elements, a combination of the Puritan and the Cavalier. That strangely split personality of diverse instincts and, consequently, innumerable inhibitions with his highly developed technique of humbug succeeded all too soon to the almost Hellenic harmony of the Elizabethan nature.

The Nation with the Oedipus Complex

The effect of these events upon political conduct can be traced without encountering any insuperable difficulty of analysis. In brief, the effect of the relaxation of outside pressure, followed by the outcome of the Civil War, was to add Puritan values to the Oedipus complex: a truly unpleasant combination of misfortunes. This may seem a surprising statement at first glance, but it can be explained with some precision. We have already studied the familiar phenomenon of Puritanism, and it is now necessary to make a brief excursion into the sphere of psychology, before marrying the Oedipus complex to that hideous bride—Puritan values—in the fatal union which begat the great Negation. The Oedipus complex, as most people know, is connected with the relationship of Son to Father. It is a relationship, as all are aware, which can easily go wrong: consequently, it was in ancient times the subject of some concern, and in modern times the topic of much study. The outcome, to date, may here be stated in terms of crudest summary without any outrage of the evidence so far collected and collated. The bearing of the whole matter on our argument will readily be observed at the end of this brief digression. In short, the attitude of Son to Father, in particular in the conditions of primitive Society, tends to vary according to circumstances. It all depends whether the Son's need for the Father's protection is stronger than his subconscious desire to succeed to his place and prestige. In a primitive society the former instincts are paramount in a period of danger, and the latter in a time of ease. Do you need strength to lead you and protect you in a threat to life and home, or, in the absence of danger, do you covet for

35

yourself the position and influence of qualities whose responsibilities, in a moment of crisis, you might not care so readily to
assume? These are the leading questions in this matter in the
analysis of primitive Societies, and we have all observed the
diverse answers which are given to them even in " advanced "
civilisations according to the different circumstances of the Time.

Do not flatter yourselves, modern generation of an all-wise
" Democracy," that you are so completely removed and
emancipated from the shameful dilemmas and ignoble motives
of primitive societies. You had more use for a Churchill in
1940 than you had in 1945. In primitive Societies, according to
psychological science, the Son element conspires to kill the strong
Father type when they no longer need his protection but desire
his power and envy his attributes. In Democracy, when war is
over, the lesser politicians ceaselessly conspire to get rid of the
Leader character, behind whom they clustered in the moment
of panic, and, in the ensuing disruption into discordant fragments, among whom are to be found many of the Leader's
nominal " party," a bewildered electorate is persuaded to perform the modern equivalent of the kill by voting him down, in
the hope of obtaining some vaguely defined booty after the
departure of the commanding presence. When, finally, he dies,
remorse and religious veneration succeed to envious hatred, and
they perform the complete " Totem Rites," recorded in the
psychological history of primitive Societies, by erecting an image
or statue to his memory with much beating on the tom-toms of
sentimental oratory. All of which might lead the cynic once
again to observe " The more it changes, the more it is the same
thing." And in a " Democracy " of Mob and Money, but only
in such a society, that cynicism is valid, because such a State by
nature lacks all real purpose and vitality of forward urge, and is
inspired only by alternating fits of hot jealousy and cold fear.

But we must now return from this brief journey into the
realms of psychology with the lesson that, when tension relaxes
and danger is less imminent, men change their attitude to life,
and prefer in Government the types which suggest quiescence
rather than achievement. They seek ease, and resent the intrusion

of any factor, or personality, which threatens to distrub it; in fact, in these circumstances, the only thing which rouses their activity is the interruption of their lethargy! So they hate alike the summons to great achievement, and the demands of that dynamic leadership, which history shows to be the essential concomitant: that character becomes identified with the exertion which they dislike.

From geographical circumstance came the insulation at this point of British History from great events of the Continent. That immunity, in its turn, produced the traditional attitude to the leadership character which summons to participate in such events. Such great men were permitted to manoeuvre small forces of professionals, in the manner of Chatham, in order to acquire an Empire and add to home comforts. But anyone at home, or abroad, who appeared likely to disturb that comfort of the whole, and particularly of the governing class, became at once the object of concentrated hatred. The one unforgivable sin was, for any reason, to ask them to exert themselves. Behind the protection of the Channel thus developed the natural lethargy of human beings relieved from the urge of life stress; from that relaxation in turn rises the Oedipus complex which resents the Father, or Leadership, presence, when it is not required for purposes of protection. Then, to lethargy and the Oedipus complex was added the Puritan character which, by reason of its own profound life inhibitions, hates the uninhibited and the freely creative, and, in accord with long habit, invents the profoundest moral reasons for its destruction on receipt of the usual direct instructions from Heaven.

Thus, the union of the anarchic Oedipus complex with the envy, hatred and malice of the repressed, and, therefore eternally jealous, Puritan spirit begets the great negation, which confronts with uncompromising opposition all affirmation of achievement. It is useless to contend that the achievement of founding the Empire is an answer to this analysis. As already observed the work was done by a tiny minority, and their activity can surely be partly ascribed to the flight overseas of lively and vital spirits from the misery which Puritanism had created at home.* For we may note here in passing a theme to which we shall return, that misery, or even suffering, appears to be as essential to achievement in undeveloped types as creative inspiration—the Daemonic, as Goethe calls it—is to the activity of developed spirits.

THE FATE OF GREAT ENGLISHMEN

The great negation operated both at home and abroad; in this respect it was quite impartial. It was not based merely on a hatred of great foreigners; it entertained at least an equal spite against great Englishmen. Not only did it strive against large designs of European construction cherished by a Louis XIV, a Napoleon or a Hitler; it reacted even more bitterly against a Strafford or a Warren Hastings. Chatham was permitted later in life to acquire an Empire on the side-line, under the condition that he left Home Affairs to the pitiful and, therefore, unprovocative figure of the Duke of Newcastle; but this belated, almost casual, permission was only granted after he had been compelled to spend many of his best creative years in an isolated opposition.

The only man who commanded the consistent favour of the negative mind in life and death, was the Jew, Disraeli. In fact, it may be remarked that Conservatism has done no thinking since he died. He knew so well how to play on their stupidity and vanity. The best instincts of the old ruling class were exploited to give him a power which was never afterwards seriously used to serve the end proclaimed. Their great love of the land and of agriculture was the instrument by which Disraeli secured the downfall of their leader, Peel, in a moment of difficulty and crisis. We can search the history of the nineteenth century, in vain, for any substantial evidence to show that his love for the simple life of the landsman was, thereafter, translated into legislative effect, when he had the opportunity. But the finest

*The exception to this rule was of course the *Mayflower* which carried the joys of Puritanism to America; hence the " sororities." The consequent conflict in the soul of America between the inhibited and the creative still rages: on the outcome probably depends the contribution of that Continent to history.

passion of the ruling class at that time, for the English country-side, was adroitly employed to win the highest office in British politics for the Sicilian theorist. Thereafter, they characteristically preferred a natural sycophant to a vital leader, and his oriental talent for devising the obscure but romantic euphony of a nearly meaningless mysticism was just the thing needed to assuage their consciences with the posture of high-minded intent, while leaving them free to pursue ever sillier amusements as their roots were gradually prised from the soil which, in practice, their favourite fakir did little or nothing to defend. His chief colleague, Lord George Bentinck, described their relationship rather differently, but very succinctly, when he observed in private " every amateur team requires a professional bowler."

A very different reception was accorded to his great rival Gladstone, who, in his efforts to solve the Irish problem and thus to forestall the Home Rule crisis, which might have cost the life of Britain in 1914, incurred such a savage hatred among the " respectable " classes of Great Britain that their children were literally taught to believe that this eminent churchman, of character as pious as it was sedate, was playing the unlikely role of Faust by having entered into a pact with the Devil. In fact, anyone of any talent or personality who ever suggested doing anything sensible in time to avert a catastrophe, let alone dared to advocate active measures to mitigate unnecessary human misery, was merely making application for a sentence of frustration, if nothing worse, from the combined malice of every dunce and mediocrity in British politics. Such small souls were never moved either by large design or fine emotion, but responded rapidly enough to the conditioned subconscious instinct which urged them to hate the " Father figure " of the man of action, and to envy the bright form that might be capable of the achievement which their own inhibitions forbade.

Never has any community been so greatly served by great men or been less worthy of them than the British ruling class. But still the supply of giants continued for use only in the recurring crises of pigmy creation, and, in our time, the treatment of Lloyd George and Churchill carries further the sorry story. The writer happened to spend most of his political life in strong opposition to these two men on account of their Germanophobe policy, so he will be acquitted of partiality. These two statesmen, in the meridian of their years, conceived and advocated measures of social reform which were large and far-reaching in the terms of a static society, such as Britain: in retrospect scarcely anyone can be found to deny that most of these proposals were beneficent. Few, also, will now be found to refute that they were the only two men of genius whom their two generations of British politics produced. Yet, their fate was to be more hated and more bitterly opposed by the overwhelming majority of the British ruling class than any two men of their time. No other men in their period were so persistently, bitterly and libellously attacked as these two. The savage vindictiveness of his own class against Churchill, in particular, recalled the observation of Mirabeau: " The Aristocracy pursue with implacable hatred the friends of the people, but with tenfold implacability the Aristocrat who is a friend of the people."

In all their large and generous proposals of an earlier period, which might have brought some stability to the State by timely reform as well as some alleviation of the lot of those who toiled and suffered, those two men met nothing but unreasoning abuse and savage malice from that ruling class of Britain, which is only roused from lethargy by the impulse to prevent something good from being done. Yet, in inevitable irony, these two statesmen in their latter years were accorded at long last, and in high degree, the favour of Britain's " elite." Those, who had vilified them the most ferociously, found it expedient for a brief space to fawn upon them the most obsequiously. The reasons were that their character and talents were required for the conduct of unnecessary wars. Having been denied the opportunity to do wise things in their maturity, they were finally mobilised to do something really foolish in their age. Any large measures of construction were earlier forbidden to them; but all means of destruction were later placed with acclamation in their hands. Churchill, in particular, who had been the most hated, became, for a time, the most beloved. The reason was that he was the only man of that calibre who was available to frustrate a man and a Movement of great achievement on the Continent. His own deeds at home would be forgiven him, if he could prevent yet greater deeds abroad. Such are the conditions of service accorded to genius by the British ruling class; and they are stamped with the authoritative seals of the Oedipus complex and the Puritan tradition.

Was it such a situation that the poet, Hölderlin, imagined when he wrote lines which may be freely paraphrased as " Deep in my heart, I despise the rabble of mob and money, but still more genius which makes common cause with them."

The Triumph of Spite

It might be supposed that the tardy admission of great talent, rendered at length necessary by some situation of crisis, would, at least, lead thereafter to the permanent recognition of such outstanding gifts, and even to some desire to make amends not merely to the individual but to the State, which had long been denied such services by the jealous resistance of most mediocre characters. Once discovered by the hard test of fact, such abilities might at least be retained in counsel and in action for the future benefit of the nation. On the contrary, the very moment that danger was passed the situation immediately recurred in which, according to the diagnosis of that shrewd observer of the English scene, Jonathan Swift, the presence of a genius in national affairs can invariably be detected by the unfailing test that once again " all the dunces were to be found in league against him." The moment they ceased to be scared out of their silly wits by the imminence of disaster, which their previous follies had invoked, they at once began again to conspire against, and chatter down, the man who had committed his final offence by saving them from the catastrophe which their blunders had so richly deserved. For, among those types the gratitude of the natural man becomes merely a bitter reminder of their sense of inferiority in relation to a person who would normally be the subject of a manly tribute.

So, a Lloyd George was summarily dismissed at the end of an uneasy four years after the First World War, during which he was the object of ceaseless intrigue and attack. The remaining years of his life were spent in an opposition condemned to be entirely sterile, because his untiring efforts to secure serious attention to the unemployment problem, which was gnawing at the roots of national life, were greeted only with the flippant derision of the complacent little men who commanded the two chief parties of the State. Churchill received even shorter shrift, and was dismissed almost immediately after a performance which was described by his supporters as the greatest service in British History. Such glowing eulogies, however, did not prevent a continual conspiracy against him directly the danger was past, with a consequent shattering of his previous body of support into a multitude of discordant fragments, which was only, in part, collected and reunited into a new Government for the purpose of dividing a non-existent National wealth; while the Empire, which, under Churchill, they had alleged they were defending, was given away with both hands to any fellow-chatterer of other climes, who made himself sufficient of a nuisance.

So it ever was, and so it ever will be, while England is hag-ridden by the dominance of such types and such psychology in her politics. Even the great Chatham died while speaking in the House of Lords in a last and unavailing attempt to avert the loss of America. In the petulant passion of their arrogance they lightly discarded a union with a poor relation; the position was reversed when the long sequence of their subsequent blunders reduced them to seeking it again. Would that great Shade feel only sorrow at the drear wasting of a century and a half of supreme opportunity for the united English-speaking peoples to lead the world in high achievement; or, would the bitterness of his earthly experience superimpose a certain sardonic amusement, when the eternally recurring figures of his old opponents lined up in that pathetic procession to beg Washington for yet another loan, because they had not even possessed the energy to hold and to develop the remainder of the Empire which such as he had left to them? For, it is difficult to deny that the face of this earth would be different if the British ruling class had devoted a fraction of the energy to doing something great in their own Empire that they gave to preventing great foreigners from doing something great in Europe. If the great negation in Europe had been instead the great affirmation in British Empire, the troubled history of mankind might have taken an upward instead of a downward path. But that would have needed the creative surge of the Hellenic-Elizabethan, which was replaced by the narrow inhibition and repression of the Oedipus-Puritan.

EUROPEAN DESTRUCTION BEFORE EMPIRE CONSTRUCTION

If even the African possessions of British Empire had been grasped and developed fearlessly and openly as a great estate, Britain to-day could be richer and more powerful than America. Men like Rhodes were not lacking to point the way. Every raw material that industry could possibly require, and every wealth potential that mankind could ever dream, were present in abundance. Just conceive the energy that Britain evinced during the last two wars against Germany as applied to the development of Africa by the direct action of a united nation, which was bent on the achievement of a higher standard of life. Remember the energy and enthusiasm evoked for the purpose of war by men who were capable of leadership even in the wrong direction; then apply, even in cursory survey, the possible results of a similar dynamism to such a project as the opening up of Africa. Just conceive what the English would have done if they had devoted to construction the same force that they gave to destruction. They could have done it, too, if they had not become hag-ridden by a strange accident of geography, which brought an immunity from the life challenge, and so played on that natural human weakness and lethargy which none but the rarest men have yet evolved far enough to overcome by force of their own spirit. As it is we have been made to witness, even in the age of the triumph of science, poverty in the midst of potential plenty together with widespread unemployment, while a large

43

proportion of the people urgently required the goods which those in enforced idleness could so easily have produced. The unemployment problem was only temporarily solved by the expedient of war, which caused such shortage of all existing wealth that all had to be employed to make it good, if collapse was to be averted; they never even learnt how to distribute their wealth: they only knew how to destroy it, and that they have now done to some decisive purpose.

No excuse of space confinement or lack of raw material could be pleaded in British politics; they had far more space than they knew how to manage, and more raw materials than they had the energy to develop. Nothing was lacking to them except the will, the energy and the Leadership to do and live greatly. But their psychology, which we have already examined in detail, was resolutely opposed to all " Doers," whether at home or abroad. The Continent need not complain that the malice of the present English life denial is exclusively directed against them; it is aimed with even greater force against England. The great negation operated even more potently, because more constantly, against the " Doers " at home than against the " Doers " abroad. In fact, the " Doers " at home could only find employment at all for the object of frustrating and defeating the " Doers " abroad. Such were the only uses of high talent and character in the service of Oedipus-Puritan mediocrity: Siegfried in the bondage of the dwarfs. Pity the strange enthralment of the English genius, rather than envy it or blame it.

THE WILL TO DO VERSUS ECONOMIC DOGMAS

In the end what matters is the will to do: paper plans merely add to the bitterness of disillusion in the absence of that quality. The globe has been stuffed with paper projects from British archives for use at home and abroad. But the will to do has always been lacking in recent times. Behind all the mass of paper and red tape has stood the spirit of denial in resolute opposition to all men at home and abroad who bore even the semblance of a " Doer." So, the policy of the ruling clique in Britain, whether it was labelled at the moment Conservative

or Labour, has been an affliction to their own country and a
nuisance to Europe, which culminated in a catastrophe. In
economic problems several solutions nearly always exist, any one
of which may succeed if resolutely pursued. What matters is to
get anything done; what is difficult is not to find a paper plan
but to get any plan put through. That is the point at which the
great force of inertia is encountered. In Great Britain there is
never a dearth of paper projects for the solution of every question
under the sun, or rather the fog; the only thing lacking is the
will to execute them, and the machinery of Government which
can only be created for that purpose by the will to do. Economic
solutions follow naturally the power to do things; if one plan
does not work, another is tried until success is wrested from
circumstance.

Such a concept offends, however, two almost religious
emotions of British politics. The first principle is that no one
should be given the power to do anything, at least, anything
constructive: this complex we have already examined. The
second principle is that economic beliefs should be fixed like
religious dogmas—in fact, in the latter day mercantile soul
economics have almost replaced creeds as the object of spiritual
veneration. All this, of course, is the greatest nonsense to the
realist mind which says—if one broom is no good to sweep out
the room, try another. We keep our metaphysics for application
to spheres other than the scullery floor. But very different is
the attitude of the British parties who kneel before various
economic dogmas, all quite obsolete anyhow, and furiously
denounce as treachery, or impiety, any suggestion even to adapt
them to fresh circumstances. As in all systems of illusion, the
one thing certain is that none of these beliefs will ever really be
put into practice. To prevent this disaster they all unite in the
maintenance of a system which, in peace time, renders all
effective action impossible by organised chatter. Now that
religion has been translated into economic terms their old rule
still holds that religion and business should be kept well apart!
The economic dogma is one thing: and the practical business of
Government is quite another.

The Labour Party

If anyone thinks we draw a caricature, let him glance at the history of the Labour Party; for, in British politics, caricatures both walk and talk. The Labour Party is the acme of the illusion world, for no one any longer even suggests that their policy will actually be applied. It is sufficient to ask the reader to contemplate for one moment the official policy of the Labour Party—" to nationalise the means of production, distribution and exchange "—all of them! and then to follow the cautious and very ineffective attempts of the Labour leaders to make capitalism work. Thereafter, no shadow of a doubt can exist that we face the final sterility of the Puritan mind in a system which keeps religion — now political economic dogma — well apart from business, which is now the practical conduct of Government. Psalm singing and religious precept used to be kept for Sundays: now Party policy is kept for Party conferences. And it is just as well when Party policy appears so foolish after experience of the first few halting experiments in Bureaucratic Socialism.

We will revert shortly to a brief survey of their few attempts to apply small fragments of their professed policy, and to some examination of the fundamental error made in their whole approach to the problem. But priority should surely be given to some study of the chief work of Labour in power, which is the patching of capitalism. In all their efforts to avert the collapse of a failing system one factor is outstanding: the measure adopted is invariably out-of-date. It is usually a proposal which was hotly debated and rejected years previously by the dominant spirit of denial. Tardily, it is then adopted by a Labour Government as a brand new project of economic thought when men have almost forgotten the previous controversy. An analysis was undertaken some time back, by others, of proposals originally advocated by the present writer, and rejected at the time, which had subsequently been adopted, or proposed again, as expedients in the desperation of the Labour Government elected in 1945. Under examination it appeared that the time-lag between the original proposal and its adoption by Government was at least fifteen years; it was only then taken up, of course, under deepening economic pressure, and was even then denounced for its novelty. But the only interest of these incidents to the present survey resides not in the fact that such proposals are ultimately adopted but in the typical occurrence that they are then completely out-of-date.

The situation is moving much too rapidly for the mind of " Democracy ": by the time it has at length resolved to do something, the measure is no longer effective. The old tag holds good in these grave matters, " a stitch in time saves nine." By the time the necessary stitch is applied by a democratic statesmanship, nine times nine stiches would be necessary to close the rent, which fast-moving and neglected events have torn in the clothing Politic. The delay is in part due to the natural lethargy of the type which emerges to power under " Democracy "; it is in part caused by the all-pervading spirit of the great negation; and it can in part be attributed to the religious nature of current economic dogmas, which have just been noted. To secure any modification in existing precepts not only the disturbing shock of events is required, but also endless mumbo-jumbo of discussion and debating ritual, before the sacred " principle " can be shifted sufficiently from its original position to make room for a little commonsense. The absurdity consists in translating purely practical things into metaphysical regions. It arises from the human urge to take refuge in unrealities if it is denied realities. So, in the absence of real action implementing a dynamic faith, artificial principles are made of economic expedients whose application should be purely pragmatic.

In fact, some of these economic devices are applicable in one period but not in another; they may work admirably in one decade but not in the next, if circumstances have changed. They should be treated as instruments of rapid and flexible adaptation to the service of men and not as " Arks of the Covenant." A fine example of this tendency from a bygone period was, of course, the Free-Trade-Protection controversy which divided Britain with the force of a religious quarrel. Without examining the merits of that sterile debate, it is clearly possible to suggest

47

that Free Trade might have been advantageous to Great Britain in a period when she was the sole producer of manufactured goods, but not so convenient during a time when she was the subject of strong competition from similar produce in home and world markets. In fact, a man carries an umbrella if it is raining, but not if the sun is shining. But, any approach on such practical lines was completely excluded by the religious atmossphere with which this bogus controversy was invested by the mercantile soul which made the daily haggle of shopkeeping practice a substitute not only for constructive achievement, but, also, for ethics and faith. To-day the Labour Party is the final reduction to absurdity of that Puritan spirit which, because it had so long been accustomed to cover sharp practice in commerce by high-faluting humbug in religious protestation, finally, made business a religion. In a particularly muddled form the complex now comes out in sweeping proposals for a complete change of economic system, which everyone knows to be quite impracticable, and none have the least intention of carrying out. But the measure is invested with such religious significance, in the name of the Labour Party programme, that practical measures, to say nothing of any real drive to the great changes now necessary, are inhibited by the constant cries and warnings of impiety from the wool-clad guardians of the rose-pink shrine, when anything real has to be done.

Nationalisation is Buying Obsolete Industries at Public Expense

Such attempts as are made to carry out the " programme " assume a most characteristic form. The really safe, established industries, now verging on the obsolescent, are selected for the first experiments in Nationalisation. Experiment is scarcely the word—for the experimenting phase in these industries was undertaken generations ago by Capitalism, and they have now settled down to a respectable and sedate senescence which, in most cases, almost certainly precedes a very natural death, as new inventions and enterprises grow strong enough to replace them. Greatly daring, Labour's brand of Socialism merely takes over what Capitalism has done, as the latter is ready to move on to new fields of greater interest and far more profit. Labour, or Social Democracy, like the classic husband of Gallic comedy, is left to hold the baby for somebody else. All this would, of course, be very diverting for any spectator who was not included in the ranks of the long-suffering British taxpayers, who are always required to pay for this pompous nonsense, which provides some outlet for the wish-dreams of the Neo-Socialist, and some pretence of implementing their completely unreal programme.

The real struggle in carrying out the Labour, or Social Democratic, programme consists not in the effort to wrest some deep secret or new principle from nature in a creative endeavour, but only in the small and squalid manoeuvres which determine to what extent the Government can swindle the shareholders, whose money long ago enabled enterprising men to build the industry. Their only hope of showing a satisfactory balance-sheet in a long-established and now declining trade is to deal unfairly with those who originally created it. In so doing, of course, they offer rare encouragement to the new brains on whom they rely to create the fresh enterprise which the " Labour " controlled state is quite incapable of initiating or conducting for itself! By swindling those who have created in the past, they kill the enterprise of those on whom they depend to create in the future. As their Government is quite incapable of conceiving, let alone undertaking, any large pioneer project, it is entirely reliant on the private capitalist for that purpose. It is, therefore, a strange inducement to this enterprise on which their " Socialist " system still depends, invariably to expropriate the fruits of these labours at below the proper value, directly the concern has been built to the point of an established success.

In practice, however, as already observed, a Labour Government is saved from the full effect of these self-defeating principles by the fact that the industries they Nationalise are nearly always verging on the obsolescent. The more enterprising capitalists have, long ago, lost interest in them and have moved on a long way ahead of the pedestrian pace of the Social-

Democratic Government. Such men are always a good many jumps ahead of such a State; so, in cold fact, it is " the widow with the savings," or a similar type, who is always left to face the shock of Nationalisation and the small swindles undertaken by the Government at the expense of the shareholders, which are always represented to their cheering supporters as a death blow to the sinister capitalist. The latter, of course, is by then revelling in some great fluctuation of prices, caused by the ineptitude of the Government, which enables a quick mind to jump in and out of the market with immense profit. Some silly speech by an unwitting Labour minister, which allows the speculator to pick up a few cheap shares or commodities, provides him with a much more profitable game than lining up, with the country clergy, to find out how much of the value of their property in a nationalised industry the " strong, anti-capitalist Government " is prepared to leave them. All of this again would be very diverting to anyone who had no interest in the welfare of the State or compassion for the poor and weak: for seldom has the gap between the " real " of what truly happens, and the " unreal " of what politicians say, been so wide and so blatant.

In passing, it is well to note the effect of such a Government and system on the psychology of the *entrepreneur*. In previous times he obtained considerable reward by building a new enterprise and conducting it, in permanent forms, through ever-widening developments as new possibilities were opened by new ideas and inventions. If he could make a real success of an industry he would reap his reward and continue to draw an increasing return from a growing success. His roots were in the industry and his whole being was interwoven with the prosperity of his firm and those who worked for it. But, in present conditions, he faces the prospect of Nationalisation directly he has done all the hard work, and the industry is established to the point where it is safe and easy for the State to take over, even under the most incompetent leadership. So the psychology of the man of enterprise inevitably changes. He ceases to be an industrialist and becomes a speculator. His inclination is to take an enterprise so far and then get out. In the final phase, which Britain is now entering, he ceases to be interested in enterprise at all and becomes a pure speculator. His whole mind and energy tends to concentrate on taking full advantage of the incessant price fluctuations with which Mob blesses Money, by the chronic ineptitude of its conduct of Government. Flux, as we shall note, is the poison of the producer but the meat of the speculator.

A NEW IDEA OF STATE ACTION

We must now observe the complete contradiction between the principle of State action under a Labour, or Social-Democratic, Government and the principle of State Action which is here suggested for any realist and dynamic system. It will appear to many minds, nurtured in sound Social Democratic principles, a paradox, verging on the insane, to suggest that State-enterprise should not play the role of liquidator to the obsolescent, but pioneer in new and great enterprises too large in scope, and even too imaginative in concept, for any ordinary private enterprise to undertake. We conceive a part for the organised and organic State under dynamic direction which is more daring, and yet more wise, than to take over coal mines just as Atomic energy begins to threaten them with complete desuetude within almost measurable time, or timidly to change a few chief clerks who conduct long-established means of transport or sources of power which, now also, live under the shadow of that natural supersession which is finally the lot of all mortal achievement.

To open up an African Empire is a worthy challenge to a New State which inherits nearly one quarter of a globe, that, for generations, has been shamefully neglected. To carry the light of Europe through the shades of darkest Africa is a mission worthy of great men in leadership and of great peoples in execution. Wealth untold awaits a new challenger of chaos who grasps in firm hands the immense weapon of modern science to wrest from nature her ultimate riches in developing the untouched wastes of British Colonial Empire, and, as we shall later observe, the whole undeveloped African heritage of

51

Europe. To open the African Continent with a new system of Power and Transport is an enterprise worthier of greater peoples than to debate little paper schemes for changing the nominal management of a too-long established power and transport system in a small and ancient Island. Why does Government not even contemplate such a project?* Is it that an order of manhood of intellect, will and courage will be required for such an enterprise very different from the qualities needed to tell the public that Government had performed a financial revolution when they had merely nationalised the Bank of England, which everyone " in the know " was well aware had been nationalised for all practical purposes during many generations past. Such great things are not attempted because they mean the end of the world of talk and make-believe and the beginning of the world of reality and deed. That postulates a different system and yet more different men.

A New Idea of Empire

It involves, also, a complete change in the principles by which an Empire is conducted. Is the mission of the European to lead

---

*When this book had been written, the Government announced, after two years reflection in office, that it intended to spend £100 millions on the development of Africa. As they had previously announced, after only one year of office, " Nationalisation " schemes to buy up obsolete industries at a cost of over £2,400 millions, the argument of this book was, if anything, reinforced by this trivial piece of window-dressing. On June 28, 1947, the Oxford Economist, Mr. Roy Harrod, wrote in *The Times,* " The Economic Survey for 1947 estimates that capital outlay plus those forms of Government outlay which use up men and materials will amount to the huge sum of £3,800,000,000 (translating percentages into figures) in 1947." Therefore, if we flattered the Government so much as to believe that their African schemes would be put through in the short space of three years, their much advertised Colonial Development scheme would amount to less than one per cent. of current expenditure on capital equipment. Even this pathetic little measure was virtually enforced by the increasing difficulty of borrowing money from International Finance to import necessary foodstuffs and raw materials. This factor alone drove them away from the Internationalism in which they had always believed to make a gesture of creative work in the Empire in which they had never believed. Even now they appear to leave the respective spheres of State and Private Enterprise undefined, except for a general suggestion mankind in creative achievement, not only cultural but also material? Is our task to provide the highest with ever greater means of high achievement? Or have we a " sacred trust " to keep jungles fit for negroes to live in? Which matter most?—the peoples who have achieved everything, or the peoples who have achieved nothing?—that is the first question and it goes to the root of the matter. Are we dealing in terms of nature, reality and history, or in the entirely false values through which the will of the British people has long been enmeshed by the fatal heritage of Puritanism's pseudo-religiousness? If we are to talk in terms of negro welfare, what is the greater benefit to backward races? Is it better for the negro to have a defined and protected function, but not the leading role of which he is incapable, in the development of the African Continent? Or is it preferable that he should be called a free man, striding forward to self-government, while, in reality, he is the entirely defenceless victim of an unbridled capitalism which exploits him as cheap labour, and a bewildered recipient of religious tracts from the missionaries whom he can seldom understand, to say nothing of the blessings of alcohol and venereal disease from the

of bureaucratic control; and no precise provision is made either for the prevention of competition with Home industries, or the protection of natives from " sweating " for such purposes.

The reader is asked to contrast this petty piece of make-believe, which is as trivial in conception as it is ambiguous in plan, with the policy defined in this book, which rests on diametrically opposite principles. This policy is a more mature and complete form of proposals which were described by the author as " Imperial Socialism " in his first election, when he was returned to Parliament at the age of 22 in November, 1918, and were further developed by him in his book, *The Greater Britain,* in 1932, which founded the New Movement in England and advocated, *inter alia,* that the " Colonies should be developed on Imperial plan."

The policy was later pressed by him in numerous speeches and articles, and, finally, brought up to date in a series of articles, beginning in February, 1947, on the policy which he elaborates in the second part of this book.

Unfortunately, no chance exists that the principles and methods of the Labour Party will permit them seriously to implement that policy: we are, therefore, merely left with the danger that their present tendency to flee from their discredited internationalism may invest real policies with something of that ineffective absurdity which attaches to anything which is even remotely connected with the Labour Party.

merchants whom he soon understands all too well. In attempting in this sphere a complete reversal of all existing values, we shall, at least, have no occasion to apprehend the censure of those 135 millions of Americans who are not observed to be exclusively engaged in policing the Red Indian Reserves, which do not still occupy the entire area of the North American Continent.

The dilemma and the alternative can only be crudely and briefly suggested at this point; full examination of this deep question will be deferred to a later chapter of constructive policy. We are now only concerned with noting that Government is completely occupied with unreal measures at home, instead of engaging in a real policy of Empire and African development, which would solve British difficulties and the problem of Europe as a whole. It is clear, also, that much could be achieved by such action even if the complete reversal of principle, here suggested as our attitude to such matters, were not adopted. In fact, a policy of action could go far even under the handicap of current cant. To such a policy nothing is lacking except the will, which can only be expressed in a new system of Government and a new type in Statesmanship. Until that deep change, Britain must be content with a Government which finds it easier to bilk the widow than to build an Empire.

LABOUR—BUREAUCRACY—FINANCE

Such types as the Labour Leaders always find it easier to tie up a bunch of errors in a bundle of red tape than to organise large measures to meet a new situation. For it is the small-time muddler who relies on a stifling bureaucracy, not the deviser of great designs. We will not put it so crudely as to suggest that Government interferes in everybody else's job because they themselves are short of a job: but the jibe would have some element of truth. If Government were occupied in the root problems just briefly discussed, and the vast enterprises which should form the proper object of state activity, they would adopt a very different attitude to existing industry. Government would seek to direct the whole along the lines of National welfare and development rather than to possess a few obsolete sections of other people's past enterprises. The part of Government is direction and not management. The former requires the highest political talent; the latter can only be done by Government through a Bureaucracy. When the former is lacking, the latter tends to run the State. But this is exactly the opposite of what should occur. A Nation requires strong and imaginative political leadership; it is the function of the statesman to see further than other men and to assume responsibilities from which they shrink. But a nation, which still retains vitality, is very far from requiring the constant and fussy interference of a silly governess in the daily affairs of life; which is the only contribution of a Bureaucracy, when it swells from a small lean band of highly trained and devoted specialists to a large machine of idle but self-important mediocrities. Social democracy inevitably produces a diminution of Leadership and an accretion of Bureaucracy: it hates big men who do, and loves small men who fuss. Thus, it shrinks from the great task of directing the State and turns for a substitute to the management of long-established businesses, which are usually better conducted by those who created them.

Government has to do something, particularly if it has obtained power by absurd promises to the light-minded and credulous. If it is inhibited by lack of character and talent from performing its real task, it is bound to do something silly. It follows naturally from failure and cowardice in all real things, that the Labour Party, which has never yet dared to mention in a programme the great International Finance houses which for years past have dominated the economy of this country and much of the world, should proudly boast that it has brought under National ownership and control a Bank of England whose Governor, in actual practice and for long past, has attended the Treasury at regular intervals to obtain his instructions from Government. So a world of make-believe replaces reality in all spheres, and particularly in the realm of Finance. In this sphere Social Democracy shudders with superstitious awe when it recalls the summary end of Ramsay Macdonald's Government in 1931, and M. Blum's Government in France in 1937, when the

Financial Power decided that they had lived long enough. To make Finance the servant instead of the Master of the State is beyond the wildest ambitions of Social Democracy; they dare not even suggest a measure to bring the Finance Houses under the broad direction of the National interest. Yet to co-ordinate all operations of Finance within a Corporation constituted for the purpose, not of conducting its daily business, but of directing its larger policies in accord with the welfare of the State, is clearly as real and effective a policy as to take over the management of a few nearly obsolete industries is ineffective and divorced from all reality. Even " the big five," whom the Labour programme sometimes menaces, are conducted by men very conscious of their duty to the country, who have always done for years past exactly what the Nation required them to do. The action of Social Democracy, in Nationalising the ever dutiful and obedient and ignoring altogether the activities of some of the great International Finance Houses, is equivalent to a police force keeping all the most respectable citizens in custody while they turn a completely blind eye to the whole community of Burglars. Some method may exist in this madness if the policeman is very small and weak, because a Churchwarden is less likely to resist arrest than Bill Sykes.

The action of the Labour, or Social Democratic, Governments in the realm of Finance is a vivid illustration of their character in whole policy. By adopting what they would denounce as the Fascist device of a Finance Corporation, through which they could direct the whole policy of Finance, but not interfere in the daily conduct of a highly specialised business, they could, in practice, command the whole field of industry in this country and much industry elsewhere, as International Finance does to-day for its own purposes. They would thus occupy a dominating height, which is a key position of real power. But the heights of opportunity, and of danger, are not for such as they; they greatly prefer the comfortable crannies created long ago by other people's exertions. So they take over a row of long-established and soon obsolete industries to which some of the less competent politicians can be sent for a comfortable retirement, in much the same manner as they were despatched to the House of Lords in the less spacious days of Whig and Tory. All this, of course, has about as much relation to reality in the Atomic Age as a gas jet in a back kitchen has to the conflagration caused by a planetary collision. But, for a little while these strange survivals must populate what are misnamed the seats of power: just until something really happens.

LABOUR HAS ADOPTED THE VICES BUT NOT THE VIRTUES OF TOTALITARIANISM

The performance of the British Labour Party, in the exercise of the complete power conferred by a Parliamentary majority, is well worthy of a world study, extending far beyond the shores of the British Isles. Here, in broad parody of a passing epoch, can now be observed the final reduction to absurdity of the Social Democratic mind. Their character may be known everywhere from their handling of the great opportunity given to them by the British public in a period of weakness and weariness at the end of an exhausting war. True to type they promptly assumed the vices of their defeated opponent, but not his virtues.

Control of many aspects of National Life were temporarily necessary in Nazi Germany by reason of restricted living space and raw materials. They had, also, to support an immense burden of armament in face of a world which they conceived with some justification to be relentlessly hostile. They were obliged at the same time to make bricks without straw, in the shape of building a new economy with scanty raw materials, and to militarise the State with much diversion of exiguous resources to such purpose. That was, indeed, a situation in which Totalitarian methods were, in considerable degree, compulsive if the Nation was to survive; and, consequently, some restriction upon individual liberty could not be obviated in the period before the war. The result was, at least, to lift a bankrupt nation from the dust of economic collapse and immense unemployment to a relative height of material prosperity while, in the same period, a tremendous strength in armaments was also created.

Contrast now the performances of the Labour Government in

Britain. They promptly imposed at least as great a degree of control upon private liberty in every sphere of enterprise and business: in fact, in daily and fussy interference of the red tape mentality, they almost certainly went far further than any restrictions imposed in Nazi Germany. The main economic measures of Labour in Britain, such as Exchange Control, were directly copied from Nazi Germany. But what was the justification for these faithful copyists, in terms of relative national difficulties? Britain had an immense Empire containing every raw material and resource that industry could possibly require. She had the advantage, too, of the rich American cousin who was ready to lend millions to carry her over the period of reconstruction after the war, until her own resources could be developed. But how was that assistance used? Was the American loan spent on machinery and capital equipment to develop the boundless wealth of the Empire territory, and thus to render Britain for ever independent of any help except her own energies? Or was the dole spent on dope? Was the American loan expended in buying American tobacco and films to keep the disillusioned people quiet? At the time of writing the outline of an answer begins to take shape.

So Britain enjoyed even after the war two advantages that Nazi Germany lacked—an Empire to develop and financial assistance to do it. The fact that both these opportunities were missed in no way mitigates the offence of the Labour Government in repressing private liberty without one-tenth of the justification of necessity, which could be pleaded by the country whom the Social Democrats professed to be fighting in the cause of "Liberty." A man who is fighting for his life in circumstances of almost insuperable difficulty has some reason for getting a bit rough. A pampered invalid, who is being propped up by rich relations until he is strong enough again to enjoy the ample meal of his own vast resources, has no such justification: and no better excuse is provided if, instead of taking any advantage of this extraordinary opportunity, he then proceeds to make a consummate ass of himself by wasting every chance in the most frivolous possible fashion.

Who now can deny the gravamen of the charge that "Labour" in power took over the vices of Totalitarianism in restriction of personal liberty, but not the virtues of that system. For none can deny that the Nazis, at least, wrested from almost impossible circumstances both a relatively high level of material prosperity for their peoples and a National strength which was adequate to resist a world in arms for nearly six years. Much may be forgiven to men who achieve, which is not forgiven to men who do not. In these conditions the mass of the people is right to say, "If we have to be bossed about, let us be commanded by a man who will get us somewhere, and not by a silly pack of little creatures who are giving orders for no clear purpose beyond the satisfaction of their own small vanities and fussy pomposities." Restriction with achievement may be hard to endure, but loss of liberty without achievement is unendurable. That is the situation of Britain under the complete power of Social Democracy; and it is a lesson for mankind to note.

TRUE CONCEPT OF SOCIALISM:
STATE ENTERPRISE NOT STATE RESTRICTION

The absurd failure of Labour is the fatality of the Nation, and a recurrence of such experience can only be avoided by a reversal of all existing values. In summary, the function of the State is neither to take over and manage obsolete industries, originally created by Capitalism, nor to interfere in the daily conduct of business with endless rules and regulations. The great part of the State is to be a pioneer in enterprise too large for private industry to undertake and, also, perhaps, too daring and imaginative to be conceived or executed by any qualities inferior to that supreme degree of will and intellect, which only a complete change in the structure of the State, and the outlook of the people, can summon to the service of a nation.

The task of the Organic State under great direction is to open vast areas of undeveloped resources by measures of a magnitude which recent Science makes possible. Thus engaged, in all main energies, the State will not indulge in fussy interference with private business. The true concept of State

Socialism is State enterprise not State restriction. It is, of course, necessary that all private enterprise shall operate within the boundaries of the welfare of the Nation as a whole; but within these limits it should be entirely free. It is vital, too, that the Organic State should secure a progressive increase in the standard of life as science and new industrial development increase the power to produce. If wages and salaries, as well as the profits of industrialists whose enterprise and energies deserve reward, are not increased in proportion to the growth of productive potential, trade fails for lack of a market and collapse ensues. The mechanism required for that purpose we have elsewhere explained in detail, and new and larger aspects of these possibilities will be examined in this book in the light of changes which experience suggests, and in view of the great developments which further and deeper thought has engendered in the long opportunity of recent years. In brief, the mass of the people can only share in the benefits which modern science can bring through the devoted service of those whom they entrust with the task of Government, and who are armed by the people with the necessary new system of the State. To secure that service they must not only create a new system of the State, but must also produce an altogether new and higher type of man, who is dedicated in whole life and purpose to the service of the people and the State; the latter is by far the harder task. But these studies belong to a subsequent section of this book.

THE PACE OF THE SLOWEST—REWARD BY RESULT

For the purpose of this analysis of failure we must now examine another factor of Social Democratic policy by which every law of nature is frustrated and the pace of the quickest is dragged back to suit the laggard footsteps of the slowest: for this is the principle on which all Social Democratic action is based. Their whole thought is in terms of minima and not maxima: their main concern is not that the efficient man should earn what he deserves, but that the inefficient man should earn what they think is enough; and " enough " is always an arbitrary figure resting on the calculation how much the " non-doer " can squeeze out of the "doers" in any given state of society or moral feeling. It may be that compassion should shelter life's ineffectives from the harsh law of nature within a civilised society. Those deep ethical questions, which react so strongly on biological considerations, will be discussed at a later stage. But we have to recognise that anything of the kind is a reversal of natural law which speedily eliminates such types by very familiar processes, and that progress, to date, in the long terms of History and Science, has largely depended on this operation. If, therefore, they are protected from the action of natural laws within a civilised society, it is all the more important that the type, which would normally replace them in conditions of natural struggle, should not be artificially discouraged.

Yet this is precisely what happens under Social Democracy; not only are the weak preserved but the strong are enchained; not only is the inefficient protected from the result of his failure to produce and to fulfil the demands of life, but the efficient is too often penalised for his capacity thus to serve the country by the removal of all incentive to exercise his ability. Nearly all reward is fixed in terms of minima, which tends naturally to be what the least efficient is capable of earning, or, in many cases, of earning with the assistance of more vigorous members of the team in which he is working. Innumerable rules and regulations are familiar to all who have studied these questions, whereby able men are actually prevented from producing more than a given amount in a given time. It is typical that, when a maximum is fixed, it is a limitation and not a target. In such instance, of course, an immense volume of production in the aggregate is lost. Further, it is plain that in practice the fixing of a limitation to production within a given period tends to fix a standard even below the average. For, if an average rate of production were made the standard, half of those employed would not be able to reach it. Consequently, any fixed standard of the kind which has become such a widespread practice in British industry tends not to be an average but a minimum. Thus every natural law is completely reversed, because the prevailing standard becomes that of the weakest and not that of the strongest.

As a civilisation tends to approximate in character ever closer to the prevailing ethic by which it is guided, a Society which considers it right to adopt such practices tends ever more to become a community of the weak and not of the strong. Consequently, not only do appeals for greater production in the short terms of practical politics become ever more futile, but, in the longer term of race and nation, the stock becomes ever more feeble. What other results, either in the short or the long view, can ensue from these practices, which inevitably follow the declared principles of those Social Democratic Parties who now rule Britain and most of Europe? Again, a reversal of all values is a necessity of progress and even of survival. The basic principle must be that reward is directly related to result. It must prevail in every sphere, ranging from the highest grade of management and technical abilities to the entirely unskilled manual worker. In a great variety of circumstances the principle is by no means difficult to work out. For instance, in any kind of team work, which excludes a precise individual assessment of effort, the appropriate reward can go to the team as a whole. The workers in question will very quickly settle the individual apportionment on a satisfactory basis, if left to themselves without interference from the now omnipresent government. The first act of effective government in present circumstances would be to relate all payment to result and make illegal all restrictions of production.

CONCEPT OF SERVICE. THE FUNCTION OF BEAUTY

This principle of reward according to service should apply not only in industry but in every region of national life. Would anyone now, in theory at any rate, deny the principles: — " All shall work and thus enrich their country and themselves: opportunity shall be open to all, but privilege to none: great position shall be only conceded to great talent: reward shall be accorded only to service." The reader must be warned against accepting such principles as plain commonsense, for they are extracted from the objects of British Union, which were first published in 1932 under a storm of denunciation. Fewer now will deny, at any rate, that reward should be accorded only to service and that it should be broadly proportionate to the service rendered.

It is obvious that the true concept of service is not limited to the production of commodities. It must even be extended so far as to embrace the desire to make life more beautiful, if such an idea is not too astonishing to the contemporary mind. In fact, it is even conceivable that in a really civilised community it would be a recognised function of a considerable number of gifted people to be wholly dedicated to the discovery and development of fresh forms of the beautiful. It would be well worth the while of any society animated by the finer values to place great resources at the disposal of such people. Their high task would be to show the world how beautiful life could be. The Artist in life would be honoured only less than the Artist of eternal beauty in music and the plastic arts. It was some rather dimly held idea of this kind which was used in earlier days to justify the main-tenance of a hereditary aristocracy which drew considerably upon the resources of the community. Any such Order which is based wholly on heredity—unqualified by a requisite standard of talent—is open to grave objection. An elite can only be guarded against a futile decadence and guided towards ever higher forms by a constant and rapid efflux of the unworthy, balanced by an influx of new vigour from any quarter which possesses the desired qualities.

Heredity can be made to play a far greater part in the attain-ing of new heights of human achievement than has yet been fully realised. But it must be tempered by selection, which discards the unfit and attracts new resources. The objection to a static and ossified Aristocracy has long been valid in Great Britain. There may be some argument in favour of a Society which shows the world how beautiful life can be, but few reasons exist for the maintenance of a Society which shows the world how silly life can be. Yet, that is the inevitable effect upon such a Society of a system which fails to discard the unfit and unworthy, and only draws to itself reinforcements from the sphere of Money, which possesses precisely the opposite qualities to those required by any Order dedicated to Public Service and the pursuit of

Beauty. But these considerations belong not to an analysis of failure but to the construction of a system of values which are a reversal of existing values, and to an Idea of Life far beyond the present concept. For present purposes, we should merely note the suggestion that the relation of reward, and manner of life, to some form of service must extend far beyond the industrial regions to embrace every sphere of existence. In industry the matter is pressing; for it is now patent that a system which reduces the pace of the quickest to that of the slowest is fast becoming a disaster. All incentive is destroyed, and all initiative slowly withers, beneath a principle which denies every normal impulse of man and violates every law of original nature.

SPARTACISM

How came it that this insane paradox became such a rigid fixture in the Social Democratic mind? The reader must forgive again a slight digression into the realms of psychology, and contain his incredulous surprise, for a brief period, when we suggest that in Social Democracy the Spartacist outlook is added to our old friend the Oedipus-Puritan complex, and that the infelicitous combination adds up to a muddle and a futility on a scale which truly approaches the perfect of its kind.

We have already analysed the origin of that great inhibition of the British ruling class which obstructs all achievement of higher forms by a resistance to any consistent policy of energy and action and, in particular, by an almost pathological dislike of the type of man who is likely to secure results, except in time of war. We have further noted that, in relatively static societies, the character of a ruling elite, or dominant minority, is likely to impose itself upon the whole community and especially upon new aspirants for place, if not power. These considerations have greatest validity in a society which is both static and addicted to snobbery, and both these conditions have long been present to the English scene. Consequently, it has often been the subject of public observation, and private merriment, that the middle and working class leadership of the Labour Party has been most concerned assiduously to ape the manners and adopt the outlook of their nominal opponents. Some of them always succumb to the last Platonic test of pleasure, directly the exertions of their supporters have lifted them within reach of opportunity. Hence, a sense of personal zest is added to political relief when, in any period of crisis, they can find excuse to escape the more onerous responsibility of office by entering into a Coalition with the Conservatives. By every inclination of public and private character they assume the intellectual and spiritual make-up— the whole colour and texture—of the force which they are supposedly out to destroy.

These tendencies have frequently reached the grotesque proportions of caricature. It is, consequently, not surprising again to find in the Labour Leadership most of the faults of the Aristocracy and few of the good qualities, such as they are. In particular, they have taken over from the British ruling class the traditional hatred of the executive character, and have accentuated that dislike and resistance to the " Doer " by attributes which are a speciality of their own Party. For, the movement behind the smooth and respectable facade of the middle class Labour Leadership has one deep-rooted instinct, and that is, hatred of the figure which it calls " the boss." The origin of this feeling was in many cases very well founded upon the treatment of the working class in the early days of the British Industrial Revolution, which was often vile beyond belief. They gradually won some emancipation by the struggles of their own early Trade Unionism which began as a liberator and, as so often happens, in later development shows many signs of becoming in turn a Tyrant. It should also in fairness be noted that earlier members of the Aristocracy, such as Lord Shaftesbury, added a sense of duty and responsibility to privilege, and played a leading part in combating the conditions which then oppressed the people.

The attitude towards the employer or " boss " is, therefore, easily understood in origin; but it was so branded on the soul of the working class that it became in the present-day another " complex " to add to the disturbed psyche of the British people. So, a pathological dislike for any commanding figure, who might be conceived as giving them orders, was added in the national character to the positively diseased dislike of the British ruling class for any executive character, who appeared likely to disturb their prosperous lethargy or disrupt their smug complacency by introducing the active creed of the " doer " to the Blessed Isles of their comfortable repose. The working class continued to resist such characters because they feared they might " boss them about "; the Aristocracy because they feared they might wake them up. From such diverse processes of the subconscious mind was built up the granite resistance of British psychology both to deeds and to men of deeds, except, of course, when they became absolutely necessary in time of wars, which were engendered by even fiercer hatreds of energetic foreigners. If any man thinks this picture is a caricature or even overdrawn, let him try to get something done in England.

In such circumstances it was only surprising that " Doers " got as far as they did in normal times in Britain; but nine-tenths of their energies had naturally to be devoted to breaking through resistance and only the remainder was left for the constructive task. So, to the Oedipus-Puritan complex of the governing class was added the " Spartacist " outlook of the man who has but recently revolted from a condition approaching slavery, and is very conscious of his still unfamiliar emancipation. This is the type on whose lips is ever the most familiar slogan of contemporary English life: " I'm as good as him "; to which the answer is quite simply: " Yes, when you have done as much " —or it would be the conclusive answer in any society which rested not on privilege but on the proved service of tested talent. This universal tendency to be animated by envy and to deny admiration was the subject of adverse comment by the leading philosophic mind which has been directly identified with the " Left " in Great Britain. This objective thinker was moved to observe that the qualities most required in the present world were " more admiration and less envy " and to quote with something approaching approval the famous dictum of Heraklitus that " every citizen of Ephesus deserved to be hanged because they would suffer no man to be first among them " (and they had not the excuse of living on a sheltered island which had enjoyed a Cromwell and been blessed by his lesser following of money-grubbing psalm-singers).

THE " AGE OF THE COMMON MAN "

This psychology has to be noted as a powerful factor in present world affairs because it is dominant in the " Left " of both Britain and America. In France too it has been a strong instinct, by reason of the execrable treatment of many of the people before the Revolution; but, it has been balanced, and often overcome, by an intermittent creative urge which has sought and supported great men and vigorous policies.

The strong phobias and deep wishes, which are associated with this psychology, entirely inhibit any realistic thinking in "Left" politics, and lead to conclusions and policies which are manifestly the result not of reflection but of desire. From such tendencies arises the slogan of the " Age of the Common Man," which in relation to current fact is plainly idiotic. The present prospect may be good or bad—for the moment that is beside the point—but that catch-cry is plainly at variance with all observable evidence of the present world. Just as pure mind, in the shape of science and a new type of political intellect which is competent to work with it to mould new forms from its discoveries, emerges as entirely dominant in terms of power realities, strange little figures of the chattering " Left " run to and fro announcing that the day of " the Common Man " has at last begun. It is, of course, obvious that the day of the common man is just coming to an end and that the day of the uncommon man is about to begin. At last mind prevails over mass, and brain replaces brawn; quality will be everything and quantity next to nothing. The people will only be able to realise their desires through the service of exceptional men. These are the terms of reality in a new age, and neither talk nor desire can alter them. Finally, too, the system of the State must be fitted to reality. But these considerations belong to the constructive phase of this study, and we must return to the analysis of breakdown in " Democratic " psychology and life with which we are immediately concerned.

CONSERVATIVE CHARACTER OF LABOUR LEADERSHIP

We were regarding the transient phenomenon of the British Labour Party whose middle-class leadership has taken over the values of the ruling class, but whose mob support impels them to go forward under the impact of Spartacist pressure. Is it too much to say that the Labour, or Social Democratic, Party alternates between Snobbism and Spartacism? Let us examine this proposition and its results, if it be established.

May we postulate that four main reasons once existed for a man of some ability to join the British Labour Party, or equivalent Social Democratic Movement elsewhere. The first has been almost eliminated by the grotesque failure of such Movements, under the actual test of experience, to achieve anything; but it was formerly a powerful factor. In Britain, in particular, no means previously existed to get anything done except through the Labour Party. It was the only possible expression of the " will to achievement," which we shall define in Part II of this Book. A man, who was animated by high idealism in politics and moved by warm compassion for the suffering masses, had no means to work except through the Social Democratic Movement. There alone, it appeared, he could express himself in great constructive achievement, as other artists express themselves in music or the plastic arts. Conservatism was too plainly a mere negation to provide any alternative for such spirits to a Party which was born of the determination of the working class to escape from avoidable evils and which, therefore, in original essence was a dynamic movement. Here was the means to implement ideals in great service, and to express great abilities in the way of nature by great achievement. In the sterile days of the old " Democracy " the " Will to Achievement " had no possible outlet except in the Labour Party.

In the present phase, of course, it is plain that such a level of will and ability will never again be at the disposal of such a party. The frustration of actual experience has been too great and too obvious to any newcomers of that calibre ever to permit a fresh attraction of such types. Also, as we shall later observe, in the analysis of the new figure requisite to the future, the " Will to Achievement " man is so far a relatively rare phenomenon on this earth; when he comes he will now be drawn, as a steel filing adheres to a magnet, towards a world of idea and action which is very remote from Social Democracy. The Leadership of the Labour Party will, therefore be dependent on the three remaining types which now comprise it and may be broadly defined. The first is the Conservative working man who can find no place in the Conservative Party; this is the fundamental character of the Labour Leadership. Such is still the structure of Conservatism that a man from the working class has little chance of making much headway in face of the absurd social snobbery of that Party; and all experience, so far, proves that he has not a hope in the world of aspiring to the leadership. In the preponderant politics of Britain the underlying prejudice against the working man is as foolish and self-stultifying as the equivalent feeling against an aristocrat in the politics of France. Realism will use every man of genius or talent without regard to the accident of birth.

As a result of this situation, the Conservative working man in Britain must go to the Labour Party because he has nowhere else to go. Since the Conservative type, at any rate until recent times, has formed the big majority of the working class, nearly all the abler members of that class take themselves and their Conservatism into the governing hierarchy of the Labour Party, and, by reason of their majority influence, command its policy. They have acquired in high degree the spirit of the great negation from the old ruling class, whose values are still stamped on the whole national life by the prevailing snobbery which accentuates, in Britain, the customorary dominance of a small " elite." The solid phalanx of Conservative working men in the inner circle of Labour consequently presents an impenetrable barrier to the dynamism of any achievement man, who, for reasons given above, is, or was, temporarily drawn to that party. It is true that the latter can sway against them by oratory and writing the mass of the Labour rank and file on some great issue which vitally affects the desire and struggle of the working class to better things. But the Conservative element in the Labour Party, who possess the machine, always have the last word by the casting of the great block vote of the " Trade Unions," which completely dominates, by physical mass, the mind and will of the political rank and file on the all-decisive occasion of a Party Conference. In fact, the Labour Party is the only party in Great Britain which is so constructed that it is physically, or mechanically, impossible for dynamic leadership, with the support of the political rank and file, to prevail against the great negation. In the case of the Labour Party that dominant factor in English life is accentuated by the addition of the Spartacist complex to the Oedipus-Puritan values which the old ruling class have imposed on the national outlook.

It is true that the working class leadership of the Labour Party is usually Conservative in instinct, but it still possesses, at least, the subconscious hatred of the " Boss," which derives from long and deep memories of working-class struggle against past oppression. Scratch but a little the smug and portly figure of a Labour leader, seated in affluent ease and automatic *bonhommie* at the tables of those whom he likes to think the great (because they possess much money), and you will find the " Spartacist." That spirit of revolt, which is never far from the surface, naturally does not express itself in terms of achievement to lift the masses from whose suffering it is sprung: any expression of creative revolt takes a man very far from the ranks of Social Democracy, as many dynamic men of working class origin have proved in recent times. No, Spartacism, in the Labour Leader, is not positive but purely negative. The object of hatred is no longer the man who may oppress his supporters, but the man who may command him to exert himself in doing something for these masses to whom he owes all. The hatred of the Boss is transferred from the employer to the leader figure; it is the call to effort the mediocrity now fears. The Labour Leader has joined the blessed company of the comfortable and complacent and his values are now those of the " Will to

Comfort." All his energies are consequently concentrated on opposing the " Disturber ": and this ordinary ruling class reflex of resistance to the " Daemon " is enhanced in the Labour Leader by the dark atavistic memory that he has once been bullied. To his eyes any sceptre of power can never be the wand which opens closed doors to reveal new visions; it merely bears the semblance of a whip. So, to the resentment of the Oedipus-Puritan is added the apprehension of the Spartacist. Yet some still believe that the Labour Party can be made into a creative instrument.

THE CHAMELEON QUALITIES OF ARISTOCRATS AND ACADEMICS IN THE LABOUR PARTY

The third type to be found in the Labour hierarchy embodies in high degree those quietest and, indeed, chameleon qualities which were acquired by the Aristocracy round the time of the the Reform Bill. From the moment that the great Duke of Wellington " thrust his hat on his head " and announced that " the Government must be carried on " the old British ruling class decided to compromise and not to fight. By his sense and realism this Aristocracy were saved from the blood-stained course of France; yet they changed, thereby, at first imperceptibly, but, in the end entirely, their own character. They were wiser than the French Aristocrats of that period and consequently saved their necks: further, if they no longer had the genius to lead their age, compromise with the new forces was really the only alternative left to them. When the dynamism of history impels great changes, high character and talent feel inspired to mould them for high creative purposes: no such constructive impulse was present in the British governing class at that time. Chatham and a few of the " Pros " had presented them with an Empire; and they had used the proceeds to frustrate Napoleon. So that was enough for the moment: now for a quiet life! The ardently desired quietism was only to be gained by assimilating the appearance, if not the qualities, of the new " Democratic " forces, to which they lacked the vigour and ability to present a more vital and constructive alternative.

So, as time went on, the old British ruling class became more and more " democratic " in manners, if not in life; the latter only became compulsory after their second world war.

Thus quietism was only secured by the assumption of a chameleon character: they took their colour from whatever was the " thing " at the moment. That was the final expression of conformity to the dominant force of an age which they could no longer impress with their own thought and purpose, because they lacked both. No doubt, that hearty good-fellowship with whatever was " going " was at first a pose designed to circumvent forces in national life which they secretly despised, but did not feel strong enough openly to challenge. The dope of easy-going nonsense to the effect that everyone could get on well together, and keep gradually moving forward, provided no one got rough and asked for too much, was originally concocted for the masses to swallow: and eagerly it is still gulped down by Labour Leaders when handed to them in a golden cup by what they fondly imagine to be a " real gentleman." But it appears to be an evolutionary law that you cannot talk nonsense for many generations without beginning to believe it yourself. A consistent habit, deliberately acquired for a specific purpose, in time alters character as surely as the habits imposed on animals by physical environment were observed by Lamarck ultimately to affect their physical structure. To put it crudely, you cannot lie too often and too long without beginning to believe the lie. In fact, the most effective humbugs in British Public Life appear usually to adopt the preliminary precaution of deceiving themselves before they deceive the people; it works better like that.

However, we are dealing here not with the occasionally delusive effects of rhetoric upon the orator, but with an ingrained social attitude, at first deliberately assumed for transient purposes of self-defence, but later fixated by over-use into a permanent and debased character. For, fundamentally, it is the character of an imitator and sycophant, and, by its acquisition, the old Aristocracy loses the last possible excuse for existence. Whether we use the term Aristocracy in the false meaning of an accident of social class or in the true meaning of the " best "—an elite selected for high function—no shadow of a reason can be conceived for the continuance of such a body if it ceases to contribute any leadership, intellectual, moral, or spiritual, but is content to be a humble camp-follower of Mobs in return for a few obsolete privileges. Such is now the position of most of the British Aristocracy as a result of acquiring the character of a chameleon in pursuit of quietism. The potion was originally brewed for the masses by the original hard and, indeed Macchiavellian, realism of the governing class, but the poisoned chalice was later handed back to their own heirs, and a spiritually, but not physically, degenerate generation swallowed it complacently with a tired gesture of life weariness, in final abdication of their only possible life function. It is interesting to note that the French Aristocracy preferred breaking to bending: yet came again, not to politics but to science, with an extraordinary efflorescence of genius which became one of the glories of Europe. They declined from the days of Louis XIV to those of Louis XVI; they could not lead, but only oppose to the end; Fate struck them down and pruned them back to the earth: then, fresh shoots of the great stock reached out in new direction toward the sun of high achievement. In the end, the line of least resistance is never the most fruitful; and, undoubtedly, it is better, at least, to strive throughout to direct events rather than for a time to become their victim. However, the quality of striving and the uses of adversity, belong to a later stage of this study.

At the moment we are concerned in tracing the evolution, or rather devolution of the character of the British ruling class from the Elizabethan revival of the eighteenth century to the quietism of the present day. In particular, we must here note the effect of this change upon the Labour Party. That strange miscellany is touched in two respects by this profound transformation of character in the old ruling class. In the first instance, the flexibility, adaptability, and general affability of manners in that class are well designed to excite the snobbism, but assuage the Spartacism, of the Labour Leaders. The oleaginous embrace leaves behind it the taste of a "comrade" rather than the impress of a master. Whether in a coalition with Conservatives, or in a closer association, Social

Democracy finds it easy to get on with these good fellows, who have such an unassuming demeanour and a great readiness to oblige in quite a variety of ways. Particularly, in moments of crisis it makes it easier to hand over effective control to the Conservative Party without those feelings of resentful inferiority which are excited by the high degree of talent and energy that labours under the democratic disability of not suffering fools gladly. In the second instance, this change in upper-class character facilitates the entry of most genuine, if mediocre, characters from that class into the ranks of the Labour Party. They have no idea whatever of large constructive purposes, and feel no call from the dynamism of the suffering mass to any real creative achievement. They contain no element of the first type we considered in this connection: the " Will to Achievement " man. But this third type—the aristocrats in the Labour Party—have usually a well-developed sense of service, and are perfectly sincere in their beliefs as they trot behind the Spartacist Mob, picking up the odds and ends it has dropped and trying, in the most conscientious fashion, to discover whether anything useful can be done with them.

They were soon joined by the fourth type in the shape of a quaint collection of Professors, who were mostly not quite good enough for the Universities. They found in the Labour Party an inexhaustible market for the more sterile academic qualities: Labour loves a " Don " as dearly as the Middle Classes used " to love a Lord "; and has just about the same capacity for distinguishing the genuine variety. This type of second-grade University Professor often carries the now prevailing middle-class sycophancy of the working class to a grotesque degree of caricature. Mr. Disraeli's historic enquiry of a nonentity in the Lobby " How is the old complaint? " was founded on the assurance that every aging politician suffers in some such fashion, and will mistake for a flattering memory what is only a shrewd surmise. So the cynical professor may to-day be heard to enquire of the Labour Member, " How is the family? " in the equally perspicacious certainty that the enquiry will evoke from the object of present solicitude (and future voting strength for the

Party executive) a flood of minor domestic anecdotes which may be tedious to hear but, at least, save the assiduous climber to favour from the exertion of further mountaineering. This new type becomes quite a classic of the time as he strolls through the eternal lobby of spiritual negation, his arm round the neck of some working-class " comrade," who is too gratified to note the negroid roll toward some more profitable client of those cold, dead eyes, which shine only with trivial lust of petty power. Is this caricature—do you say young Englishmen? My answer is—go into the Labour Party and try to get things done. But it is a pity to waste good years in finding out. Can you not judge them by results and save the time?

LABOUR AS PACE MAKER FOR COMMUNISM

The purpose of this brief survey of the character of the Labour Party is to illustrate the essential dualism of that Party, and of all Social Democratic Movements in all lands, which results in a great variability of conduct in differing circumstances and in an inevitable instability. It is unnecessary to add that the Labour Party need not even be considered as a possible factor in any real and conscious achievement: the significance of that Party resides only in the forces for which it prepares the way by the chaos it is bound to create. The dualism of the Labour character consists of the Snobbism and the Spartacism: the first factor is paramount in normal times, but the latter becomes dominant in a period of stress and collapse, as the rank and file passes, under the pressure of events, towards Communist leadership. The ordinary leadership types in the Labour Party, whom we have just regarded, are well enough content to sit comfortably in the seats of Whitehall respectability as long as they can, in a perpetual posture of affable surprise at having so unexpectedly attained an eminence so entirely undeserved. All goes serenely and sedately until things begin to happen: the "things" are, of course, the angry stirring of the masses to whom they owe their position.

Soon the latter begin to demand the implementing of foolish and dishonest promises, as they suffer the economic pressure of the gathering crisis, which the ineptitude of their leadership accentuates.

75

The response of the Labour Leadership is two-fold and characteristic: some feel an irresistible desire to " run to father " in the shape of a Conservative coalition: others feel impelled to angry resentment at the harsh strokes of Fate, which they can never ascribe to their own failings, and move further to the " Left " for a link up with the Communists. The bulk of the Party feel pulled in both directions at the same time, and are, consequently, at once paralysed by fear and rendered hysterical by anger. So, the opposing tension of Snobbism and Spartacism, during crisis, results, in terms of Party fortune, at best in complete immobility and, at worst, in final disruption and fragmentation. As the one coherent instinct of the Leadership at that time is to keep the Party together—no Party, no jobs— they are inclined just to sit tight before crisis like a rabbit in front of a boa-constrictor. But, not so the rank and file: they have been filled with promises and their stomachs are now empty of anything else: no sitting tight for them; their economic position will not permit it. In growing despair the masses look for new leadership and they find it in Communism; if no effective alternative is in a position to enter the field.

The latter possibility must await later consideration in this work, with the passing note that the emergence of any truly vital and really constructive alternative to Communism will in Britain encounter the maximum possible initial difficulty by reason of the deep-rooted complexes and phobias of the ruling class against any effective force of real achievement, and still more against any dynamic personalities who are necessary to implement it. These tendencies have already been analysed at length together with that impress of the " elite " on the present character of the Nation, which is still more marked in Britain than in most countries. It will need a very great pressure of events to change their psychology sufficiently to remove their opposition to anything except entirely bogus movements and still more bogus men of their own creation, who might mollify the usual jealous animosity by their fundamental ineffectiveness of character, but would leave the national situation even worse than they found it, despite every effort of the Press, which might lift them to high position, but could never hold them there.

The interest of the matter rests not in the consequent suicide of the ruling class (which is immaterial, except for the loss of a strong stock that still holds great possibilities for the future if it were redeemed from false values) but in the irretrievable ruin, moral and material, which the victory of Communism must entail, with particular force of disaster in the case of these crowded Western Isles.

Our task at this juncture, in a survey of the composition and character of the Labour Party, is merely to record the ineluctable fact that a party so misconceived in whole structure, and so perverted in every value of life, can only in the ultimate analysis of crisis perform one of two roles: the first is to be a sycophant of Conservatism and the second is to be a pace-maker for Communism. In practice, Labour begins by playing the first part, but ends by performing the latter. In ordinary, the arriviste working class and middle-class leadership of the party, of course, prefer the first course as the natural expression of their comfortably ambitious quietism, and in normal times they can hold fast to the desires of their type. But the will of the suffering masses to better things is a force deeply opposed in real nature to the smug wishes of the Bourgeois leadership. In time of crisis that dynamism of the mass breaks through to true expression in some creed of reality, and the quaint small figures of gilded straw and painted cardboard vanish overnight, as the great wind blows through the little places that once knew them —in search of truth.

SOCIAL DEMOCRACY ALWAYS BRINGS CHAOS

The question of Truth belongs to the second part of this book: we are here concerned with an analysis of Failure, and particularly with that final *reductio ad absurdum* of Social Democracy, which is a Labour Government in full power in Great Britain. It passes from Snobbism to Spartacism under pressure of the discontented masses as the results of its errors begin to mature. The Nationalisation of obsolete industries has no effect on national life, except that they are run rather less efficiently by the Bureaucrats than by the Capitalists who created them and had to stand or fall by their success. The mass of the Party supporters are amazed and disillusioned to find that the golden panacea of substituting State-paid clerks for big-business-paid clerks in long ossified concerns has no immediate effect except a slight deterioration in service: particularly the workers in those industries become shocked to find that conditions are little different, but the conduct of business is less efficient by those who have no personal interest in the results. So the State concern is either subsidised by the taxpayer, with further strain on the general economy, or is the subject of universal discontent. Labour then turns to the only method by which it can obtain immediate, if temporary, results for its supporters. The chief organ of the Labour Party, the *Daily Herald,* once wrote " We have learnt, not that a reforming Government cannot make a system of partly private enterprise work, but that it cannot make it work to-day without a constantly inflationary pressure . . . " The present writer put it rather differently at the time: " Any fool can inflate, and, appropriately enough, this is the only remedy now left to the Labour Party " (*To-Morrow We Live,* published 1938). The result is plenty of money but no plan to direct it to useful channels. Spending of the most foolish kind becomes rampant while the Black Market flourishes and goods are short. Prices outstrip wages, and demands from the workers become stronger for increased purchasing power to secure goods which do not exist. The spiral begins, and leads to the classic inflationary catastrophe unless speedily checked by the opposite folly of a deflationist monetary policy, which is gradually forced upon the weak executive, despite every asseveration that they would never again adopt it. Whether it be inflation followed by deflation, or inflation to the point of crash, the only result is a more or less extreme fluctuation of prices.

We observed in greater detail in previous books, that the only beneficiary from price fluctuations is the speculator who lives by buying at the bottom and selling at the top, with all the fancy variations of that theme which financial ingenuity has devised in a variety of zoological similes. The big racketeers make vast profits by legal financial speculation, and the small racketeers make commensurate profits from the illegal black market: the game is, in essence, the same whether played in full light at the " big table " or in twilight under the counter. Speculators alone benefit from the muddled weakness of a Labour Government: however admirable the personal probity of individual ministers may be it is no coincidence that " Stavisky " accompanies the final expression of Social Democracy in Government. The policy and method of such a Government is bound to create a paradise for the racketeer and a hell for their supporters. When business is paralysed by the universal interference of a governing bureaucracy, unaccompanied by any plan or real grip of Executive Government, production slows up and goods are short. In the end this means suffering for the worker and an opportunity for the racketeer in shortages: in cold fact: hell for the worker and heaven for the speculator.

There is no other result of a Labour Government by reason of its principles, policy and practice, and, above all, by nature of the personnel produced by values which are deeply false. The time and degree of catastrophe may vary for many reasons, such as the presence or absence of foreign financial support: but, over a short or long period, and in large or small measure, according to contemporary circumstance, such is the only end of a Labour, or Social Democratic, Government: which is left to itself and is not temporarily saved by one or other of its two guardian angels—High Finance or War—or that blissful union of the two which saves Labour Leaders and their Spartacist Mobs from the painful necessity of any further thought. Thus, whether it be peace or war, the role of most Labour Leaders is to " make the pace " for Communism once they have ceased under mass pressure to be the mere sycophants of Conservatism.

DIFFERENCE BETWEEN COMMUNISM AND FASCISM

We shall observe in the next chapter that Communism benefits as much as Finance from price fluctuation: instability is essential in the first phase to the profit of Finance and in the final phase to the triumph of Communism. Consciously or unconsciously these two forces are eternally complementary, because the basic requirements of their success begin by being the same. They are entirely antithetical to any stable system in which the producer of every type can thrive and prosper by his contribution to the commonweal. They are yet more hostile to those calm and abiding values of the spirit through which alone the tradition of European culture can aspire to grow, deep-rooted in the soil of two continents, to the further and limitless glory of mankind. It was always a superficial folly to contend that Fascism and Communism were, in any degree, identical: it would be yet more absurd to assert that the ideas of this book, which reach beyond both Fascism and Democracy, have even the remotest similarity to Communism, because they prefer plan to muddle and grip to drift. The only thing which Fascism and Communism have ever possessed in common was a very diverse answer to current chaos: but the answers were fundamentally different and the alternatives sharply antithetical. Fascism was the answer of the West and Communism was the answer of the East; the first was conceived by Europeans; the latter by an Oriental. Fascism swept to power within a few years of its birth in three of the most advanced countries in Europe, directly they felt impelled to find an answer to disaster which was a natural expression of Western Man. Communism, after a century of struggle, failed to approach power in any European country; and only succeeded in the oriental land which borders Europe, by employing many of the commonplace methods of Eastern despotism under a veneer of Western propaganda forms, which the leaders had picked up in exile and invested with some of that euphonious but meaningless jargon of pseudo mysticism that comes so readily to their racial type.

Between these two creeds lay the vast gulf which divides the West from the East. The divergence is, of course, rendered greater by recent history: and the idea beyond Fascism, which this book formulates, passes into a sphere which is inconceivable for Communism and the whole psychology that gave it birth.

The old differences were plain enough; the new differences go deeper still. It was ever the practice of Communism to destroy everything before attempting to build anew: as all technical ability was wiped out in the insensate fury of class war, such capacities had later to be purchased from abroad, and the work of construction was impeded and retarded. Fascism, on the other hand, was prepared to assimilate everything that was good and vital in the State it took over: high abilities from any class were used if they were prepared to leave the faction and serve the State. All existing capacities and merits of the nation were not discarded, but woven into the pattern and fabric of the new design. Only the outworn, the useless and the corrupt were eliminated; the dead wood was ruthlessly cut away, but the live and the good was carefully preserved and nurtured. From this profound difference in method followed inevitably two factors, which were entirely to the advantage of Fascism in this comparison. The first was that any results were obtained far more quickly by this technique than by the clumsy surgery of Communism. The second was that it, thereby, became possible for Fascism to govern a highly developed state without producing that collapse which the Communist destruction of all existing abilities would inevitably entail in an advanced community.

It is one thing to take over a backward Eastern State, resting on a broad basis of peasant population: it is quite another to be given power in a highly evolved industrial organism, resting on a basis of skilled technicians. In the first it is possible, although at great loss, to begin by eliminating the few specialists who exist: the rural masses still carry on in a primitive society, even if breakdown and famine wipe out many millions, as in Russia. In the second, it is impossible arbitrarily to discard all existing skill without bringing immediate and total collapse. For that reason it was only possible for Communism to succeed in Russia without complete disaster. The only modern movement in 1939 which could have succeeded in bringing fundamental changes to the highly developed communities of the West was Fascism. (It is interesting to note, in this connection, that the basic difference between Spartacism and Caesarism in the classic

81

world was to some extent reflected in the modern scene.)

In every practical matter the methods were sharply anti-thetical. All that mattered to Fascism was that industry and management should serve the whole nation and not the anarchic selfishness of vested interests. Within the broad boundaries of the national welfare the actual method could be infinitely flexible. Power resided in the State at once to change management if it conflicted with the national interest: on the other hand, management was completely free from interference in daily business, provided it recognised that responsibility. The direction of industry was responsible to the Government which represented the Nation; on the other hand, that Direction could require a like sense of responsibility to its authority from those engaged in the industry. The power of the State was ever present to intervene on behalf of the national interest or of the welfare of the workers on whose support it rested. But the chain of responsibility and authority was always clear and rested, above all, on the principle of individual, not Committee, responsibility. When breakdown arrived it was, consequently, easy to fix individual responsibility and rapidly to make the necessary change.

Communism, on the other hand, began with the theory of Committee methods and mob tactics. In practice, of course, this violation of all realist principles of action led to immediate and almost complete collapse, as in the early days of Soviet Power, which would have been the end of any State except a primitive rural community. Under an elaborate make-believe that such principles still existed an iron despotism of a small clique was then introduced; which ruthlessly salvaged what remained of the State and built up a limited technical efficiency with the dearly purchased aid of foreign technicians, who then directed great masses of virtually slave labour. Mob rule gave way to chaos followed by oriental despotism; but enough of the propaganda forms of Western Spartacism were preserved to deceive many outside the " Iron Curtain."

So the practical genius of the West confronted in this realm of reality the destructive lust of the East. The former contained the germ of a limitless success as the reply of the West to chaos. The latter held nothing for the West except the internal collapse which alone could make possible the triumph of the Orient. It is not entirely surprising that many powerful elements in the Western countries preferred the latter alternative. The stupid did not fear it because it looked so inefficient that they believed that it could not master them: the clever perceived something which could be used to serve their purpose, which contained, at least, an initial affinity with the Soviet genius of chaos.

The New Idea Versus Communism:
The Spiritual Conflict

Such were a few of the practical differences between Fascism and Communism, which struck deep roots into the diverse natures of the European and the Asiatic. The ever-widening spiritual conflict goes much further and, in the ideology of our later study in the present work, will be considerably developed. It is sufficient at this stage to observe that we begin with the premise that values of the spirit oppose those of pure materialism. None can deny that the latter are the values of Communism. They learnt from Marx the Materialist Conception of History, and from their early atheist teachers a denial of any element of truth in any religion: that negation, itself, soon assumed the force of a religion. All was material, whether the past, present or the future of man; he became a mere conditioned reflex to material things. The soul of man as an eternal force became a quaint illusion for analysis in Soviet laboratories, or humour in the comic papers. Any higher striving, in harmony with a higher purpose flowing through earthly things, was reduced to an animal urge to fill the belly with material satisfaction for the brief and finite mortal span of a limited generation. To that fixed end, discipline and a compulsory co-operation were necessary to an extent that should replace the religious urge. The busy diurnalism of the Ant Heap became, at last, the substitute for the Greek Phusis reaching out from Hellas through three millenia of European growth and culture to the achievement of ever higher forms in union with the higher purpose which directs all earthly existence.

Here we come to the root of the matter: our values are those of the spirit, and their values are those of materialism. No religious controversy is posed in this: a simple difference is stated. If our values are not spiritual values, our struggle and our sacrifice have no purpose. We strive, not merely for the material satisfaction of a transient generation: we strive for the emergence of ever higher forms upon this earth. It is not merely a question of changing material environment, important as this work is: even more it is a question of changing man himself. We reject alike the Communist conception of man as a material animal and any faith of complacency which treats him already as a perfect image or reflection of the Deity. Man is neither an animal nor a God; he is a striving being in a world of flux and becoming, who will either revert to a final nothing or win heights of achievement and of being whose divine sunlight would dazzle present eyes to blindness. He must lose all or win all; he has no alternative: and his redeeming achievement is to transcend himself in a higher form. To stand still, or even to remain himself, is to fail.

That simple fact is writ across the map of the contemporary world and is stamped on every feature of a generation which is failing: the will of man must conquer not only material environment but must also surmount the weakness and smallness of his own character. His earthly mission is to surpass himself in deliberate striving for a higher form in harmony with the only observable revelation of the Divine purpose in this world, which is presented by evolutionary nature as an expression of that purpose.

When we conceive the earthly mission of man as a conscious striving for a higher form, we challenge every fundamental of a creed which is not only material but denounces as the final crime any effort to create, or even to preserve, forms above the ordinary.

The main purpose of Communism is to reduce all to the ordinary, or below it to that lowest common denominator where even envy becomes exhausted: our main purpose is to surpass the ordinary, because we believe that an accelerated evolution of a higher type is essential to man's survival in face of present circumstance. We believe, too, that only through the emergence of ever higher forms can the Divine will be served, and that it is our task to serve this purpose. So, in the final clash we oppose the idea of the higher man to that of the Mob: the values of the striving spirit to the values of an all-reducing and imprisoning Materialism. To his final Empyrean shall reach and soar the Gothic soul of Western Man in an eternal striving for harmony with the infinite. In the end he will be bound neither by these chains of gold nor by these bonds of anarchy, which symbolise the revenge of the defeated Orient upon the bright figure of the Western genius, whose final triumph is still the hope of the world.

COMMUNIST HOPES REST IN VIOLENCE AND WAR

Communism is in essence a creed so alien to the Western mind that it has no hope of success except in violence. A realistic understanding of this fact dictates its strategy. The method is to develop military force in Russia, and mob force in other countries. Communism seeks to turn itself into an army and its opponents into a mob. An ever more rigid discipline is imposed within Russia and the party structure, while an ever harder drive towards anarchy is launched within the countries of the West. From their standpoint, it is a well-conceived plan, because any man who succeeds in turning his own force into an army and his opponent's force into a mob is bound to win. This is clearly the aim of the new Communist Imperialism which thus combines the worst features of the old aggression and the new anarchy. At present it plays for time with the endless manoeuvres and tergiversations which bear the unmistakable hall-mark of the Oriental mind. The reason for this is equally plain: Russia seeks time in order to build that equality of weapons with the Western Powers, which she now lacks. The relatively backward Oriental country would have no hope of doing this without assistance from Western Science and technical ability.

With their usual readiness to oblige a mortal enemy, and serve the most foolish purposes which the human mind can conceive, the British ruling class has hastened to provide Russia with the scientists and technicians who alone can give her world dominion. Their insensate fury against all things German drives some of the finest technical abilities in the world into the arms of Russia. A level of ability, which she could never herself produce or attain, is thus placed at Russia's disposal for the final attack upon the West by the energetic stupidity of the intended victim. From Russia every inducement is offered to German scientists, and from Britain every insult. They offer Germans of high ability any reward the world can give: to their eternal honour most still refuse. But Britain sends an occupying force which, in part, appears to be deliberately composed of some of those types who have long been all too familiar in Britain. The true Englishman may well say to the German: we can feel for you because they " occupied " us before they " occupied " you. Let *Deutsche Treue* to the West stand fast against scheming bribe or silly insult: the day of truth and honour will come again and find yet higher expression in yet greater achievements of the Western spirit. Meantime, I here brand before History a crime and an insanity without parallel in the long record of mortal folly. It is the gift of the German genius to the purposes of Russian Communism by the rule which now disgraces the name of Britain. Through such insanity alone can Oriental Communism triumph: it can never win either by the consent of the peoples of the West or by its own skill in a clash of arms. But a fuller study of the menace of Communist Imperialism, which comes from Russia to challenge the new Europe, must await the second part of this book and the formulation of those constructive ideas which can give strength to overcome it.

In passing we note the tactic of Communism to arm itself and to divide us, because it can only succeed by successful violence. Fascism, however, in brief career proved an ability to win mass support in the Western lands on a scale which brought it to power in Italy and Germany, and would have brought it to power in Britain and other lands if the war had not intervened.

Still more will this creed, which is born of a deep and bitter experience and is destined to stride forward beyond even Fascism toward new vistas of the striving spirit, evoke the strong support and passionate enthusiasm of the peoples of the West when gathering storm impels them to seek the only alternative to chaos. Communism can only win by violence and the West must be ready to meet it. But, we have shown that we can win by the consent of the peoples, and we note the one merit of the present system in the fact that it enables this consent to be given when the time comes. The British Constitution, in particular, provides for any change, however great, to be made in peace and order by the vote of the people. The British people and the peoples of the West can command by their votes even changes so vast as those proposed in this book. The realism of the British led them to change from oligarchy to what is called " Democracy " without a shot being fired, when the time came and necessity beckoned. That same realism will carry them far beyond Democracy when the hour of its passing strikes, and they will change to a new system in peace and order with that calm commonsense which recognises a fact when it becomes a necessity. The British never move before they must: but, then, they move fast. They possess the ultimate realism.

The force which menaces any such peaceful transition in Britain and throughout the world is obviously Communism. It will clearly try to fight rather than lose, and it may strike before the intended hour if it sees that it is losing. In the hour of decision, when they seek and find their way out of ultimate chaos, all lands of the West may be attacked internally and externally by Communist violence. In the end they will have to face that attack in any case, if they decline in lethargy to a weakness which invites its success. It is better to meet it, if necessary, while they still retain their vigour, before it has been sapped by the long and stealthy approach of the Oriental assault which is now being prepared. Whatever happens, it is better to die on the feet than lying down, and, on its feet the West will win. In fact, if the West awakes in time Peace can be preserved, because

the overwhelming strength, which can only be derived from
the timely awareness of the European, alone can present Russian
Communism with the accomplished fact of a force which makes
hopeless the intended assault. The West must arise in time if
Europe is to be saved from anarchy and the world from war.
Once again must realism organise for the best but prepare against
the worst: to this end certain lessons of realism from the last
conflict will be noted later in this volume. The blood-stained
annals of mankind so far record the dynamism of History in
terms of violence rather than of Peace. Let us, at least, mark the
lesson that the only guarantee of peaceful achievement is the
possession of overwhelming force. That is the gift with which
modern science must first endow for his survival the aspiring
spirit of European Man, who will repay in terms of a constructive civilisation that will be the glory of science.

APPEAL TO THE BRITISH

We come to the end of the analysis of that failure which led
to this sombre scene. Chaos looms, and the peoples of Europe
and the Americas seek the alternative. We shall turn in the
second part of this book, to regard the radiant possibilities of
superhuman achievement with which the material possibilities of
this great age challenge the will of man. Let us face it with a
full sense of the superb moment in which we live. It is true that
" danger shines like sunshine to a brave man's eyes "; yet it is
now a brighter sun than even Euripides could conceive, because
from it is reflected not only danger, but the possibility of a
civilisation beyond the dream of the ages.

In the last words of this survey of failure, I turn to my own
countrymen—to the real people of England whom I have known
in real things, in Agriculture, in the great Professions, in the
back streets of East London, in the industries of the North, in
the Army and " Royal Flying Corps " of the 1914 war, to whom
are now added a new war generation of similar ideal—and I
ask them this question: " Will your genius live again and in
time to make its unique contribution? " Too long has it been
enchained to serve purposes the opposite of those you desired.

Once again the dark technique has used the best instincts to produce the worst results. Their politics persuaded you that you were a Knight Errant going to the aid of the oppressed: in present society you had no means of learning the truth. Your fine and generous instinct to help the " under-dog " was, exploited to make you the instrument of European frustration. In the misery of the post-war period how strange and darkly mysterious appears the metamorphosis by which the under-dog becomes a money-lender to whom you owe your world. That conjuring trick of fatality still bewilders you, while Mob and Money laugh and dance on your generous ideals. The finest and the best in a new war generation sink beneath the wave of bitter cynicism which submerged our few companions, who still lived in 1918. Deceit was the end, but yet the means were noble. You gave all for high purposes and, in so doing, you made your own high character. That remains, when the ends for which you fought dissolve in dust and ashes. Nothing matters now except that you should use the character you gained in the hard experience of that great illusion to serve new ends of reality and truth.

Again and again I have been brought down in the service of high things by the triumph of the small, the mean and the false; but, each time, the experience has made me stronger. All that matters is to rise always from the dust, with will and character even stronger from the test—that you may serve yet greater ends until relentless striving brings final victory. Such has been the character of the English in their sunlit, creative periods, and that nature still lives in the real England. The great river still flows in deep and calm, if latent, purpose; but the scum on the top is thick. Beneath, are still the great qualities of the English; your kindness, your toleration, your open-minded sanity, your practical sense, your adaptability in plan, your flexibility in action, your steadiness of spirit in adversity, your power to endure, your final realism, even your ultimate dynamism; all the great qualities are still there, which took you out from the Northern Mists to see with the Hellenic vision of the Elizabethan bright lands which you held and moulded with firm, Roman hands. Will you rise and use your genius in time? Will you away with the spirit of denial and negation before it is too late? Will you fulfil your destiny in a harmony of the European spirit, without end in expression of beauty and achievement? Or will it really be too late? For this time it will be the last " too late." I have given many warnings to my fellow-countrymen which were true; but they were not heeded. I now give my last. . . . There will be no Channel next time. . . .

Chapter II

THE FAILURE OF GERMANY — PROPAGANDA AND REALITY

No subject is more necessary to the study of the future European than the failure of Germany after so many and such great achievements. What lessons for the task of construction can realism derive from the frustration of that great life urge, which has led to the bitter experience of the German people. As usual, it is necessary to clear from our path the debris of illusion before we can perceive reality. The illusion is contained in the propaganda explanation of the German failure, and the reality will be found in an analysis of the actual mistakes in German policy: we will examine both.

The propaganda of the " Left " states that Germany was impelled to a disastrous war by the Marxian laws which must govern such an economy: the propaganda of the " Right " states that Germany was inspired to such a catastrophe by the desire for World Dominion: many people ascribe the fatality to both factors, in that comprehensive combination of every available muddle which constitutes the " Democratic " mind. So, we will dissect firstly the Marxian, and, secondly, the World Dominion fallacy, before advancing to meet the more interesting truth.

Marxian Theory: Or Interaction of Finance and Communism

In an analysis of failure, which is a necessary prelude to the construction of a system of Achievement, it is, in any case, essential soon to study the dominant forces of the present time and their origin, with particular reference to the supreme disaster of the last world war. Such a survey must lead us along devious and tortuous paths which pass through such arid territories of the mind as the Marxian theory. The reader, who is not an addict of economics is, therefore, advised to skip to page 85, where we enter a livelier world. On the other hand, no apology should be made for such a dull beginning, as it is impossible in modern life to avoid the dullest of subjects. The Marxian Theory grips physically an immense area of the European Continent, holds in mental thrall a large proportion of the remainder, and menaces with spiritual subjection to an oriental creed most of the western world. The great power of its spiritual appeal is perhaps confined almost entirely to those who have not read it; like certain " mysteries " of old its command over such types may even rest in its incomprehensibility to them. But, tedious and fallacious as Marxism may be, we cannot ignore it as an established fact, in terms of power, and as a creed which is influencing the minds of millions in a manner comparable to the earlier impact of Christianity. Before the true may live, and grow to full stature, we must destroy the false in the minds of men: and we must do so in terms which most men can understand.

Prior to some consideration of the Marxian analysis, however, we should observe a natural relationship between Communism and Finance, a mutual thriving of Mob and Money, which was very far from being noted by Marx. Yet it is, at any rate, difficult to deny the similarity of the conditions in which they both prosper. They appear to represent the opposite poles of life, but, in reality, are not antithetical but complementary forces, because they both depend on the same basic conditions for success. The circumstances which assist both Finance and Communism are flux and chaos. The profit of Finance depends, in broad terms, on buying at the bottom and selling at the top. Continual flux is, therefore, essential to Finance; the opposite condition of stability provides neither a bottom nor a top and, therefore, no speculative profit. The advance of Communism depends also on that continual flux which destroys all social stability and leads to the ultimate chaos by which alone it can achieve success. Even the clash of the two forces supports the interests of both. The threat of Communism to an existing order produces the tendencies to flux, by means of panic, which enhance the profits of finance. The speculations of Finance accentuate the conditions of chaos which accelerates the triumph of Communism. It is unnecessary to accept the thesis of a conscious conspiracy between these forces in order to observe their effective interaction; although, on occasion, Finance has given sufficient assistance to Communism to provide much evidence for that theme, and the same type and race can, of course, often be found in the leading positions of both these organisms.

We have already observed in this volume that the subconscious often plays a greater role than the conscious mind in social and political tendencies. Such forces as Communism and Finance naturally pursue, whether consciously or subconsciously, the policies which serve them best, and they remain complementary to each other, even if the relationship is obscured in the conscious mind by apparent antagonism rather than attraction. Chaos serves both and that condition is provided more effectively by their clash than by their overt co-operation. Each serves the other and must so act, because they have the same fundamental values. This is even more true in the spiritual than in the material sphere.

Mob, Money and the Division of Europe

The obstacles to the progress of both these forces is the higher type of European; so he and his values must be destroyed before their victory can be won. The great stock, which derives from the soil of Europe and is animated by the ideal of service and not of profit, stands like a rock of stability across the course of Flux and Chaos. Personally incorruptible, because he has values beyond money and is a representative of steadfast continuity in nearly three millenia of culture, the higher European is the final enemy of both Finance and Communism, because he can neither be bought nor frightened. Further, in any straight conflict he cannot be overcome by these forces. It is inconceivable, if we eliminate for a moment in imagination the effect of the last two wars, that the massive figure of the European man could be defeated and subdued by these weak and alien forces which possessed nothing approaching the material means or imaginative genius which were so clearly at the disposal of the accumulated wisdom, scientific skill and vital energy of a united Europe. In fact, the only resources they could acquire with which to fight their great opponent, belonged to him, and could only be obtained by the treachery of the natural parasite.

When the alien forces of Finance and Socialist-Communism began their long and persistent attack on the spiritual values and material prosperity of Europe it would appear *a priori* that every factor of strength and skill favoured the defender. How then was he reduced to his present plight? The answer is that Europe was divided, and thus alone the men of Europe could be conquered. They were overcome by a method which played upon their best and noblest instincts: their love of country was used to destroy their continent. Too late, they learned that without their continent their countries could not live. The best elements in Europe were divided by love; the worst elements were united by greed: in that strange paradox lies the tragedy of Europe. It was the fine instinct of a love of country which divided the best manhood of the Continent and hurled it to mutual destruction. How did it happen that a motive which is altogether good led to a conclusion so fatal? Did any real reason exist whereby Patriotism must inevitably impel the European to a Continental disaster? On the contrary, every reason founded on reality, as opposed to the passions engendered by Mob and Money, postulated Union and not division in a policy of national self-interest which should coincide with the wider harmony of the whole continent. How then occurred the disaster of these two wars in a continent not yet ready for Union? If we set aside for later examination the reason, "world dominion," presented by pure propaganda, the answer usually given is economic. And, indeed, if no man or nation can be believed foolish enough to attempt the subjection of all others through a crude old-fashioned tyranny, by means of a transient superiority of arms, and without any clear purpose of personal or national advantage, it would appear at first sight that the answer can only be economics.

Marxism Contrasted with the Old Orthodoxy

Let us, therefore, briefly examine, in relation to the foregoing question the two economic theories which commanded the thought of the old world; they can be broadly described as the Orthodox, or Liberal, and the Marxian. In the pure theory of the former no economic cause for war can arise. Germany, for instance, was the second best customer of Great Britain and, in the old Liberal theory, the destruction of the former could be nothing but an economic disadvantage to the latter. Other countries were, in fact, regarded as customers and not as trade rivals; the prosperity of other lands beneficially contributed to an ever-increasing world market in which every efficient nation would obtain ever-growing sales of its own goods, balanced by the purchase abroad of desirable commodities which it could not so easily or cheaply produce at home. So, in orthodox economic theory of the old world, economics could only unite and could not divide; trade was not a cause of war but a bridge over all differences of nationality. In practice, that theory was soon and greatly altered by the operation of the finance which accompanied it. Directly sales were not balanced by purchases, and Finance became something more than the medium by which that exchange was effected, a new situation arose. When countries were lent money in order to buy goods, quite different tendencies developed. These new countries became a sphere, almost a possession, of a particular financial combination which might be physically resident in another country or in several. Competitive groups of a similar character would soon enter the picture, and the smooth exchange of goods, in the economic idyll of the old theory, soon gave place to the harsh clash of International financial interests, which, in some circumstances, could command power diplomacy and national armies in their support.

Where then, the reader may enquire, is your union of International Financial interests if, in fact, they can oppose each other and even promote wars in their rivalry? The answer is paradoxically that their union can only prosper in the division of the world. Strife and War, with consequent flux and chaos, bring opportunity and profit to the gambler, but depression and ruin to the producer who, above all, requires stability and peace. In the maintenance of that system the big speculators are all united; it is only in the profitable game which that system permits that they are divided. The various gamblers may be united in the maintenance of the Casino, whence they all derive profit: but they are divided when they sit at the high table and play against each other for high stakes. The interests of the fundamental union are the deeper, and the profitable fascination of the game is the greater, if they play with other people's money—and lives. Let us never confuse the system with the game.

It is at this point that the perversion by Finance of the old Liberal orthodox theory enters the Marxian sphere, and it is here that we begin to see the operation of the Marxian analysis. Rival capitalisms begin to fight for markets under the leadership of Finance; wages are beaten down towards the subsistence level to assist the keen competition of the struggle; diminishing wages yet further reduce the home market and pile up a bigger surplus of production for disposal abroad, which in turn intensifies the struggle for foreign markets. Industrial systems are driven by the lack of purchasing power in the hands of their own people to concentrate on the struggle for foreign markets which Finance began. When every great industrial country is trying to dispose of a surplus by selling abroad more than it buys, a clash becomes inevitable; because it is a clear, mathematical fact that they cannot all do it at once. Ever keener becomes the international struggle of all national industries under the lash of competitive finance, and ever more deeply committed are the whole economy and life of nations.

In such conditions the struggle for foreign markets, which advances behind the battle for financial spheres of influence, may, at any moment, involve first Diplomacy and then the armaments of Nations. How far we have now travelled from the old Liberal Orthodox theory of economics in which Finance merely oiled the wheels of exchanges! At this point, our facing of facts as they are coincides almost entirely with the Marxian analysis; but let no vital spirit, therefore, deduce that we accept as final that dark defeatism of the human mind and will. A doctor may recognise a tumour in a body as a fact, but, if he still possesses the skill of surgery, he does not surrender to it. He does not admit easily that the patient must perish, together with the accumulated wisdom of his mortal experience, so that all the long labours of his earthly mission may return to dust and, in his place, some hideous parasite may arise, which has no relation to the human body, mind or spirit. On the contrary, the surgeon notes and acknowledges the symptoms; then operates before they can go too far. At least, that is his course if the vigour of life and faculty are still within him; if he is a " conservative " type of course, he merely denies the existence of the tumour, which Marx observed, until the patient is dead. It is not necessary to question the validity of much of the Marxian analysis in order to deny its conclusions. What we challenge is not the necessity to change the present economic order but the permanent tendency to those " death instincts," revealed in the economics of this old Jew, which were so shrewdly analysed by his co-racialist, Freud. Those instincts may be very appropriate to certain exhausted sections of the Orient, but they are very far from being an expression of the will of Western Man. To the European, and to the related American, a recognition of such facts is a challenge to action and by no means an invitation to resign ourselves to the end of our life and tradition, still less to welcome the Slav marching across our culture to impose on us the dead uniformity which so well suits his flat Levantine soul—as dreary and as featureless as the dull waste of his native steppes.

The answer of vigour to the Marxian analysis was the insulation of an economy from world chaos.

INTERNATIONAL SOCIALISM'S RESPONSE TO MARXISM

In the entirely unpractical theory of International Socialism it was held possible finally to overcome the fatal laws of an anarchic Capitalism when the whole world decided to go Socialist. What happened to the advanced countries who took this step, while the backward countries remained under the exploitation of financial capitalism, was never very clearly explained. How could a high standard of life in a Socialist country subsist, within the Internationalism which it supported, in face of free competition from lower wage standards, which were supplied with equal mechanical facilities and technical direction by Financiers who were engaged in exploiting the lower life of backward labour for greater profit? This question was posed in very acute form by the development of Westernised industries in such countries as India, China and Japan before the war of 1939. The impact of a far lower standard of life was driving from many world markets even the highly competitive products of European capitalism whose own labour was living little above the Western subsistence level, and whose technical skill in management remained superior to the new Oriental competition. What hope then had Western Socialism to take over from Capitalism in advanced countries, with all the inevitable dislocation of efficiency at first inherent in such a change, and then to face in the world markets of international trade a yet more dangerous capitalism which was supplied with labour at a fraction of the European labour costs that prevailed before Socialism took over in a welter of promises to raise labour standards?

In fact, European Socialism of the old international brand had not got so far as even to think seriously about these matters. Their chronic incapacity even to face the problem how an International Socialism in one or two countries could live and advance in a world dominated by International Capitalism was one of the prime causes of the development of National Socialist thought in the economic sphere. The leaders of International Socialism never thought about it seriously until the war, and are now paradoxically only able to live for a brief space in the seats of power because the heritage of war has placed in their bewildered hands a few instruments, such as Exchange Control, etc., which enable them to improvise expedients to protect themselves from the shock of the International system, which they have spent their lives in recommending. Even then, they find ever-increasing difficulties in discovering markets, in face of Capitalist competition, for the exports which are necessary to their international system, despite the fortuitous assistance which was again afforded them in the elimination of previous cheap labour competitors such as Japan.

NATIONAL SOCIALISM'S ANSWER TO MARXISM

The new National Socialist mind, on the other hand, advanced consciously and deliberately to meet this problem as basic to the solution of every other. We shall observe now the close bearing of this economic digression upon the causes of European division and war. Under analysis, it will appear that this new concept of economics entailed not an intensification of the factors underlying war, which Marx and others observed, but the withdrawal through a new type of economy from those prime causes. We shall, therefore, be obliged once again to look elsewhere for the deeper origin of the late war which these considerations render at first sight yet more inexplicable.

To the National Socialist mind it appeared inconceivable that a much higher standard of life could be built in an advanced country while labour was exposed to the full shock of competition from backward countries, and both the raw materials and markets of industry were assailed by the incessant flux caused by the operations of Finance in the sphere both of supply and sale. In fact, it can be argued that National Socialism in this respect started from the Marxian premise that these things exist, although it faced the situation with a vital realism and inherent vigour of action which was entirely lacking to the " death instincts " of the Marxian school. Characteristically, the latter could see the menace but could not summon up the decision and energy necessary to meet it. They knew a deadly snake when they saw it, but were too far sunk in the lethargy of a declining type to retain the use of their hands to defend themselves from its attack.

The answer to the world chaos, which suited so well a predatory Finance Capitalism for reasons already given, was the organisation of the National or Organic State. Behind the barrier of insulation from the rest of the world labour standards could be raised with impunity to any level which national production could justify. The allocation between wages, capital reserve, and profit could be settled deliberately and scientifically within a planned economy. It is not necessary in such a system to impose the stifling grip of bureaucracy in constant interference as it is in an international Socialist economy, which becomes a series of desperate expedients to repair a method which is basically wrong, and to patch up a system which is fundamentally rotten. We have already observed that it is the improvisor not the organiser who needs the fussy little bureaucrat to bind together a jumble of blunders with endless bundles of red tape. A planned and organised system lays down the main principles on which industry is based, and the boundaries within which industry may operate; but within those limits enterprise is entirely free.

But, we are here considering only the bearing of the new economic thinking upon the origin of the late war. For our present purpose it is only necessary to note that such a system involved not an intensified thrust into those conditions which are admitted to produce war, but a withdrawal from them. An economy which is self-contained, or autarchic, is independent of world markets because the only market it seeks is the high purchasing power of its own people, deliberately raised to a point where it can absorb the maximal production of National Industry. Such a structure of industry is also independent of world markets except in so far as it must purchase abroad raw materials which it does not itself possess. To that extent alone must it export and be dependent on international exchange. If such a state were in the fortunate position of British Empire or America, and contained within its own borders every raw material which industry could possibly require, all that is needed is the vigour to develop its own supplies. From the struggle for world markets, and the machinations of the speculative Finance which controls them, such a state can be entirely free. But, a nation which does not possess adequate supplies of raw material is driven either to acquire territory which contains them, or to dump a sufficient proportion of its own production on world markets to secure the necessary industrial supplies. Either process brings it within the danger sphere of world war unless other nations are prepared to meet it in a very co-operative spirit. To the extent that such a Nation possesses raw materials, or can easily acquire them by special arrangement, it is immunised from risks of war.

THE ABSURDITY OF MARXIAN DETERMINISM:
AUTARCHY AND ARMAMENTS

Such an autarchic economy was in fact created in pre-war Germany, which was singularly deficient in natural resources by reason of the previous war. It was early days in the realm of such thought, but a series of experiments on these lines succeeded in producing an extraordinary aggregate of production in relation to natural resources. That experiment at least translated some part of such economic theory from the realm of speculation to proved practice. The most childish of all the comments upon this fact is the remark that this production was largely devoted to armaments, and that the system would, consequently, have broken down if the armaments race had been ended. Such statements reveal a complete incapacity even to conceive a planned economy. If a State is insulated from world competition it can allocate the results of production exactly as it wishes. By raising wage rates through an organic or corporate system it can give Labour the power to absorb the whole production of industry if it decides upon so extreme a course. Theoretically, too, it can force down wage rates to the subsistence level and give the employer, shareholder or organiser of industry the whole margin of production over mere subsistence wages in the form of profits; or it can throttle down both wages and profits in favour of capital reserves and consequent production of capital goods to such a point that production outstrips demand and falling prices result in an all-round deflation; or it can force up wages and/or profit at the expense of Capital reserves to a point where demand outstrips production and causes inflation; or it can pursue the sensible course of a planned economy by a fair allocation between wages, profits and capital reserves, based upon the desire to give the maximum incentive to both management and workers that is compatible with the development of new technique through new capital goods. Finally, it can, of course, allocate such proportion of the national production to armaments as Government considers is required by the Foreign situation. If the position is critical guns may have to take precedence over butter. If the situation progressively improves the allocation to armaments can be continually reduced and, *pro rata,* applied in the form of higher wages and a steady increase in the standard of life.

These considerations are, of course, elementary to any planned and directed economy. The argument that a nation in time of crisis is devoting a large proportion of its production to armaments and, therefore, must collapse when the strain relaxes and armaments are reduced betrays a quite remarkable incapacity to comprehend the A.B.C. of modern thought and the executive mind. On the contrary, the strain on such an economy in having to support the burden of armaments, particularly when resources are limited by an exiguous supply of indigenous raw material, is immediately relaxed, when the armaments allocation can be reduced in favour of an increase in the standard of life. To argue that this cannot be done is to contend that a planned economy cannot arrange for the production of rifles to be reduced and the production of saucepans to be increased. Really, we should not have to waste time in dealing with such argument, but in such imbecilities resides the contention that an autarchic economy must inevitably result in war. On the contrary, such a system entails a withdrawal from the struggle for markets which is a prime cause of war according to Marx himself. Further, behind the barrier of insulation the " iron law of wages " can be broken by executive national action and the production of industry apportioned between wages, profits, reserves and other national requirements in any degree that is desired.

In brief, the factors causing war in the Marxian analysis can quickly be smashed by the executive will of man in the conscious plan of the organic state. The Marxian laws had a measure of truth in the same sense that the laws of gravity, discovered by Newton, contained the basic elements of truth. They retained much the same degree of practical validity when confronted by the brain and will of developed man. If we go up a high tower and jump off it we receive a vivid impression of the force of the Newton law. Having observed this fact, man did not content himself with merely jumping off high towers whenever he felt a little life weariness. On the contrary, the continually striving and aspiring spirit of Western Man invented first the balloon and then the aeroplane with which to overcome the laws of gravity; never content, and eternally reaching upward to his Gothic Empyrean, he now labours with jet and rocket to pass beyond even planetary limitations.

So much for gravity, said intellect and will. So much for Marx said National Socialism; his paper laws were an easier task. New men came—they saw the laws of chaos—they strove —they conquered. Why then was that economic victory such anathema to the rest of the world? In particular, why should it object to a process which took Central Europe not toward, but away from, the international markets which the old world so greatly cherished. If the old countries had even arranged that Germany, anywhere on the earth, should have access to the world's surplus of raw materials, their precious international markets, with all their hoary mechanism of foreign exchange, would have been entirely relieved from the pressure of the power they regarded as their greatest competitor. If, on the other hand, they decided themselves to advance into new paths, the raw material potential of Britain, America and also France provided them with an opportunity of reaching heights in a new civilisation which the limitations of German circumstance were far from offering.

GERMANY AND WORLD DOMINION

Why then this phobia and why the conflict? It is unfortunately necessary further to analyse the past before we can clear the debris from the road of the future.

The reason given, of course, was that Germany aimed at world dominion. Even at first sight this thesis contains something of the fantastic. Can it be seriously envisaged that any

sane man in the year 1939 even contemplated the permanent
subjection by force not only of all Europe, including Britain,
but also of both America and Asia, with the administration of
Africa thrown in by way of recreation and diversion? If it be
replied, in the usual didactic and arbitrary fashion of a victor,
whose arrogance in triumph frees him from any necessity for
argument or serious analysis, that these men were not sane, it
may be retorted that only sane men are dangerous in great
affairs. If the realist has a most cherished wish, it is that his
opponents may be impaired by a madness sent by the Gods
as a preliminary to their loss. That is why he sometimes regards
with a measure of reassurance the antics of the leaders of
" Democracy." So the brief answer to the concept that the
leaders of National Socialist Germany contemplated the government of the whole world from China to Peru by means of a
highly centralised administration in Berlin, which local non-
co-operation would have rendered necessary, is that only idiots
would nurture any such design and that the plans of morons
are easily frustrated. If that were their design, the Gods had,
indeed, made them mad, and it would not have required much
assistance from man to secure their permanent disappearance
from the mortal stage.

It is true that present conditions are fundamentally different
from those of 1939, and that to-day it is conceivable that one
great power for the time being, at any rate, might dominate
and terrorise the rest of the world with one of these completely
novel weapons which a revolutionary science, stimulated by
the stress of the late war, appears now to be providing. For
instance, even the traditional courtesy and knightly restraint
of America does not altogether mitigate the influence in international affairs of that country's possession of the Atom Bomb.
But, in 1939, the whole premise of power strategy was completely different. Then, it was not a question of dropping
something on the chief cities of a dissenting country which
in course of seconds could wipe their effective civilisation from
the face of the earth. Conquest entailed the occupation of
countries in considerable force, and the problem of 1939 must

always be regarded in these terms. So it may be asked, can anyone, in his senses, have contemplated the German Grenadier perpetually marching in pursuit of eternally dissident underground movements over every great space of the earth from the Steppes of Russia to the Prairies of the Americas, across the deserts of the Sahara or the Gobi until at length his devoted figure was chasing some non-conforming Lama in the remotest fastnesses of Tibet. For, in the conditions of that day, this must have been the exhausting destiny of the German soldier if his Leaders had cherished the idea of world dominion, and had achieved the considerable initial success of overthrowing by force of arms the established government of every great country in the world. German troops must have occupied the entire earth and the whole manhood of Germany would have spent their lives and vital energies in incessant guerilla fighting.

Such were the conditions of 1939, and no German could have imagined world dominion without envisaging that prospect. Is it then very extraordinary to believe that the German Leadership preferred the entirely rational concept of German manhood staying at home to build their own country and living space, once sufficient resources were at their disposal to create a civilisation which was independent of world anarchy. In fact their whole doctrine had exaggerated that possibility according to prevailing British standards.

Contrast Between British and German Colonial Theory

The Nazi Party concentrated on the idea of bringing all Germans living in Europe together in a homogeneous block within a geographically united living space. To this end they had largely if not entirely renounced the Colonial idea. Except as a means of obtaining raw materials Colonies had little interest for them: they believed that practically everything they required could be developed in Eastern Europe. Granted sufficient raw materials to build an autarchic economy, which was free from World Finance and concomitant chaos, the Nazi theory was inclined to regard Colonial Empire as an actual disadvantage. They preferred young Germans to stay at home among their own people rather than to dissipate their energies in educating negroes to a white standard of life which they believed such peoples could never attain. Their only interest in space, outside Germany, was a desire to secure the necessary measure of raw materials to serve the purpose of building, within Germany, a high standard of civilisation. The " White Man's Burden " was an English invention and was almost entirely alien to the German mind. Whether it was inspired by the Bible or the Bank (Holy Book or Pass Book) it had no interest for them— not even if it contained a little bit of both. They were definitely interested in Germans and not in Negroes, and reprehensible as such perversity may appear in the eyes of both British merchants and missionaries, it remained one of the basic and ineluctable facts which statesmanship should have recognised. For, it obviously presented the basis of agreement by providing a natural division of interests which could eliminate all cause of conflict.

It is much easier to avoid a quarrel with someone who wants something quite different than with someone who wants the same thing. Before the war the Briton and the German wanted entirely different things; the former wanted a world Empire and the latter wanted a united German population with outlet for development towards the East of Europe. So far from these two ideas clashing they should rightly be regarded as mutually complementary. A main factor in the peace and stability of the world outside Europe was the British Empire, and a main factor in the peace and stability of Europe would have been a united German people in Europe naturally forming the classic and traditional barrier to any incursion of the alien force and culture of the Orient. The true vision regarded British Empire in the world, and German power in Europe, as the twin pillars which would support, through an aeon of material development and cultural achievement, the stable edifice of order and of peace.

THE FOLLY OF 1939

However, the contrary view prevailed with results which can

now be measured in almost mathematical terms; one-third of
Europe is lost to Russia and the triumphant Orient stands in
towering menace above the exhausted remainder, which is protected only by the Atom Bomb in American hands. Further,
in terms of pure statistics, 74 per cent. of the population and
16 per cent. of the territory of British Empire* has also been
lost and, in terms of real strength, what is left of that superb
body, after the shattering effects of a second world war, staggers
forward for the time being on the crutches of Foreign Doles.
Such is the situation that Britain's War Leader in the House
of Commons on November 12, 1946, was moved to refer to
" the former British Empire "; an observation which, according
to *The Times,* was strangely greeted by the " laughter " of the
House.

Was it all worth while? Had the sacrifice even an element
of reason? It could only be justified on the one ground that
Germany planned world conquest and had to be fought. The
reader will make up his own mind on that point, remembering
the fact which surely cannot be disputed that German leaders
in 1939, if they embraced that idea, must have been mad, and
that in the end madness is ineffective in great events. He must,
also, consider whether, in fact, men could have been so mad who
had started with nothing and after nearly twenty years of struggle
in and out of power had already achieved so much. Such madness
does not really quite fit the facts of their achievements; madmen
do not achieve. The heights of human attainment are not reached
by the abnormal but by the supernormal, as we may observe
later in some study of the type of Statesmanship which the future
will demand. But let us, for the sake of this argument, assume
the contrary thesis that it was possible for Germany to have
made a bid for world dominion after she had developed as much
strength as possible by the absorption of German populations,
together with territory and raw materials, in the East of Europe.
Suppose she had then turned West in a drive not only against
France and Britain, but also against America. What was the
answer and what was the policy in face of the suspicion that

*On the assumption that the loss of India is directly due to the war.

this might occur? The answer was not to rush in without arms before it happened but to wait until it did happen and, above all, to use the interval in the intensive production of arms. In the material balance of 1939, Britain, France and America could not have been defeated by Germany with any resources which that power could command, provided that their vast industrial potential were developed to provide armaments which in the condition of that time were decisive. In the material terms, which most military critics now admit were determinant in the conditions of the last war, the three Western powers could have deployed an overwhelming superiority to Germany without any reliance on, or regard for, Russia, one way or the other. In the state of military matters in 1939 the weight of material produced by industry alone counted, and that preponderance was on their side.

The only way the Western Powers could secure their own defeat was to rush in before they were ready; this, of course, was precisely what they did. In fact, despite their vast superiority of material potential, they very nearly managed to get themselves defeated by this serious error, from which they were only saved by the mistakes of their opponents.

SETTLEMENT OR WAR

Is not the course of realism in such circumstances always to strive for the best but also to prepare for the worst? Translated into the actualities of 1939 that principle entailed, on the one hand, trying to remove all real causes for a German explosion and, on the other hand, preparing to meet it if it came. The first effort meant a constructive act of statesmanship in providing Germany with access to the world's surplus of raw materials which existed at that time; either in some territory adjacent to her Eastern borders or in some colonial concession. The former, both from the German and the British standpoint, was the more desirable, but it required a degree of realism and decision which, *ex hypothesi*, cannot be found in a " Democracy." Such a suggestion is, of course, entirely outrageous to the " Democratic " mind, but the whole question of living space and raw material, together with the facts of natural and racial capacity to develop backward territory, will be frankly faced in a later stage of this argument, when the worst suspicions of our opponents concerning our " depravity " in such matters will, I trust, not only be confirmed but surpassed! The issue will not for a moment be shirked: it is high time we had a full dialectical show-down with one of the most absurd postulates which now impedes the progress of mankind.

Other methods, more in keeping with the prevailing mind and temperament of the " Democracies," were also available if a real will to settlement had existed. Germany would probably have accepted any form of international organisation in which raw materials could be afforded to her industries from the existing surplus of the rest of the world, even by trade or barter rather than by direct access, provided it had been free from any condition of outside financial control. Britain's chief contribution to such a solution was to buy up the Rumanian wheat crop to prevent Germany getting it, while refusing a market to our own Dominion of Canada. Otherwise, beyond improvised aeroplane flights to meet crises as they actually arose from the confining of Germany within too narrow a space, what persistent and consistent effort was made by " Democratic " statesmanship thus to eliminate the cause of an explosion? What response even was made to the various earlier proposals from Germany for disarmament which History has placed on record that cannot be erased? Surely, elementary sense and justice entailed at least an attempt to remove the admitted grievance of German restriction in a cramped area without adequate raw materials. Surely too, if they suspected that Germany really desired not a full life for her own people but a fight for world dominion, they should still have made every effort to secure such a settlement, while using the time so gained to develop their vast industrial resources to a point where the armaments of Britain, France and America could have outweighed any German armament and speedily frustrated the design they suspected, if, in fact, it were ever implemented. If war had to come and the Allies had been ready, it would not have lasted nearly so long, or caused more than a fraction of the loss of life and devastation which arose from the protracted muddle that the " Democracies " called policy and preparation.

The writer is as convinced now as he was then that a real effort at settlement would have succeeded, and that Britain and Germany would have become not conflicting but complementary powers to their own advantage and to that of Europe as a whole in the peaceful and ordered development which that free and natural association would have brought to the world. But, if that view had proved wrong, was not the dual policy then and now suggested clearly right? Is not to strive for the best, but to be ready for the worst, always better than to make neither effort for the best nor preparation for the worst? Was not the actual policy pursued the height of folly, in that it was a combination of war and weakness—interference without strength? Had not the contrary policy anything to be said for it—a combination of peace and strength—an effort to settle accompanied by vigorous armament in case it failed?

An Explanation of War

If such an attempt to win peace had succeeded the " Democracies " would have returned to their ardently desired international mercantilism under the auspices of their presiding deity of High Finance. They need no longer have been threatened or trammelled by Germany either as a military menace or a trade competitor, because her energies would have been absorbed in her own territory by the building of a self-contained civilisation. If her effort to create such a system had succeeded, Great Britain and America might even have been inspired to make a similar attempt with the vastly greater resources for the purpose available to them in British Empire and the American Continent.

Perhaps, at this point, for the first time we approach a rational explanation in a sphere which has hitherto appeared to be dominated entirely by the irrational. Such an example of success must have been highly dangerous to the paramount position of the presiding Deity. What would have happened to High Finance if a nation with limited resources had made such an evident

110

success of a system which was not only free from its control, but free from any necessity for its operation? The nations with unlimited resources would plainly have been impelled toward yet more fruitful experiments by popular demand of their peoples. Finance simply could not afford the success of the German experiment, because the eyes of its subject peoples in the " Democracies " would have been opened.

So mob was mobilised by money for world catastrophe! In terms of underlying reality that was the dominant fact. But, let no one think that the fatality can be altogether grasped in terms of the conscious mind. In such matters the subconscious is almost entirely prevalent in mob, and is largely in control even of those highly sophisticated circles in which money and the ruling classes interact. Only so can we account for a fact which we must all, at some time, have observed with distress, that people, whom we know personally to be of good and honest character, pursue in public life the vilest and most selfish policies. Beneath the conscious mind operates every atavistic impulse of class, self-interest, and the highly developed herd instinct of the ruling elite for preservation of power and position, with a violence and a fury of which the personally pious members of this largely hereditary sect are usually quite unconscious. We are all subject to such dangers in some degree, until our study of the new Science has immunised us to the point of being able at once to observe such tendencies in ourselves; but such considerations belong to a later stage when we consider the type that the future demands.

For the moment, let us observe merely that Money could not have mobilised Mob for world disaster if deep subconscious instincts had not been available in many quarters to produce a catastrophe which was entirely irrational, and traversed several possible solutions that the rational plainly indicated. When every interest of the two initial protagonists, Britain and Germany, were complementary, and the national characters, as we have earlier noted, possessed the same related qualities; when, in fact, they had nothing in the world to fight about, how could it occur that their clash should wreck Europe and threaten the world with the consequent triumph of Barbarism? Something so essentially irrational requires analysis: we must probe this matter to the depths and understand it, if we are to build surely in a future which demands a union of Europe that can only rest on the full participation and friendship of these two peoples, together with America and France, as a prerequisite of human survival in this new age of Science.

LESSONS OF THE PAST

How did it all happen? How did war occur, and the European disaster ensue? From this preliminary analysis, it would appear that the origin of war was, at any rate, not economic in the Marxian sense, and could not be ascribed to a deliberate attempt by Germany to establish a world dominion. The writer faces the future as a European striving for the Union which alone can bring life to this Continent. We look now to the future, but must first survey the Past to mark its lessons, because they must be learnt if the future is to be won. We have already examined the contribution of English policy to the clash and turmoil of this world disaster and we will now analyse the errors of German policy. How did it happen that two peoples, who, by every fact of material circumstance and bent of national character, should have been complementary rather than anti-thetical factors in the European scene, became embroiled in an antagonism which wrecked their Continent? My views on the part played in that catastrophe by the ruling Parties in Great Britain have been expressed many times, and as many times misrepresented. For the expression of these opinions, as a matter of principle, in face of an inevitably hostile public opinion on the outbreak of war, I and a large number of my colleagues spent five years in gaol, concentration camps and house arrest, and suffered the destruction by law of a Movement which had been built in seven years of striving from nothing to an effective contender for power. At that time, we directly challenged the action of the Old Parties, and their supporting interests, in the political field with the foreseen and unavoidable result of their victory in the conditions of insane passion which the outbreak

112

of war had engendered. These material things are nothing in the scales of the spirit; for principle and honour sometimes demand a struggle which circumstances from the outset have rendered hopeless. It is better to give all and to risk all than to acquiesce in what seems dishonour; it was an occasion to return upon a shield. Such then are our credentials for the possession of, at least, a fair mind in examining the German part in that catastrophe.

THE POLICY OF GERMANY IN RELATION TO THE LAST WAR

The purpose of the ensuing study is two-fold: in the first instance, to essay an objective analysis of various factors relating to the last world war in the interest of historic truth; in the second, to show that the lethargy and ineptitude occasioned by their system would have led inevitably to the defeat of the " Democracies " if they had not been saved by an extraordinary combination of political-military mistakes on the other side. The necessity for this warning can be briefly stated: Western Europe may quite soon be at war with Russia. The lessons of the last conflict have surely been noted by the Masters of World Communism, and they are unlikely to repeat proved errors. If, therefore, their present search for decisive weapons yields any result, they will eventually attempt some form of surprise attack in the hope of securing a rapid decision before the " Democracies " are awake. Such a strategy in the last war would, undoubtedly, have led to the defeat of these powers: the weapons of the next war will afford far greater opportunity to such method. The Western Countries will, consequently, run great risk of an early and complete defeat if they still retain their old system and psychology when the conflict with Russia begins. For these reasons I ask the peoples of the West to note and consider these lessons.

To obtain a complete picture of the pre-war position we must first survey that German policy which was wrecked by the errors we shall later examine. Finally, we may derive some additional advantage from the study of these great events in the elucidation of various general principles of realism,

113

which may serve the New Europe in affording some instruction to the new men who must save and re-build our Continent.

For the purposes we have described, the policy of Germany must be regarded purely from a realistic standpoint of German interest, in terms of historic objectivity. The policy and interests of Britain, and of Europe as a whole, has been reviewed in the last chapter: at a still later stage we will consider any contrasts which moral factors may present to the purely realistic. Let no one, therefore, complain that other interests, or moral considerations, are lacking from this chapter. The argument will be unfolded in successive stages: it is necessary in writing, as in speech, to remember that everything cannot be discussed at once (except between " Democrats "). If anyone thinks that we redress the balance of current thought too sharply to produce a true equilibrium, may the fault be in some measure ascribed to the present distortion of fact, which has prevailed too long to be corrected without such emphasis of contrary considerations that this possibility must be incurred.

THE PROBLEM FACING GERMAN LEADERSHIP

German leadership was confronted by a great problem which was described to the world in speeches and writings of the greatest force. In brief and crude summary, German policy was moved by two main factors: the necessity to secure the return to the German Fatherland of exiled populations and to obtain living space for a great, vital and expanding people. The demand for these two things would appear by nature so reasonable that they might be conceded by the reason of the world. In fact, ever since the Treaty of Versailles, which was the main cause of these conditions, the world had been prepared to admit the validity of much of the complaint, but had done little or nothing of a practical kind to remedy it. Until the arrival of the Nazi Movement, in power, reason had failed, and reason did not appear much more successful in obtaining a response to the long series of conciliatory gestures—disarmament proposals, etc.—which followed the arrival of the new Germany, and heralded a higher degree not only of will but of political skill in charge of the destinies of Germany. In face, therefore, of a blank wall of negation three courses appeared open to the German Leadership. The first was to use what resources they possessed to build a German State which should be a model of achievement to the world in the hope and expectation that the new spirit stirring everywhere in Europe would later bring to power in other countries movements which would possess a greater realism, and also a greater sympathy for German aspirations within a new harmony of the European spirit. The second course was to draw from History the sad lesson that reason seldom operates in human affairs unless it is at least supported by force, and so to proceed as far as possible in regaining populations and acquiring raw materials and living space without going so far as to produce a war. For a considerable period this second policy was actually pursued according to the evidence of such historic facts as the occupation of the Rhineland, Austria and the Sudetenland by a measure of force which was insufficient to awaken the fear, anger and fighting will of the sluggish " Democracies."

The third course was to draw from History the bitter lesson that nothing is ever conceded to reason but only to triumphant force and so, with cold and deliberate calculation, to prepare for the inevitable war in circumstances the most propitious to Germany—which were, of course, surprise. An impartial reading of History would indicate that the third course was never consciously pursued; such long, cold and deliberate decision of the mind and will are very rare in human affairs. In any case, it is clear that the third course conflicted sharply with the second, which was obviously pursued for a period. The deployment of the second course would clearly be almost fatal as a preliminary to the third, because, if it is held that war is inevitable, the last thing a realist should do is to give his opponent continual warning of his intention and approach: particularly if the potential enemy is a strong but sleepy fellow who is formidable by reason of his latent strength when he is awake, but almost helpless if he is not stirred out of his condition of habitual lethargy. It is also, on the other hand, clear that the pursuit of the second

115

course must traverse sharply the development of the first; because, if it were hoped that Movements would grow in other countries which were more sympathetic to the aspiration of a New Europe than the existing Governments, it would be obviously undesirable from this standpoint to create continual tension which made their position difficult to the point of the impossible. In fact, three courses were open to the German Leadership, any one of which might have succeeded but which were mutually exclusive. In such circumstances a confusion between conflicting aims and methods is " human, all too human," but supreme achievement requires a realism in union with idealism, which might be held to approach the superhuman. Yet these attributes must be possessed by that " Thought-Deed " type whose character, so vitally necessary to the future, will be the subject of a later study in this work.

As a lesson for the future, our task is here confined to a review in a little detail of the problems confronting the German Leadership and the three courses which might have presented it with successes of a very diverse character if any of the three had been the subject of concentrated and single-minded pursuit.

COULD GERMANY HAVE LIVED WITHOUT THE USE OF FORCE?

As time passed it became increasingly clear that the National Socialist and Fascist leadership of Europe was experiencing a progressive disillusionment with the prospect of an early solution by consent through process of reason. Germany, for better or worse, turned her back on the first course outlined above and moved towards a reliance on the second, with ultimate embroilment in the third. In the first instance this brought disaster to the friends of Germany abroad and, in the second instance, doom to the Third Reich.

It may, of course, be argued that, if Germany were either to build a state which might be an example to the rest of the world, or to avoid a war for living space, it was necessary for her by all means short of war to secure the raw material and room requisite to the achievement of the former and the avoidance of the latter. In fact, this argument could postulate that within the area to which she was confined Germany could not develop or even live; therefore, it was necessary by some acts of force, whatever the disadvantages, immediately to remedy the position, at least, in some degree. This is, of course, a very difficult question for anyone outside the inner German circles to judge fairly with anything approaching a grasp of the facts. But some comment may be made upon it. In the first instance, not only the cultural and spiritual achievement of the New Germany but also the material successes were amazing in relation to the resources at their disposal, even before additional room of any kind was secured. The impression made at that time on any impartial visitor to the country was enormous, and this fact lends weight to the view that a standard of civilisation might have been achieved in Germany which, in relation at least to her previous condition, would have been an almost decisive factor in the world argument even prior to her obtaining the full and fair opportunity for development which would have followed the universal adoption of a new Idea. If this course too, had been pursued with the concentration of a single purpose, a large part of the production devoted to armaments would have been available for its fulfilment. In these circumstances for instance, our Movement in Britain could have argued with overwhelming force " if they have done so much with their resources, what could a National Socialism of British character achieve with Empire resources?" That situation would have greatly assisted not only the urge toward a change of system in Britain, but the emergence of a Europe united in friendship with Germany in place of a Continent continually divided by the antagonism of old and new creeds. Both Britain, drifting to a deeper economic catastrophe than she had ever known before, and France, racked by financial scandals and torn by the deep cleavage between her great traditions and the current condition of her politics, would have advanced to a very different alignment of European thought and power if the fear of Germany had been replaced by an example of industrial achievement and spiritual regeneration which faced the rest of the world with an argument of accomplished fact.

117

Admittedly, this is a somewhat idyllic picture which in face not merely of a stupid and conceited world, so far unchastened by any break in the smug prosperity of the dominant powers, but also of the coldly scheming hostility of a finance, which, naturally, feared such a success as fatal to its own position, must have been difficult of achievement to the point of the impossible. It must, at any rate, be conceded that the progressive winning of ever higher standards of civilisation, which is rightly expected of and desired by a dynamic movement, could not have been secured without expansion of Germany beyond the narrow space to which she was confined by Versailles. Any development within that area was clearly limited and could only be regarded as a relative achievement in comparison with the miserable condition of the country before the new Movement won power. The limit of that work might soon be reached and, if opinion in the rest of the world had not moved in time, a standstill in progress would be experienced. In face of such considerations and the uncertainty of events outside Germany it may well be difficult for the Historian of an unprejudiced future to blame the German Leadership for proceeding as far as possible to gain space and raw materials without incurring war; in fact, the long series of coups before 1939 could claim the justification of success in default of any alternative in a world which had long turned a deaf ear to any appeal to reason. But, it cannot be denied that the effect of this second course of policy, which was pursued by Germany at this stage, imposed naturally and inevitably the maximum possible handicap on all Movements in other European countries which were friendly to her. On the one hand, the fact that they stood for peace and friendship with Germany could be turned against them with the vilest misrepresentation when every move of Germany excited fears of war on a German initiative. On the other hand, their success as National Movements clearly depended, as had previously the triumph of National Socialism in Germany and Fascism in Italy, in large degree on the collapse, or semi-collapse, of the Financial Democratic economic system. In fact, the one thing which could prevent this occurring was first, the alarm of war

118

with consequent armaments expenditure, and, second, actual war with a riot of unproductive effort for the full employment of labour which the " Democracies " had utterly failed to achieve for the constructive purposes of peace, even in sufficient degree to avoid widespread unemployment in a world urgently requiring the goods which the idle hands could produce. Nothing could save the " Democracies " from the disgraceful doom occasioned by their failure to bring together their vast material resources and their unemployed labour to end the poverty and distress which was a blot on the face of a civilisation possessing a potential of wealth without parallel in history. Nothing could save them except one event—that was war—and their last chance and only salvation was provided by German policy. Well may the spirit of the Roman poet whisper to the soul of Europe, " these are the tears of things."

So the " Democracies " seized the traditional and effective, if temporary, escape of all bankrupt systems from the inherent rottenness of their economic system and the decadence of their principles of Government. In a paradox, which is all too characteristic of the relationship of current propaganda to the realities of History, the desire of Germany to secure sufficient living space to begin the building in peace of a new civilisation was represented as the attempted escape of a Dictatorship from internal difficulties by means of war. In fact, war came just in time to save the " Democracies," who had staggered through successive economic crises, from their final economic crash, which would have given our new Movement in Britain, for the first time, that same opportunity of obtaining power with the ardent support of a disillusioned people, which elsewhere had been turned to the triumph of new causes.

In the ultimate paradox of History, it was the cause of Fascism which was lost by war, and the cause of " Democracy " which was temporarily saved. If anyone doubts that let them just watch for a while longer the efforts of " Democratic " statesman-ship in present circumstances to meet deepening economic crises. Despite the " totalitarian " powers which war has left in their hands—despite their vast resources and a world-demand for

119

goods—the inherent weakness of system and character will soon
operate.

PRE-WAR MISTAKES OF GERMANY IN TERMS OF REAL POLICY

However, in face of all such considerations it may still be
argued that the German Leadership was right from the purely
German standpoint to pursue an exclusively nationalist policy,
as, for reasons already analysed, all National Socialist and Fascist
Movements of the world were then conceived and organised on
purely national lines, which followed rigidly national policies.
What mattered to the German Leadership in the German interest
was quickly to win living space for Germany, and to regain exiled
populations at whatever cost to the position of their friends in
the world. Germany must come first; that was natural to the
Germans; it was both the strength and weakness of an ultra-
nationalist philosophy. We must grant this premise in studying
German policy for the purpose of this section, purely from the
standpoint of the paramount German interest, in the hope of
deriving some lesson for a future realism in a policy of European
achievement. It is at this point that serious criticism of German
policy may begin under a realistic analysis. Let us deal with
the matter at this stage in terms of pure " Real Policy " without
regard to any sentimental or even moral considerations. So, bear
with me a little in these " immorally " realistic considerations,
British moralists of the Puritan School. We will later consider
most seriously whether you correctly understood the direct
instructions of the Almighty in one generation to blow Sepoys off
the end of cannon, because they resisted what they thought was
an interference with their religion, and, in a subsequent generation
to resist, if necessary by force of arms, the rough handling of
Jews in Berlin or Vienna, where, for diverse reasons, they had
made themselves for many generations past highly unpopular
with the local population. Remember all the charges of wholesale killing, etc., only arose long after the Declaration of War,
and this subject, too, in due course, will be frankly examined in the
interests of truth, historic perspective, and the attainment of the
European future on a solid foundation of unprejudiced fact.

We have already observed that the second course, which was actually pursued by Germany for some years before 1939, must not only have the effect of destroying the first course, which has already been discussed, but must also adversely affect the prospects of the third course if that ever became necessary. The third course was a war of surprise. The purpose would have been to win living space and liberate German populations if the fixed hostility of the rest of the world, under the effective leadership of the Money Power, should continue to refuse any appeal to reason until the final breaking point was reached. In the event of that contingency arising it must have been clear that a series of armed coups would alarm and arouse the opponents, which is the last situation any real policy should produce if a war of surprise be necessary. These considerations are yet more relevant if success by surprise is essential in the event of war, because the industrial resources, and, consequently, the war potential of the opponent in the conditions of 1939, were far greater. Germany was faced by possible enemies with enormous latent strength but relatively slight available, and mobilised, power. The first dangerous opponent was a giant fellow, but well covered with the blubber of fat and loose living engendered by the " easy " principles which governed his usual existence. Germany was in the position at that time of a far lighter man with nothing approaching the opponent's muscular resource, but fit, wiry and trained to the last ounce of possible achievement by a system and spirit of resurgent manhood. If war had to come everything depended for Germany on a quick win. In these circumstances it would not appear wise constantly to prod and slap the fat fellow with the continual warnings that he might get a hiding if he did not wake up; which were provided by the series of coups between 1936 and 1938. Against this view it might be argued that these strokes were necessary to provide Germany with extra resources if war should come. Again, without access to any of the facts which were then at the disposal of German Government, it is difficult to give an informed judgment upon the relative merits of the additional striking power thus obtained and the paramount factor of surprise. But it is difficult to believe, for reasons which will shortly be examined in the political and psychological field as well as the military, that in the German situation of 1939 any factor can have transcended the desirability of a quick win if war had to come; and that clearly could best be secured by surprise. *Prima facie,* at any rate, the German coups in the years which preceded war broke the first principles of real policy.

Those rules in simple form are habitual to any experienced swordsman—make a move to hit an opponent—make a move to deceive an opponent—but never make a move to show him what you are going to do next. These ancient laws of men in real things have always had, and ever will have, a direct bearing on the most complex questions of strategy and all great forms of life struggle. The same traditional wisdom of men who have lived with real things should teach us, also, that sabres are meant to thrust, or to cut, but never to rattle. The effect of rattling a sabre is to say to an enemy, " on guard," and, while that formality is considered essential to the courtesy of a *salle d'Armes,* the harsh necessity of reality may have to dispense with it in war. The simple truism is too often forgotten that in war it is foolish ever to indicate to your opponent what is going to happen next. All display of strength, all public playing with the glittering toys of armaments, all brandishing of weapons, all marching and counter-marching without definite military objective, can only have this effect. Where strength exists it should always be concealed if, in fact, it is intended to use it. It should only be displayed if, in fact, it is not intended to use it; when it is believed to the point of certainty that the objective can be obtained by a bluff, or a threat, without recourse to arms. But, in that event, before the display of strength is given it should be clearly decided whether or not it will be fully effective for the purpose in view. If any doubt exists on this point and it is possible, let alone probable, that an actual conflict must occur, it is vital to conceal strength and never to display it, because the element of surprise in the ultimate decision will transcend every other factor. These considerations were of vital importance in the War of 1939: they will be paramount in any war of the future. Such lessons of real policy must be marked with care, because the next conflict with Russia really may decide the fate of Europe—and the world.

To what conclusion, therefore, do these principles lead us in a survey of German policy prior to 1939? For reasons already sufficiently examined the first course is excluded, although the writer is convinced it would have succeeded by reason of the ultimate collapse of "Democracy," and the victory of new movements with popular support. But, in the remaining choice between the second and third courses, the condemnation of German policy is clear under the test of realist thought. Before adopting the second course, they should have made up their minds not to proceed beyond it to the third course. They should have decided either to go as far as they could without war in the winning of living space and the liberation of exiled Germans, or they should have made no move to warn their enemies and have concentrated on breaking their bonds by a war of complete surprise. That is the real criticism in those terms of historic objectivity which must ever survey history in the first instance in terms of pure realism, without reference to moral or human considerations.

No greater problem confronts the human mind than the interaction of the moral, as man conceives it, and the real, as fact and nature present it. This grave matter will certainly not be avoided; but in this section we are engaged in an historic survey of the real in the sense by which not only the military but also realist-political minds of the past have studied these affairs. In terms of such "reality" the criticism of German policy prior to 1939 was that it hesitated fatally between two opinions. Having embarked upon a policy of obtaining as much as possible by a limited measure of force without incurring war, it finally drifted, or was goaded, into a policy which, in the last stage, clearly would be made a cause of war. From the outset, in the light of such considerations, policy should have said " so far and no farther "—the limit being the outbreak of war; or, alternatively, war it must be; so no warning but all preparation. Always in life is needed the clear-cut plan which is the result of

123

profound reflection; comprising the weighing of all known factors and the study of the opponent's psychology. Once formulated and decided it should be pursued with the utmost force of will and passion of purpose. But never should irritation with opponent or circumstances, and certainly not the impulse of the moment, which is not related to reasoned plan, deviate the purpose from the preconception of reason. Only fresh facts and evidence should postulate a change: otherwise it is not mind and will but the conduct of the opponent which forms policy. Flexibility and readiness to adapt plan to new circumstances are ever vital; such changes are inevitably forced by unforseeable factors upon the man of action; but ice-cold should be the mind that conceives and fiery only the will which executes.

The science of thought and decision is eternal in human affairs, and lessons may be derived from a situation which may never recur in the same form and are only applicable in future, if at all, to totally different spheres of action. The " Thought-Deed" man of the European future should study all situations in which human mind and will have interacted with great events, because, only when we understand the circumstances in which even the strongest minds and wills have failed, can we hope in new spheres of human activity to transcend those human failings which have brought vast conceptions to ruin.

If the world is to live man must surpass himself; in a dark scene it is a source of hope that many of the realist qualities required for the future have already been adumbrated by history in what may be described as the Caesarian type. At least, the mighty shadow of the " Thought-Deed " man has already appeared on Earth.

MISCALCULATIONS OF GERMANY IN WAR

But it is necessary before considering the future, to pursue to some conclusion the study of those factors which brought to the dust the extraordinary spiritual and material achievements of National Socialist Germany. How was it that an urge of the mind and will, which for years was so superbly evoked and led, failed in the clash of arms, despite the creation in the year 1939 of the most formidable instrument for that purpose which the world had yet witnessed. How was it that the magnificent vitality and self-discipline, loyalty to cause, power of organisation and detailed realism in working and planning combined with every capacity for sacrifice to the ideal, and innumerable other noble qualities of the German people at that time, could end in the most bitter frustration of History?

We have already examined some of the faults of policy prior to the outbreak of war, and they will appear to be accentuated in the light of our earlier study both of the greatness and weakness of the English character; for the psychology of a people which has so far always been an enigma to the outside world was a decisive factor in these great events.

Some brief survey should now be made of those main decisions by the German Leadership during the war which appeared to violate every principle of realist policy. For reasons already stated, it was not only desirable, but necessary from their standpoint, for Germany to win quickly. In any case it is elementary to the point of the trite to suggest that the plan by which a war can be fought to a conclusion should be, at least, envisaged from the outset. It was clear that Germany could only end the war either by decisively defeating Great Britain, or by forcing her to accept peace by measures which made her further effective conduct of the war impossible. To believe that the British would stop fighting while they were still able to fight was a grave misreading of the national character. If, in fact, that view was held, despite all evidence on which a contrary opinion should have been based, it was a blunder of the first order. A reading of history without any study of the national psychology would, at least, prevent an error so egregious. If, then, the premise be granted that the British would only stop fighting if they had to stop, what measures were available to Germany for compelling this end? Three possibilities appeared to present themselves: (1) The Submarine; (2) Air Bombardment; (3) Invasion. A realistic and historic sense, reviewing the prospects of the submarine in 1939, would surely doubt whether the repetition of a menace which had nearly brought success a quarter of a century

125

before was likely to bring any great results again. If ever an enemy had been warned of danger this opponent had been notified by bitter experience of this possible disaster. It says much for the quite remarkable lethargy of the British system and Leadership between wars that, even after the experience of 1914—18, the submarine weapon was able to get the results it did in the war of 1939—40. Yet, in great events, no one can reckon as a gift of nature upon the laziness and stupidity of opponents, even when they are the leaders of " Democracies ": Fate is rarely so kind as that. In the light of such considerations, therefore, it should have appeared highly doubtful from the outset whether the submarine weapon could again approach a decision.

As to the weapon of Air Bombardment, unaccompanied by military measures, it was, except for minor experience, an almost entirely unknown factor. It might or might not be decisive; it was impossible to judge definitely because success depended on so many imponderable factors, such as the bearing of the civil population, which are difficult to analyse in advance in the case of another country which has not been at war for a number of years. Air bombardment would appear, in any case, too uncertain a weapon at that stage on which to rest a calculation upon early success, which the time-factor made almost imperative. These considerations must have been particularly cogent, as it appears that the limited resources of Germany tied down the available Air Force very largely to Army co-operation, and they had not the surplus of supply available for the task of developing an independent striking force on the lines later adopted by the British. This restriction brought two disadvantages; the first that the Air Force was not primarily designed for the purpose of such air bombardment, and the second that the use of the Air Force for such ends beyond a certain point of loss might jeopardise the position of the Army, with which it was designed to co-operate, in the by no means unlikely contingency of that Army being called upon to perform further tasks of the first magnitude. In fact it appears that this point was reached in the attempt of the German Air Force to reduce

Britain by bombardment, and the requirements of the Army in the possible, and, later, probable, clash with Russia would have been imperilled if the Air Bombardment of Britain had continued.

GERMANY'S DECISIVE WAR BLUNDER

The conclusion, therefore, seems unavoidable that the only effective means open to Germany of eliminating Britain from the war was an invasion and occupation. No one has held more firmly than the present writer that such an invasion would have been out of the question if Britain had possessed the Air Force second to none in Europe, together with the modernised Navy, in front of a small but effective and mechanised Army, which he had advocated for years before the war. The experience of 1940, at least, justified this view entirely. Britain possessed no such Air Force; no such Army; and little of such a Navy. Yet, to put it no higher, the Germans found the greatest difficulty in invading Great Britain. The Englishman resolutely refused to wake up, despite every warning, and yet was saved by his Channel and a tiny handful of Airmen. Nevertheless, despite every traditional heroism, that small Air Force must surely have been overwhelmed at that time by sheer weight of men and material from any mass attack planned and organised in advance from the Continent.

The enigma of history is now made the more mysterious by ever-accumulating evidence that no such attack was ever really envisaged, let alone worked out as a decisive plan of paramount importance from the German side. Yet, on that attack hung the whole issue of the war for Germany. History presents no more extraordinary phenomenon than the attitude of the German Leadership towards the forcing of a quick decision with Great Britain. A large body of evidence appears now to be available which was collected from German Generals, without contact with one another in various prison camps, by one of Britain's leading military thinkers. All the evidence seems to suggest that the problem of invading Britain was never seriously faced, and that the planning of the undertaking on a large scale and in

127

requisite detail was vetoed by the higher political direction. It is even suggested that a decision with the British military forces on the Continent was deliberately not forced at Dunkirk. Prior to this evidence, it was generally assumed by military critics that the invasion of Britain was exhaustively examined but abandoned as impracticable in face of British Sea Power, etc. It was always difficult to follow this view in consideration of the practically helpless position to which previous neglect had reduced the defences of the Island in the Air and on Land. It was, in fact, impossible to believe that an Air Force, as numerically powerful as the German Air Force was in relation to the British at that time, could not give air cover to an invading army against any Navy in a narrow sea only twenty miles across; provided that the German Air Force had been concentrated on that problem, and their General Staff had been wholly dedicated to attaining this objective. Even a rapid improvisation on the lines of an inverted evacuation of Dunkirk, by which an advancing army would follow the same course as the retiring army in a medley of small craft, would surely have landed and supplied, under strong air protection, sufficient German forces to secure a decision in a country where they would have been faced with little except a Home Guard undergoing its first few days of training.

Why the first principle of the pursuit was not applied in these circumstances remained one of the mysteries of History. Now it appears that not only was it not attempted but it was not even seriously contemplated. The mystery deepens to the point of the inexplicable. Was it that some extraordinary idea existed that all could be settled by political skill alone when passion had reached such a point? Was the illusion nurtured that the British mind in such circumstances would move as logically as the Continental mind, which knew something of military matters? If so, both the invincible courage and the yet more invincible ignorance of the English were profoundly underrated. Did some extraordinary sentimental consideration traverse the mind of German Leadership to the destruction of every realistic consideration? It is almost unbelievable that any such feeling should have influenced so far; but it is one of the tear-laden paradoxes of History that the man, whom the mass of the English learnt to regard as their greatest enemy, cherished a sentimental feeling toward a " sister nation " which, in the eyes of historic realism, must border on the irrational, and, in the test of fact, was pregnant with the doom of all he loved. This view seems too fantastic in such circumstances of life-or-death decision to permit any credence, but it appears to be supported in large degree by the sober testimony of diverse German General Staff Officers.

Whatever the underlying cause—and it is doubtful if the full truth will ever be known—it is clear that in the German conduct of the war at this point every rule of real policy was broken. And who can deny the eternal truth of these basic principles? In war, when the enemy breaks, the relentless pursuit is vital, to the exclusion of all else; until a decision is reached—pursuit —pursuit—pursuit—nothing else matters until he is down and it is over. Every text book they had ever known or studied taught them this. In all real things which concern the clash of body, mind and will the same eternal reality holds: when the big fellow staggers—attack—attack—attack—no other thought until it is done. If it was not contemplated that the attack on the French front in 1940 would succeed, it should not have been undertaken. If it was considered, as must have been the case, that it would succeed, the pursuit to a conclusion of the war, which could only mean the invasion of Britain, should have been prepared in advance by express and urgent instructions of the political leadership. Nothing should ever be put into execution which has no chance of success; if success is won the opportunity which it presents should never be neglected, particularly if that opportunity is the chance of a final decision. To exert yourself to achieve a result without reaping the benefit is a denial of all realism; it is to sow but not to harvest. Unless these simple principles are denied (and to such ultimate clarity the infinite complications of real policy, in the final analysis, can be reduced) the German conduct of the war in late 1940 must be regarded as the prime cause of her ultimate defeat.

What strange enchantment brought the long pause on the German side after the fall of France until they again violated every principle of real policy by turning their back on an undefeated enemy to advance upon Russia. They turned their back, too, on an enemy still resolute. He was mortally weak, it is true, but he had vast latent resources available to him for slow building into effective operation, and a long array of friends and relations—including the potentially strongest country in the world—who could be gradually cajoled and manoeuvred by a great traditional political skill, in alliance with the incessant intrigues of the Money Power, into a world coalition of overwhelming force. Did the tomb of Napoleon, enshrined in the vast bitterness of that same and, then, ineluctable experience, never whisper again in the Paris of late 1940, " ask me anything but time."

The Duplicity of Russia was Main Cause of War

The subsequent clash with Russia has often been criticised as a fatal error, both in origin and in some of the detailed conduct of the campaign, which stretched both the German lines and resources much too far. But it can be argued with force that at most this fault was only a subsidiary error in relation to the failure to settle with Britain in 1940. It would have been a very uneasy strategic position to wait indefinitely for a possible Russian attack in the East, while British strength slowly mounted in the West and drew on another hemisphere for aid in the final encounter. A military power with an offensive tradition might well hold it fatal to sit passively in the shadow of the gathering storm. The oriental cunning of Russian policy must then have been as plain to German eyes as it later became to the vision of the further West. Then, as now, Russia was playing to win time for the next move. Already Russian policy had set a match to the whole powder magazine of Europe. The abrupt change of policy which took her over from an alignment with the Allies to a close understanding with Germany, which culminated in the carve-up of Poland, will probably be regarded by an objective Historian as the biggest single factor in the origin of war. If

Russia had stood calmly and patiently with her Western associates and had not double-crossed them to do the deal with Germany, which led to the disappearance of Poland, would a realist policy in Germany have challenged that combination in 1939? On the other hand, if Russia had declared from the outset, plainly and clearly, her solidarity with Germany on the Polish and cognate questions, it is doubtful whether even the hotheads, which followed a condition of cold slumber in Britain, would have challenged by force of arms they did not then possess so massive and decisive an array in so remote a territory. In fact, if Russia had been steadfast and faithful in anything, straight and loyal to her engagements to either side, it is highly probable that war would not have come.

It was this manoeuvre by Russia, which appeared to take her over to the German side in 1939, that encouraged German Leadership to think that expansion in the East could be secured by agreement with Russia without serious interference from an unprepared West, even if such a preventive war should be attempted by Britain and France in these circumstances. The subsequent and second change of attitude in Russia came after Germany was committed to war. The cunning Oriental only demonstrated his friendship until his friend was finally committed to the path of danger: the faithful companion withdrew his succour directly his comrade had been lured into the morass. For, at once he began to move away to his original position with a good load of booty in his pocket from having double-crossed first the Western Powers and, later, Germany. It was at this stage a probably reasonable calculation on the German side that Russia's next move would have been to assail a Europe exhausted by internecine conflict, after an interval in which she had grown stronger and the West had grown weaker. In view of the record of that time, was it unreasonable to discern a Russian intention to grow fat while Europe bled, until the strength she had derived from Continental war could overwhelm the weakness to which all others had been reduced. At that stage in 1941 it is quite possible to follow the logical working of the German mind: it is 1940 that presents the enigma which contradicts every consideration of real policy. From the German error of 1940 followed almost inevitably the situation of 1941. To lose the opportunity of 1940 was to bring Germany to ultimate fatality: Destiny seldom beckons twice. So it is possible in terms of pure realism to understand German policy in 1941 but not in 1940. The clash with Russia was the cause of ultimate German exhaustion, but the failure to pursue in 1940 was the first cause of that cause.

The struggle with Russia may therefore be regarded as a secondary factor which merely implemented the causal sequence of fatality begun in 1940.

The decisive importance of the Russian factor rather belongs to the phase of 1939. It was her habitual duplicity that produced a catastrophe well calculated to end in a European collapse; which would expose the whole life, culture and tradition of the West to the triumphant advance of that Oriental and, consequently, alien form of Government which is known as Communism. It was only her perpetual double-dealing and constant shifting of position, in the manner best calculated to produce war, that finally lured the West to that fratricidal struggle from which only the Orient could gain. In this case, the Siegfried of the Western genius fell a victim to the wiles and trickery of the spiritual dwarf who emerged so cautiously from his Oriental underworld to win by cunning what he could never achieve by intellect or strength.

The Decisive Part of Science

Only one force other than speed could have brought Germany victory, and that was Science. It is now a commonplace that the stress of the last war brought the greatest advance in Science that History has witnessed. A consideration of the tragic paradox that a convulsion of destruction seems always more fruitful than the creative urge for the purpose of such achievement, belongs to another place. That study goes to the root of things, and must pass through the sphere of human psychology to the realm of almost pure metaphysics in order to discuss whether the force, which is commonly regarded as evil, can be discerned as performing some function in the fulfilment of a higher purpose on this earth. These matters have long concerned the philosopher and the intuitive poet, and must engage the deep reflection of the system builder of the future in a world consciously directed by Thought-Deed men in the service of a higher purpose. Therefore, we must dare to wrestle with these high things before this book is ended. But, at present, we are only here engaged in a brief historic survey in terms of realistic objectivity. So, we merely note the fact that Science made an enormous advance in the last war, and the further fact that, if the weapons available at a later stage of the war had been at Germany's disposal at even a slightly earlier period, she would have won the war. Not only a speedy decision before her sluggish opponents were ready would have brought her victory, but, also, a slight lead at any stage of the war in decisive new weapons of Science. It has already, for instance, been observed by military commentators that if Germany had possessed the Atom Bomb even a few weeks before her defeat she yet could have wrested complete victory from imminent disaster. It was clear in the later stages of the war that such considerations greatly engaged the mind of German Leadership from the constant appeals to the German people to hold on until new weapons were ready. And it later became plain that many striking new inventions were at their command, or, on the verge of being completed, when the end came.

It is not clear, however, from anything yet published, whether they had anything in near prospect so decisive as the Atom Bomb. But it seems to be established that the effort to produce such weapons was the almost exclusive preoccupation of the German Leadership in the last stages of the war; and for the obvious reason that, when speed had not been used to secure a decision when it was possible, only Science could bring victory, or even avoid defeat, in face of the enormous material superiority of their enemy. Speed in the earlier days, and Science in the later days, alone could win. The combination of speed and science at an earlier stage would, of course, have brought success beyond the wildest dreams of Germany. If Science provided weapons which the opponent did not possess, and speed and decision of political will and intelligence were used in their application, for the first time in history the numerical and material superiority of these established Powers would have been useless in face of the new striking power of their challenger. In such circumstances, all the vast industrial strength of the old world, even with the addition of the Communist hordes, would have been useless in face of the energy and will expressed by a new science in combination with a higher type of political direction, which could grasp new factors and use them with decision. New politics were the sling and Science the stone, with which the resolute hand and steady eye of a young new world could have reduced all the great, but lethargic, strength of the old world of things as they are. In terms of realistic objectivity Science for the German statesman and strategist was, in the new phase of History, the key to all. The Thought-Deed type of politics, together with the scientists of technical achievement, could have opened the door of the world.

In our historic enquiry, therefore, we ask the essential question why these two types did not come together in the hour of decision which preluded Germany's mortal agony. A political leadership existed which, in thirteen years of struggle and nearly seven years of power, had accomplished in terms of material and spiritual achievement a renaissance which had lifted Germany from the dust to the heights. Men may argue as they like whether that achievement was for good or evil, but they cannot deny the achievement. The political leadership was there which had done these things. A Science was, also, there which was second to none in the world; no Scientist can deny this. Political leadership was there, and Science was there; did they never come together before it was too late? Above all, did they ever come together before war began? The answer appears to be that they did not.* For, it is now clear that these things

*The complete division between scientists and politicians in Britain was well illustrated by an incident within personal experience. As a member of the Executive of the Labour Party before the election of 1929 I was requested to prepare a draft programme as an alternative to a draft presented by Mr. Ramsay MacDonald which some of us had strongly opposed. My draft included a proposal to allocate

were at least living in the air of science before war began. It is even suggested, with the support, apparently, of considerable evidence, that the original researches, which made possible the Atom Bomb, were being done in Germany before the war began. Was it possible that the German Leadership would have permitted war to come in 1939 if they had been at all seized of these possibilities? Could they have failed to possess, at least, a presentiment of such potentialities if they had used the vast resources available to them in their Government to acquaint themselves with what was happening in the world of science. Should they not have made it even their chief concern, to study with eager enquiry the immense vistas which science opens to the constructive mind, ever striving for great purposes of peace, but also, ever conscious, in the sad, harsh reality of mortal things, that a strife of arms may be compelled.

Would not Thought-Deed men in German Leadership have lived in the company and inspiration of scientists, as a Medici lived in the company and inspiration of artists? By their life with, and understanding of, the artist, and their genius for organising and co-ordinating his work, these men of the Renaissance left to posterity works of art which are the glory of the ages. By a similar companionship, understanding and co-ordinating executive genius, the Thought-Deed men of politics could work with the scientist to achieve a new world. Surely things had gone far enough to suggest to men with absolute power of

annually large sums for scientific research in both medical and industrial sphere. This suggestion was vigorously combated by Mr. MacDonald, who shortly afterwards became Prime Minister for the second time, on the ground that it would outrage every canon of sound finance to ask the Treasury to provide large sums of money without a precise explanation in advance of what results would accrue from the expenditure. If I, or the scientists I desired to assist, could not say with certainty what would be discovered, the money would certainly not be provided. Such was the understanding of pure science by States-manship in the year 1929, and little progress was made in subsequent years. To reduce the discussion to the level which even a Labour Prime Minister could understand, we must comment that on this principle a father would reply, when asked to pay for his son's school fees for the term in advance, that he would not pay unless he could be sure the boy would get a scholarship ten years later, or at least, until he could see what result was obtained in the exam at the end of the term.

government, and with all information and resource of the kind at their command, that science might give them the key to all these countless problems, whether of Peace or War. In fact, Science may one day provide some people even with the means to accomplish all without war, by possession of unanswerable strength. Thus may the final contribution of Science be both the worst and the best.

It may be that things had not gone far enough and that in trying to draw the lessons of realism from that period we press matters too deeply. But may we not say with justice that, if great Politics and great Science had coincided in Germany in 1939, the fate of mankind would for ever have been changed.

From the standpoint of Germany forces, which contain the true dynamic of History, would have come together. For technicians, who could provide the means, would have been united with a people, who willed the end, under the direction and co-ordination of a political leadership which possessed both thought and will. Germany would have echoed with the words of a German genius " Seinen willen will nun der Geist; seine Welt gewinnt sich der Welt verlorene."

CHARACTER OF THE GERMAN PEOPLE

No less vital to great achievement than political and technical skill is a people that wills great ends, and can stand in union through long endurance to achieve them. Not even the most bitter enemy can deny to the German people that quality. They have been, and ever will remain, a factor in world History which cannot be ignored. From their own character and historic experience, derived from geographical facts, they have drawn these qualities. For centuries they have stood sentinel on the Eastern Marches of Europe against the Oriental invader. The Barbarian was ever at the gate. If they had not possessed great character, they would have succumbed centuries ago; if they had not suffered these experiences they would never have acquired the mighty instinct to cohere into a granite column and not to splinter into soft fragments. Their great quality contains a natural urge to unite and not to divide, a longing for great leadership and a desire to lift it when found to a place where it can greatly serve their great ends: in short, a solidarity, a conscious and deliberate self-discipline to secure high things, which their high intelligence and industry enable them very clearly to understand. These qualities are the result of experience imprinted on a character which has been rendered harder and more definite and effective by the experience. " Was uns nicht umbringt, macht uns härter." If you live ever in face of the foe you tend toward the solid ranks of a dedicated and knightly order rather than to the flighty discords of a debating society whose discussions can be diverting in periods of ease and plenty, but fatal in circumstances of strife and hardship.

Such are the supreme qualities of the German people which have lifted them to the heights where they belong. What defects then have cast them again to the depths? What errors of character or judgment have robbed them of everything which their immense abilities and energies deserved? No people could plan, organise or execute so well in detail; or bring to the task a greater power to endure in combination with a superb energy and fiery idealism. But few peoples have suffered from greater errors in the profound judgment and long planning of future action which were necessary to use these great qualities to the best advantage and bring them to material triumph. Their policy lacked lucidity in design and all finesse in application. Industry and knowledge were never lacking; only clarity in great decision. " Intellect, proportion and clarity " exclaimed Schiller—" There is Hellas." The supreme direction of Germany has often lacked that combination of qualities which, in the world of action, was, also, the guiding genius of Imperial Rome. That calm, cold clarity in far plan; that power of flexible adaptability to fresh circumstance combined with rigid inflexibility in root principle; that deep realism in harmonious union with high mysticism; that perfect balance and control of character superimposed on fierce but persistent energy; that still regard for nothing but facts combined with the passionate onrush of a nature wholly dedicated to a higher purpose; that mind of ice but will of fire— in short, the qualities of the Caesarian Man. The absence of this eternally indispensable factor in great achievement has been the tragedy of Germany, which brought to the dust all her supreme attributes. The presence of some of these qualities on occasion in the war statesmanship of the British people has often brought to them extraordinary fortune, despite the intermittent energy and incredible frivolity of the British ruling class. In strange repetition of Buonapartist History, the immense energies and capacities of the German people were twice defeated by the great political skill of a rare but recurrent type in British statesmanship, which is only permitted to attain effective power in Britain for such a purpose. Men of genius have thus frustrated a people of genius.

The history of this negation is now writ stark on the anguished face of European man. The world pays the penalty when artificial division overcomes a natural union. History indicates that Germany requires some of the finest qualities which England has produced in order to reap that great harvest which is deserved by the character and capacity of the German people. No less does every fact of this age prove that the English need the complementary qualities of the Germans in an equal partnership which can only be denied at the cost of further and, probably, irretrievable disaster. The qualities of Germany may be regarded by the rest of the world as a menace or a merit—judgment depends very largely on the question whether you want to get things done or to keep things as they are—but they must be recognised as a fact. The affirmative mind says—here is something great with which great things may be done; the negative mind says—here is something dangerous which may destroy our comfort and complacency. The ruling mind of Britain was negative because Britain was ruled by the comfortable and complacent. When the mind of Britain changes from a great negation to a decisive positive, Britain and Germany will come together as naturally complementary and related peoples. When America and France, too, under the creative necessity of this age, move from a negative to a positive, we shall be within reach of a new harmony, leading to a new dynamic of achievement, in which German qualities will be regarded not as a danger, but as an essential of world survival and advance. In one way or another the Germans will come back; and, in the end, no power on earth will keep them apart or hold them down.

PART II

THE CONSTRUCTION OF ACHIEVEMENT

CHAPTER III

THE UNION OF EUROPE AND THE DEVELOPMENT OF AFRICA IN RELATION TO AMERICAN POLICY

DYNAMISM has become a necessity. Previously it was a matter of choice; those conditions no longer prevail. No one can believe that the present situation may be overcome by immobility. Science has altered every premise of existence; the structure of civilisation must, also, be changed to fit the facts of a new conclusion. The spirit of the Denier must yield to the Dynamism of the Doer. For this reason I have analysed at length in Part I of this book the forces which have created the great Negation, and the circumstances and psychology from which they were born. The analytical and destructive task is done: the dead wood of the mind must be cleared, before new life can come. Now we face the task of construction, and are no longer concerned with critical analysis of existing things except by way of contrast, or as illustration of a difference in principle or method.

The problem has often been stated with much authority and some clarity. It can be reduced in essence to a complete simplicity. The world has shrunk, and man has found the means of complete self-destruction. From these recognised facts it follows that power must extend, and must reside in hands that will prevent the final catastrophe. But it is not enough to enlarge the basis of national power; the extension of patriotism is, also, necessary to support that power. The mind and the spirit of man must grow with the problem. A new spirit must move the peoples, and a new type of man must emerge in Government. Above all, the union of the best must replace the division of all that is vital in Europe. They can only be united in a constructive task for the rescue of our Continent from chaos and misery: men only unite and act together for a real purpose.

143

Thus, survival now depends upon development, which, in turn, awaits a new dynamism in Statesmanship. Let us, forthwith, face the realities of this situation. The future of the world depends on rapid action by those who are capable of achievement. The nations possessing that capacity are those which have produced great science. Such countries hold the scales of Fate —complete destruction, or construction beyond limit of present concept. In the reality of the present day these nations are America—Britain—France—Germany, and the Latin countries of Europe and South America. In the new conditions of science, which are now the only reality, they contain the future of mankind; in present terms of fact and power the rest is meaningless.

Quality is now everything and quantity is nothing. This statement may offend many, but it remains true. It is necessary now that fact should be stated; unless facts are faced the task is impossible. It is, for instance, difficult enough to unite these nations in a constructive task; it is out of the question in the short time remaining to unite the whole world. Yet, time is now wasted in the attempt to unite the fundamentally divided, and to draw into a new harmony the finally inharmonious. The effort would obviously have to be made if it were necessary either to survival or development: but it is not. If the great countries of the West were united, survival would be assured, because none could challenge their strength. If the same great nations were resolved on a new development of their resources, that achievement could be secured without let or hindrance by any other power; which, indeed, it would not concern. Nothing inhibits them except their own division.

But, before we consider present divisions and inhibitions, let us turn for a moment to the beckoning and enchanting possibility of a constructive work beyond the previous dreams of man. May I postulate, at once, two necessities of the future? The first is that Europe should unite, and the second is that Europe should develop Africa to secure the foodstuffs and raw materials which the Home Continent lacks. Both these propositions are no doubt highly debatable: in present politics the obvious has usually to be debated until it becomes obsolete.

144

May we, therefore, consider first the wide issue whether the Union of Europe is a necessity, and, later, the further question whether the appended Continent of Africa should provide the natural solution of our present economic troubles, and the best hope for a future development of our new civilisation to a full and complete life. The first proposition that Europe should unite now commands a wide measure of acceptance; it is as old as the thought of Napoleon, or older; so, people have had time to think it over! Once again we observe that a constructive idea, which is intrinsically desirable, only enters the field of the practical when the alternative is complete disaster. The second idea that Africa should be regarded as an Estate of the European, and should be vigorously developed as the chief enterprise of our Continent is so novel, in any practical form, that it is contrary to the whole trend of present thought and inimical to that current conception of morality which, *inter alia*, this book is intended to challenge. The latter must clearly be discussed at some length; the former suggestion that Europe must now unite should scarcely be seriously disputed in the light of present circumstance. It is not a matter of volition, but of compulsion; if we accept the elementary premise that it is desirable that humanity should survive, and reject Mr. Bernard Shaw's very reasonable suggestion that the recent performances of mankind warrant a contrary opinion.

Within Western Europe, and the related Americas, resides the answer to the basic question whether the human species will continue. There dwells the answer to the riddle, because, in any estimate of probability based on historic experience, within that area alone will be found the political energy and scientific capacity either to build a new era or to destroy the world. Is it conceivable that ultimate survival is possible, if science is not only permitted, but encouraged, or compelled, to hurl the thunderbolts of new discovery from nation to nation which are organised in present alignments? Such a picture of future life is as tolerable as a previous vision of the City and the rest of London, or Neuilly and the rest of Paris, organised as independent powers with their private armaments, and able to open a heavy artillery barrage on the adjoining suburb every time the local Mayors failed to agree on such daily problems as the disposal of the municipal refuse. Once the fact is grasped that the world has shrunk this analogy appears as apposite as it would previously have seemed fantastic.

THE END OF ISOLATION

It is no good saying, " Mind Britain's Business," as the writer said in 1939, or " Isolation," as able and patriotic Americans said, if, at any moment, a man somewhere the other side of the Channel, or somewhere the other side of the Atlantic, may press a button which releases a projectile that knocks London or New York flat. In the new circumstances what was plain commonsense becomes equally plain nonsense. Profoundly as I believe that we were right in our general view in the conditions of 1939, for reasons explained in my book, *My Answer,* I am, if possible, yet more convinced that in the new conditions the Extension of Patriotism from nation at least to Continent is an absolute necessity. We were right then to believe that an invading army could not cross the Channel if Britain had a strong Air Force and a modern Navy: we were not invaded although we possessed neither of these assets, and our argument appeared in practice even stronger than we claimed. We were right to say that we should Mind Britain's Business by concentrating on the building of a high standard of civilisation from the neglected wealth of British Empire, because the circumstances of that time gave Britain freedom to make this choice rather than to be drawn into the cauldron of European wars, where only financiers had interests. America, too, had an even greater case for saying the same thing in relation to the Western Hemisphere, because she had an even greater freedom of choice. Britain and America both had freedom of choice at that time if they had rested on their own strength and minded their own affairs; because they could not have been successfully attacked with the weapons of that period if they had been sufficiently armed against any such eventuality. In fact, they were not successfully assaulted even when they had no arms.

146

So, in my contention, we may claim to have been right at that time; but we should be obviously and absurdly wrong if we adopted that attitude to-day. Since that time every relevant fact has changed. Britain and America can be attacked with success from a remote distance by any power with the technical capacity to deliver the assault. Therefore, they have a vital interest in the area of the world which alone possesses such a standard of science and technique; it is not enough to say they have an interest, their whole life, their very existence is inevitably and irrevocably bound up with the destiny of Europe. Every premise of life and action has changed; not to recognise this is to step over a precipice in the belief that you are still stepping off the pavement. Only cowards surrender their beliefs when they are true; only fools cling to their beliefs when new facts render them no longer true. To live in the world a lifetime without learning anything is a waste of time, even when circumstances do not greatly alter. To live in the world without learning anything, during years in which all things change, is simply to be a fool. It is not now even a question of what is desirable; the situation has become a fact of necessity. Is it sense to sit comfortably in London, talking about British Empire, while the conduct of your politicians drives some despairing German to teach Russians, in a remote retreat behind the Urals, how to complete the Nibelung Saga of our times by blowing up the world? Is it realism, in such conditions, to sit in New York or Chicago with no eyes except for grain prices in the Middle West, or the movements of Wall Street? In 1939, to concentrate on the affairs of your own country was patriotism: in 1947, it is to serve the interests of the one country which desires to destroy your country and, indeed, the civilisation of the world. For, such an attitude can only have the result of giving Russia time, and a free hand, to prepare for the imposition of Communism by force upon all mankind. So, the attitude of a patriot in earlier circumstances becomes the conduct of a conscious, or unconscious, fifth columnist of to-day. It is one of the ironies, by which Fate has brought retribution to the last war's hypocrisy, that the old world has really got its Fifth Column at last; and Com-

147

munist Parties are so operating in many countries of the world.

THE EXTENSION OF PATRIOTISM: A NATURAL PROCESS

We must realise that the Universe has shrunk and none are safe until Patriotism has extended, and the precaution of a wider rule can impose inspection wherever destruction may be prepared. The practical method to eliminate these risks will be considered shortly: at present, we are engaged only in regarding the necessity for a wider union of present nations. We should surely not be required further to argue this necessity when the range of weapons has suddenly jumped from a few to several thousand miles and, at the same time, the force of explosives has been vastly increased by a new and revolutionary principle of science. Nevertheless, such is the obscurantism of human nature, and the selfishness of political vested interests, that a protracted argument is almost certain before the elementary action, which the new circumstances demand, is implemented in some form of European Union. But that necessity is now clear —at least to the stronger intelligences of our time, and it should command rapidly increasing support. The writer is always more concerned to argue propositions whose present necessity is not yet so clear, and to suggest solutions, which are not yet sought, but the near, or remoter, future will certainly demand. So, we can leave shortly the question of European Union to the clatter of present politics, and move forward to regions which such thought has not yet reached.

But some further comment may be added with advantage to the controversy on European Union at this stage. We may enquire whether this Union, which is dictated by necessity, is so unnatural or undesirable at this stage in human affairs. It is simply an acceleration of evolution; it is the speeding up of a natural process which has been evident throughout history. It would be startling, if it were not so familiar, to reflect that the union of England and Wales only took place in 1543, and the union of England and Scotland only obtained in 1707 after centuries of bitter warfare: even so late as 1745 the last Scottish invasion of England succeeded in reaching Derby. Every child

148

knows these things, and familiarity has robbed subsequent development of its surprising character. The fact remains that the extension of patriotism to embrace the present area of nations is of recent origin even in Britain, and over large regions of the Continent it came later still.

Throughout history the process has been natural and inevitable. As the mind of man grew and his circumstance enlarged, his sense of patriotism extended always in the same natural manner of first embracing his nearest kin, unless the process was traversed by conquest. The village merged with the next village until small kingdoms emerged to cover roughly the area of present counties: only a long and fluctuating history of internecine struggle and savagery, as well as intrusion from the outside world, finally stretched the region of a kingdom so far as to include the territory of a Wessex or Mercia in Saxon days. Only in the eighth century did these Kingdoms begin to lose their "particularism" according to Oman, who observes: "Local patriotism died hard, but it was definitely on the decrease in this age, though the union of all the kingdoms would undoubtedly have taken a much longer time to achieve but for the Danish invasions which taught Angle and Saxon that servitude to the heathen Viking could only be avoided by combination." The moral for the present age need not be pressed further. It is interesting to note that the previous Celtic civilisation had failed to save itself in like manner by some measure of union, and was consequently defeated. According to the description of Lingard: "The population was divided among a multitude of chieftains whose crimes and dissentions had rendered them too attentive to objects of personal feeling or aggrandisement to act with any combined effort against the common enemy." To this may be added the comment of Gildas that such chieftains after defeat used to be "slaughtered . . . not after any examination of their true merits" but because others had triumphed. From the failure of Celtic civilisation it appears that the spirit which leads to Nuremberg leads also to defeat: but these primitive societies possessed, at least, the merit of stripping such occasions of their hypocrisy.

149

In the wars of the Greek City States, and the civil conflicts of the Roman Republic, it is also possible to trace some ratio between the increase of internecine savagery and the decline of the ability to resist the external pressure of the barbaric challenger. But in those days, at least, the stranger was not invited to the board while you decided the fate of your relations. Rhythmic are the repetitions of History but not always ascendent.

Setting aside these embellishments of human " progress," we can note from history that an extension of national feeling took place to embrace and to unite with the nearest kindred as necessity dictated such a development. That has been the way of nature and of history; attempts rapidly to combine larger or stranger areas by the artificial processes of politics have not evinced the same durability.

THE BIOLOGICAL APPROACH:
THE ACCELERATION OF EVOLUTION

The difference between our biological approach and the political approach of internationalism is fundamental. For instance, the union of England and Scotland in 1707 was biological and natural, but the union of Britain and Timbuktu at that time would have been neither biological nor natural: in short it would have been that artificial and self-defeating process which has become known as internationalism. For such reasons, the idea of the Union of Europe may be placed in an altogether different category to attempts at internationalism like the League of Nations or the recent United Nations Oganisation. The first is biological, and in harmony with all nature and history: the second is purely political and, in large degree, a violation of both. All lessons of the past indicate that the Union of Europe is likely to succeed; while the political attempts to secure artificial combinations for power politics under a cloak of pseudo-idealism are likely to fail. The inhabitants of Europe and the Americas are related, and have all history and much nature in common. You may blend like with like, but you cannot mix oil and water; these simple facts have, hitherto, been overlooked by the politicians. Their myopia is not a peculiarity of the present day, because these same realities were, also, not observed by the industrious planners of the Tower of Babel.

We shall return later to the biological problem in an effort to restore some perspective of realism to a question which has been the subject of much nonsense, both in affirmation and negation, but is pregnant with rare possibility for the future. For the moment, it is only necessary to observe that the Union of Europe is merely a continuation of a process which has been manifest throughout History in the tendency to unite with related peoples of adjoining territory, in larger areas of rule and power, as new circumstance and development suggested or compelled. It is clear that the great leap in scientific potential also entails a quicker movement than the normal in the evolutionary unfolding of human relationships. For, science everywhere postulates this increasing rapidity of evolution, if humanity is not to be outstripped by pure mind. We have reached the point where nature must be assisted; the Mother of all in her present conception needs midwifery of Destiny. Deliberately we must accelerate evolution. This may well become a root thought of this Age; it is plainly a necessity. How many have said that man is not equal to the present creations of his mind; has anyone yet dared to say, in what are called practical politics, that we must, therefore, make new men who are equal to such development? It is not only in the relationship of States and their rapid enlargement to a wider unity, that we need more speed. Also we must accelerate the evolution of man. We must lay before humanity, as a religion, the deliberate striving for a higher form upon this earth.

Only higher men can match, and dwell with, the forces which the mind of present man have created. The world will not last long if we flatter the latter into believing that some neo-mythical " age of the common man " has arrived, and that he is a perfect " image of God " under no constraint to surpass his present condition of complete self-complacency, which is as pathetic as it is absurd. The present creed of reducing all to the ordinary, or below it, is not merely a denial of normal nature which works slowly to higher forms of the future, through the outstanding of the present. It is a complete negation of the first necessity of this age, which is to accelerate evolution by increasing the numbers, and intensifying the gifts and character, of those who are above the ordinary. To such consideration we will return in due course. At present, we need record only the fact that the clamant requirement of this age is to accelerate the evolution of man.

So, when we urge the Union of Europe we are only demanding at once something which all history shows would come in the end by ordinary process of nature. The Englishman, who regards us with fury because we ask him to unite with Frenchmen or German, must be gently told that his glare of patriotic passion merely reflects the equally inspired light in the eye of the Mercian when he was told to stop killing his hereditary enemies in Wessex and to unite for resistance to the Dane. It is true that in the ordinary course he would go on killing Germans or Frenchmen for a few more centuries before his mind enlarged. Unfortunately, however, we cannot spare the time as a new and strange species, called scientists, are making very odd things happen in the world which require a rather quicker tempo in the stately step of evolution, and, painful thought, in the intelligence of man. Therefore, as man has had a thousand years to think the matter over since Wessex and Mercia reluctantly abandoned their traditional pastimes, is it too much to ask him to make the effort to do now what his great-something-grandchildren would do in any case? If not—well —nature has tried and discarded in her striving prodigality many types and species: a lethal chamber, on the latest atomising model, seems to await those who are not quick-witted enough for modern life.

DOER VERSUS DENIER: THE "COPERNICAN" FALLACY

We postulate, therefore, that the Union of Europe is a first condition of human survival, and is not so revolutionary a step as may at first appear in that it only anticipates by a short space a process which is bound later to occur. In fact, already a considerable measure of support has been obtained for this proposal; as usual the main difficulty is not so much to propound paper plans as to get anything actually done in face of that great force of inertia which prevails within the " Democracies." In a more acute form than ever, and within a wider field, the old alignment between the Doers and the Deniers is beginning to take shape. The Doer type, as usual, tries to anticipate disaster by constructive action; the Denier exerts himself only to frustrate the Doer by impeding all action until it is too late in the interests of a *status quo* which he cannot realise is doomed.

This eternal clash of deeply divergent characters will, of course, continue whether or not the Union of Europe takes place.

A view of some *naivete* is advanced in America which suggests that the abolition of present national centres will almost automatically solve all human problems, and eliminate nearly every form of strife from mortal affairs. This standpoint is popularly known as the " Copernican ": and rests upon the thesis that the present divisions of mankind originate through regarding world problems from the different angles of the various national capitals, with the result that reasonable men see things quite differently; whereas, if they were all in the same situation, they would see all problems in much the same way. So, the argument appears to run, all that is necessary is to remove the distinction of nationality and thus make the angle of vision the same in all cases: then, at once, and without more ado, something like the millenium will arrive with universal agreement and acclamation.

Unfortunately, real life is not quite so simple as that; in fact, we shall later study certain tendencies which indicate that the purpose, as well as the phenomena, of life is a good deal more complex. It is quite true, as we have long contended, that an enlargement of national boundaries at least to Continental dimensions is a prerequisite of survival. But a further, and eternal, dynamism is no less a condition of continuing survival: on this earth there is no repose, and each triumph of the mind presents fresh and greater challenge to the will. It is one of the fallacies of a certain type of neo-religious reformism that at some given point a stable and perpetual condition of blessed repose is reached. The feeble wish is always father to the feebler thought, and the achievement of the magic state is usually to be reached through some incantatory word like " Socialism "; which the votaries often cannot even define. In this case the word of enchantment is " Internationalism," and the world of complete repose is usually to be obtained by such a wide embrace of such completely conflicting and diverse types, in such an entirely unnatural union, that the prospects of the desired quiet life are almost as probable as the " peace " which is to be obtained by locking up a tiger and a wild boar in the same cage. We have dealt elsewhere with the fallacies of the old Internationalism, and will not repeat the argument that attempts to introduce universal brotherhood by too close a blending of the completely incompatible can have no result but universal conflict. Setting aside the manifest illusions of the old " Internationalism," which have been amply demonstrated at innumerable " conferences," we have yet to admit that even the natural biological approach to a Continental Union among related peoples will not mark the end of human problems or the necessity for effort. In fact, as in the development of human character, each fresh achievement brings greater problems to evoke yet greater exertions of the mind and will.

More than ever, in the new age of science continued development is the condition of survival. Europe must unite to avert imminent disaster; but the great argument will still continue. More than ever will the division between the mind of the Doer and that of the Denier by accentuated. On the victory of the former in the hearts of the peoples will depend the future of the world. Survival and development will be increasingly interdependent; dynamism will become more than ever a necessity. But it may be generally anticipated that in a wider union the prospects for dynamic action will be improved: much that is static and inert will plainly have to disappear in the process, and the necessity for new and constructive thought will be obvious to many who are not normally moved by a yearning for change. A new period of flux and becoming is inevitable before a new civilisation crystallises within new boundaries: this will provide not only an opportunity but a demand for the dynamic in thought and in character. The Denier will be at a certain disadvantage in a society within which something plainly has to be done, and for that reason would, of course, be inclined to resist any move towards it; if Fate had not been so harsh as to place an Atom Bomb under his present seat, with the result that this limited space will shortly feel untenable even to his yet more restricted intelligence. So, reluctantly, the Denier will transfer his resistance to life and achievement to a wider sphere, where, however, his prospects of successful lethargy are unlikely to be quite so roseate as they were in the island of Britain until the recent war.

Both history and more recent experience combine to teach us that any view is much too ingenuous which holds that a larger union will mean the end of argument; the most that we can ever hope is that it will mean the elimination of conflict between scientific nations whose new capacities provide them with the means of national and, indeed, of world destruction. The great argument between the Doer and the Denier will only be translated into a wider sphere in a yet more vivid form. It will almost certainly cut right across the previous division of nations, and men from all the previous national alignments will be found on either side of the discussion directly the existing boundaries of the main European nations have been removed. The Division of the Soul will replace the Division of the Soil: in the conditions of the present time it has become more natural. This is bound to happen directly the peoples decide to merge in a larger union and so to extend patriotism; and, when that is done, it is right that it should occur. From this great shake of the dice of destiny will be thrown a new dynamism in the service of high achievement.

"THE DEVELOPMENT OF AFRICA"
THE ABSENCE OF ALTERNATIVE

In present circumstances it can hardly be contested that a new spirit of construction is needed. The great and decisive task, which awaits such an effort of new constructive energy from a united Europe, is the development of Africa. Those, who are accustomed to think in terms of old world economics, and of a situation which no longer exists, will no doubt deride the suggestion of any such necessity. If they think such an idea is unorthodox to the point of the bizarre let them suggest any alternative which will work. They have had more than two years already since the end of the war in which to think out their answer, and it is not yet forthcoming. So far, their only action in the matter has been an alternation between international conferences, which have produced nothing, and requests to America for loans, which have so far been more productive than the Conferences, but cannot be expected for ever to obviate the necessity for fresh thought and self-help.

In basic terms, Europe must develop Africa for two reasons: the first is that Europe requires food and raw materials, and the second is that within the limits of the existing system we cannot find the means to pay for them. Each of the great nations and, in particular, France and Britain, have made great appeals for export drives to provide the foreign currency to pay for the needed exports. Britain set a target for an immense increase in pre-war exports in a world which presents less opportunity for her export industries than the conditions prevailing before 1939. During the six years of war previous customers developed their own local industries in an intensification of a process which was becoming marked in the decade of 1930. If a great export nation denies its customers all supplies in order to fight a war over that period of time, it cannot be surprised if they take steps either to supply themselves or to obtain the goods else-where. The first process means the development of local industries, and the second entails the formation of a habit of buying from other exporting nations: neither event was good for British exports. Both these factors clearly mean a great diminution of export opportunity for nations which were long engaged in the European war. Yet such countries as Britain and France set an export target far above their pre-war figures. It should not be surprising to any mind capable of analytical thought that the results proved disappointing. Moreover, the full shock of the new situation clearly could not be felt until American home needs had been fully satisfied, and the immense surplus of a war-increased American productive power had washed into the remaining export markets of the world.

A temporary, but only partial, offset to these factors might provide a delusive reassurance in a mistaken policy by reason of the absence for the time being of ex-enemy countries from world markets, and the provision of a short-lived sellers' market in the post-war shortage of goods. The latter factor was bound soon to be eliminated by a war-stimulated productive power, and the former would not endure for ever. Sooner or later the war-exhausted nations have to face the fact that their war-neglected markets have shrunk as much as their own energies have been reduced. Within the limits of their system they have to solve the problem how to sell far more exports to obtain their new raw material requirements than they were able to sell before the war, and how to sell this larger volume of exports in a market of smaller capacity. To this problem so far their only answer is bigger and better international conferences to persuade former customers either to scrap their own industries, which they have recently developed, or to break their new habits of trade connections which they have formed over years while we were busy elsewhere. The former request will plainly be treated with derision, and the latter will only be considered if we can provide better goods at cheaper prices: men do not break habits except under strong inducement. Therefore, the only hope that can emerge from such a situation is success in a desperate price-cutting competition in the production of cheaper goods. As all the war nations would enter the game together, under the declared lead of Britain and France, it is not difficult to imagine the results. The end can only be a bigger scramble than before the war for a smaller prize. The nations all want to sell abroad more exports than before in order to obtain more imports; but this available market for these exports must be smaller rather than larger for reasons given above.

All this, of course, does not even take into account a factor which the writer analysed at length in previous books: namely the development of cheap oriental labour by Finance Capitalism to undercut European labour in the markets of the world. For the moment, that factor is mitigated by the temporary absence of Japan and the destruction of much oriental productive power by war. But, just wait until " Free India " as well as " Free China " and other newly " emancipated " oriental countries, as an inevitable result of weak governments and corrupt social systems, pass more than ever under Western financial exploitation, or another and worse exploitation conducted by men of similar aspect, but longer whips, who are entitled Commissars. If present world tendencies continue, we shall witness from these sources a growing stream of competition in sweated production such as the West has never previously had to face. The experiences of Lancashire and Yorkshire from Japanese competition, in the decade of 1930, will be negligible in comparison with the part the Orient can play in undercutting Western industry in the decade of 1950 under the operation of the international system to which all the great " Democracies " adhere.

THE LOSS OF OLD MARKETS AND RESOURCES

But, setting aside for the moment all question of oriental competition, can any serious hope exist of our import requirements being satisfied by selling on world markets a far greater volume of goods than we were able to sell before the war, particularly when the much needed imports come from America, and we can only pay for them with goods that country does not want and will not accept? As noted above, our only hope of exporting so much is by succeeding in a price-cutting competition with all other great nations in a scramble for world markets. A price-cutting competition can only be won either by great efficiency or by cutting wages: the first cannot be achieved under the bureaucratic controls of a Labour Government, and the second would not be permitted by the Trade Unions which control the Labour Government (and in the second respect the writer experiences the rare felicity of being on their side). So, what hope have we in such a competition, and what prospect have we of obtaining thereby the raw materials and foodstuffs which we cannot produce at home? Even if we win, some other nation must lose. It is doubtful, for instance, whether even Britain and France could both succeed in implementing their programmes, which are antithetical rather than complementary, in the restricted conditions of this competition. Room for all does not exist in the old world market which has been reduced by local production, and for which more countries are producing more exports.

This world situation is becoming more and more like a macabre game of musical chairs, played for the prize of food by starving men: on the one remaining chair of the shrunken world market will be found in the end the strongest player, who least needs the prize of food—America. Let no smaller player be reassured by the fact that the big man has not yet entered the game; he has been kept busy at home for the time being, but the rules which govern his present existence will impel him to enter the export game to some tune when the home work is exhausted. And what of the prize for which all contend?—the raw materials and foodstuffs of the world? They are not so plentiful as before the war, and the reason is not only the dislocation of production caused by war; which could be repaired. Can we be sure that these supplies from the old sources will be available as they were before the war? Before giving any confident answer our opponents should glance, for example, at rising figures of soil erosion. In this sphere the folly of man has again made a contribution to the destruction of recent years. Even America has been warned that this single factor of erosion may prove an Achilles heel to her great strength. All over the world many of the old resources have been just fooled away. And the reason?—precisely that frenzy of international competition which prevailed before the war, and is bound to be intensified in the new conditions if the same system and psychology is permitted to operate. The soil was neglected and exploited, because cheapness for competitive purposes governed all. It was cheaper to farm badly than to farm well, and cheapness in food production was important to the international dumping game by which quick profits were knocked out of agriculture in some countries, and ruin was knocked into agriculture in other countries. Now the world pays for past follies as it contemplates a repetition of the same mistakes on a greater scale.

So, in summary, we ask two questions. Can we find means to pay for our imports by increasing exports for a diminishing world market: can we be sure that these raw materials and foodstuffs will always be there to import, even if we can manage to pay for them? It will take a good many international conferences to talk down these two questions! Even if such a Conference unanimously accepted a Heaven-drafted resolution, proposed by Great Britain, to the effect that every nation in the world would stop doing foolish things and start doing wise things, would cease to be selfish and would work only for the good of all, would stop chattering and start building—even if all lions agreed to lie down with all lambs, if all diplomats grew wings and all swords turned by magic to ploughshares—some little time would elapse before even a Committee, headed by the brightest lawyer in the Labour Party, could provide every nation with all the food and raw materials it required. May we, therefore, not be thought too cynical if we do not await this millenium, but turn our backs on the methods of Babel Internationalism which have wasted the time of mankind for the lifetime of more than a generation. In terms of realism we cannot sell in the old markets sufficient exports to buy the raw materials and foodstuffs we want: and, moreover, it is very doubtful whether the old supplies of foodstuffs and raw materials will long be available in sufficient quantity to satisfy even a fraction of requirement.

The Illusions of the Old Internationalism

We are, therefore, driven to seek a new area which can produce such raw materials and foodstuffs as we cannot produce, and is also able to accept in return our manufactured exports. A new region is indicated for such a purpose, in which extensive local industries have not already developed: a planned economy is only possible with a fresh start. If such a thought is still rejected, let us consider a little more the difficulties and delays of the economic policy of the present British Government, which aims at securing a larger world market by what is termed " the division of labour and the development of specialisation " in existing industrialised countries by means of international conferences. If this phrase, which was used by the spokesmen of the Labour Government at Geneva in April, 1947, in opening a series of international conferences, has any any meaning, it implies that all great nations will agree to scrapping existing industries which do not comply with the formula. For example, if a conference decided that certain goods could be more appropriately developed by the " specialisation " of British labour than by " specialisation " in Canada or the Argentine, the latter countries must close down such industries in order to provide a balance between their primary products and Britain's manufactured exports. Since the Free Trade economics of last century's Manchester School have long ago ceased to operate, the body of world trade has to be carved up and sewn together again to conform to this model. If this is not the meaning of this policy, what does it mean? And what conceivable hope of success does it possess? Quite apart from the stimulus of the war to many many great countries to develop their own manufacturing industries, great and capable nations would never in the long run be content merely to be producers of foodstuffs and raw materials.

The diversification of industry became a very necessary precaution after their unfortunate experience of " putting all their eggs in one basket "; which was then used as a football in financial speculation. So, the process of local industrialisation was replacing import of manufactured goods in all great countries long before the war: it was merely accentuated and accelerated by war. Preposterous is now the suggestion to reverse the whole process by a series of resolutions at international conferences in the hope of persuading all industrial nations to scrap, or develop, existing industries according to some academic international plan, which is based on some theory of appropriate " specialisation and division of labour " by each nation. Just conceive the delays which would occur before even the first of the vested interests, in the first of the affected countries, had been overcome. Yet it is suggested that the policy can be implemented in all countries simultaneously and quickly: the awkward squad of the whole world is to fall in at Geneva and march off in quick step to the millenium under the gentle persuasion of a little economic theorising of a very obsolete kind. All this, also, has to be done in time to enable British exports to find a far greater market than pre-war, before America gets tired of lending money! On such fantastic illusions Britain, and Europe as a whole, are requested to rest not only the hopes of an industrial future but their hope of avoiding early starvation. We have spent the lifetime of a generation at international conferences asking other nations, in effect, to scrap their own industries and distort their economies in order to restore Britain's long-vanished export hegemony; because British statesmanship has been incapable of fresh thought to meet fresh facts. After the last war and the further development of local industries we have about as much chance of success as the classic petition of the candle-makers for the suppression of the Sun in the interests of their business.

THE OBSOLESCENCE OF CONSERVATIVE EMPIRE POLICY

Conservative Empire policy is faced with almost exactly the same difficulties in " Imperial Preference "; any prospect of large-scale success, which that policy ever possessed, has been greatly reduced by the development of local industries in all the great Dominions during the war. This process had begun in the Dominions, as well as other countries, long before 1939: it was also accelerated by the cessation of British supplies during a period of over six years. In any case, it is as idle to hope that the great Dominions will remain for ever in the relatively primitive state of simple primary producers as it is to desire that other advanced countries will inhibit the development of their own secondary industries in order to provide a perpetual market for our exports in exchange for their foodstuffs and raw

162

materials. As already noted, in another aspect, all white countries tend more and more to a diversified and balanced economy. This trend is bound to increase rather than diminish as science provides means of producing almost anything, nearly anywhere, with but slight variation in any factor of cost which does not derive from wage and skill. For instance, the particularly humid climate of Lancashire originally provided an exceptional capacity to produce cotton goods which gave Britain a virtual hegemony of world markets. Science can now artificially produce such conditions even in a climate so dry as Australia. The old argument of the " Manchester School " that goods should only be produced in places particularly suitable for their production has long been largely vitiated by science, and will soon be entirely obsolete. The place and local conditions are already a very minor factor in relation to the question of skill and capacity for organisation; how many industrialists would now contend that climate was nearly as important as stability in labour conditions?

The industrial policy of the old Parties rests as surely on the industrial conditions of the last century as their system of training for the next war is always based on the conditions of the last war. All their efforts to persuade advanced countries, whether Dominions or Foreign, to check the development of manufacturing industries in order to provide a balance for our unbalanced economy can be reduced to a simple absurdity— we are asking them to ruin themselves for our benefit. Their resistance to that suggestion withstood the sonorous platitudes of the elder Labour Leaders, and the younger Conservative Leaders, at international conferences, for twenty-one years between the two world wars. After the inevitable development of their secondary industries, during the long and rude interruption of international conferences while the second war proceeded, they are still less likely to be responsive to the speeches of the new generation of Labour Leaders, who suffer both from a worse case and less eloquence. Whatever temporary alleviation of the position may be brought by such devices as Imperial Preference, it is plain that in present conditions we cannot find a market for a great increase in our pre-war volume of exports either in the Dominions or in any other advanced countries which are interested in the development of their own industries, and do not wish to remain entirely rural populations or simple producers of primary products.

Britain should seek every opportunity of developing Dominion trade by direct bargaining; but in a manner which takes into account the natural and inevitable development of these advanced countries. It is in the sphere of mutual security, and cultural development, that blood relationship will draw Britain and the Dominions ever closer together in the future; that great communion is vital to the service which both Mother country and the Dominions can render in building the new civilisation of the future. But, rapid new trade developments can more easily take place in the Colonies, where existing industries would not be adversely affected.

It is necessary to sweep away illusions before any real prospect can be cleared to the vision: when this is done we are faced with the plain fact that we have to find a place which can supply us with raw materials and some foodstuffs in exchange for our manufactures. It must be an area which cannot supply these manufactured goods itself, and it is better if it is a region under our own control within which we can plan in advance a balanced economy, and thus prevent a repetition of the events which have reduced us to our present position.

Africa the Key

Africa is the key to all, for the following reasons: (1) It can produce any foodstuffs and raw materials we require; (2) In our African colonial possessions local industrialisation so far scarcely exists; (3) We control these regions and can thus plan a permanent economy by which their primary products are developed in exchange for our manufactures. We start with a clean slate, in our own possession, and can write on it the plan of the future. All development is within our own power and awaits only our own ability and energy. The relationship of the British effort in Africa to that of the rest of Europe will be discussed shortly. Let us first consider the method of African development I propose for Great Britain, which is equally suitable for adoption in Africa by other European countries. The subject has, so far, scarcely been touched by any practical development or even by any theory of a plan. The effort of the Labour Party was wholly concentrated on international conferences to restore pre-war markets with hopes of success we have already analysed. The younger Conservative Leaders have received their only political training in the same school. At this time of writing the only suggestion of the Labour Party for African development is to use 150,000 acres in the whole of Africa during the first year of a plan to grow Ground Nuts! The ratio of their abilities to the potential of Africa is about the same as that acreage to the total dimensions of that Continent!*

Yet, a survey of modern tendencies in all the old world markets, whether foreign or Dominions, can only reach the conclusion that in Africa alone resides any substantial hope of obtaining the foodstuffs and raw materials we cannot produce at home in a natural balance of exchange with our manufactured goods. Moreover, in Africa we shall be able to obtain these primary products far more cheaply than in the Western Hemisphere, with the consequence that it will not be necessary to send in exchange nearly so large a proportion of our home production, and that our home standard of life can be proportionately higher. Both the practice and ethics of this conception will be considered shortly. Let us first press to a conclusion the enquiry what practical policy either of the Old Parties possess to meet the economic crisis?

LABOUR AND CONSERVATIVE FUTILITY IN COLONIAL DEVELOPMENT

In the region of Colonial development, what improvement

*See footnote on Page 52 (Part I) concerning subsequent proposals of the Labour Party, after two years of office, to spend £100 millions on African development as compared with their previous proposals, at the end of one year, to spend over £2,400 millions on buying up obsolete industries in Great Britain.

is offered by Conservative policy on the complete inhibition upon all effective development in Africa presented by the official policy of the Labour Party, which declares that the " native inhabitants " must be able, " in the shortest possible time, to govern themselves "? Conservatism begins by affirming the same governing principle as the Labour Party, which was expressed by the leading organ of Conservative Imperialism in the words, " for the Colonies self-government is and always has been the aim." Beyond this inhibiting principle, the nearest approach to a constructive policy was advanced by a Conservative spokesman in the House of Commons on March 24, 1947: in the words "a much more fruitful course for us would be in the development of the Colonial Empire and its industrialisation. Markets for machinery could be available there in no very distant time. In Nigeria alone there was coal in formations which extended for 500 miles." This speech followed shortly after a recapitulation by the writer of that constructive policy in relation to Africa which we shall now consider at greater length. Let us note first the Conservative sense of urgency when confronted by crisis: " markets could be available there for machinery in no very distant time." May we ask, what market? Nigeria is inhabited largely by a species which became known to newspaper fame as the Ju-Ju men. Is it suggested that their executive capacity, and capital resources, are going to develop Nigeria? If not, who provides this vague market for British machinery in " no very distant time "? Is it suggested that British industrialists will buy the machinery and throw their energies and resources into the development of that territory, and of Africa as a whole? If so, are they likely to be attracted by the principle which governs Conservative policy as well as that of the Labour Party: " for the Colonies self-government is and always has been our aim "? It is an alluring prospect to devote a lifetime of energy, and every stake of fortune, to the development of Africa, in order at the end to be placed under the Government of the Ju-Ju- men?

British enterprise has already experienced the result of being placed under the government of a far higher type than the

Nigerians, who possess at least a very high degree of spiritual civilisation. After generations of developing India, British enterprise is now reaping the fruit of such principles. Will this experience encourage the energy of British industrialists to enter Africa in the certainty that at the end of all their exertions they will be placed under the " self government " of complete savages? If Conservative, as well as Labour, policy does not mean this, words have no meaning. In fact, it must mean this, if all the silly cant which the Old Parties have turned out for years, in a competition of humbug, is not to appear as a huge hypocrisy to a generation whom they have educated in principles of complete absurdity; which must lead to the final frustration of all executive action. So, Conservatism is left in the position that no individual in his senses would develop Africa under the limitation of the principles which they lay down; while this Party, in addition, rejects all State Action, on principle. Characteristically, they can only think of the State as a negative and never as a positive. Action by the State can only mean to them the grabbing of other people's money in the manner of the Labour Party. The concept of a creative State is beyond their furthest imagining. While, as for the Labour Party, the action of the State means to them merely the buying of obsolete industries which others have created, at the taxpayers' expense. That limited task alone they feel to be within the range of their capacity, as we have already noted in the first chapter. The concept of the Creative State as a great Pioneer of vast new enterprise demands an altogether new order of mind and will.

Yet, we must advance to this new conception of State Action, which is truly revolutionary in terms of present thought, but is plain sense in terms of reality. The State should be concerned with great things; not with small things! The task of the State is to create, not merely to appropriate what others have created. The mission of the State is to be a Leader in new enterprise, not just a parasite on old enterprise. The work of the State is to construct, not to restrict. The true function of the State is to create new things: not just to take over old things. To such end the State needs Doers and not Deniers; the State needs

Executives and not Bureaucrats. The latter may still be used to look after old drainage systems; but the former are now wanted to make a new Continent. In short, our Idea of State Action is the exact opposite of the present idea of State Action.

PRINCIPLE AND METHOD OF CREATIVE STATE ACTION

The action of the State in such an enterprise differs fundamentally from bureaucratic action in the conduct of a nationalised industry, or in the regimentation of private industry for official purposes within an already industrialised community. Also, it varies greatly and inevitably from the usual practices of private enterprise in a developed but free economy. In the pioneer work of opening up virgin territory the action of the State should resemble much more an operation of war; and must be governed by something of the same principles. It is an enterprise beyond the scope of any private enterprise, and is very different to any normal condition of trade. It possesses a definite and limited objective in the primary development of a new territory; just as an operation of war has the definite and limited objective of defeating the enemy. Neither are concerned with the niceties of marketing: a study of the customers' tastes is not relevant to their business. All that delicate finesse in adjustment to, and service of, varying demand, which is one of the main functions of private enterprise, does not enter the picture either in war or in the large-scale development of new territory. Demand is unlimited, until the task is done, for a type of material and construction which can be produced *ad hoc* and on a large scale. In practice, it has been found in war that it is not necessary to " nationalise " every industry which produces the material to be used: in fact, it has been found so undesirable that not even the most doctrinaire Socialists have been known to suggest it, when their lives, and that of the Community, were at stake. The luxuries of universal nationalisation and bureaucratic management are reserved for infliction upon the nation in times of Peace, with results which are now beginning to be observed. War is too serious a matter to be left to Bureaucrats, and an altogether different method has to be employed. The principle

168

is the co-ordination of private enterprise by the State. Our new concept of State Action in peace is neither " Nationalisation " nor undirected private enterprise.

Let all the doctrinaires reflect for a moment on practical things. It was not laid down that no component of a Mulberry harbour should be produced except in a State-owned factory. It was not ordained that the project should not proceed until some non-existent private enterprise on the coast of Normandy had provided a " market for our machinery " by placing a private order for a Mulberry with a private British firm at " no very distant date." It was an operation of war; the State gave the orders; the various tasks were allocated to a variety of responsible people, in a hierarchy of order and discipline; in fact, the State directed and co-ordinated, but did not conduct the whole work itself : yet the job was well done and quickly done. But no one could call it, in the doctrinaire sense of the old Parties, either Socialism or Private Enterprise. It was real State Action of a creative character, and on a great scale, which used every existing resource for a real end of achievement. Why are such things only possible in war? It must be admitted that such method could be used with far greater effect in the calmer and more deliberate atmosphere of peace, which makes possible organisation, in place of the improvisation which is necessary in war. And it is insufficient reply to say that the English people can only improvise and not organise; that is equivalent to saying that they are only active under compulsion, in other words that they are idle. A new generation may disprove this charge in a deliberate act of great creation.

In this connection, too, it may be commented that an ultra-sensible people does not exert itself until it must. The mass of the people are immersed in diurnal matters, until the necessity of crisis compels attention to more serious things and, in the circumstances of a war whose approach has been unnoticed, they turn to improvisation because they were not awake in time to organise. Such is the inevitable result of a prosperous absorption in small things, until a sudden danger arises. But the failure of a civilisation, which is a crisis of peace, and not of war, does not come like a thief in the night. A long, slow, ever-developing pressure of suffering on the mass of the people heralds its approach. Such an event is different to any previous experience of a people who are as famous for their capacity to improvise as they are notorious for their incapacity to organise. In such circumstances, it may not be too much to ask them seriously to organise in advance to meet a menace to their life and to find a way out from disaster.

THE ANALOGY OF WAR

The plan which we suggest is the development of Africa, and we propose that the resources of the nation should be mobilised for this enterprise on the principles just outlined. It is equivalent to an operation of war, and the methods employed should resemble those which experience has proved to be essential to the conduct of successful war. But, in such a long-term project, the improvisation and muddle with which war usually begins could be eliminated. In Great Britain, in particular, it always takes a long time at the beginning of a war before bureaucratic methods are abandoned, or even reduced, and the executive type is called in for the employment of an efficient method. In fact, it takes so long that the war is nearly lost before the necessary change takes place. Even armies are strangled in red tape until gradually the stress of circumstances enables the executive individual to cut through. Generally, the red tape persists, in large degree, to the end, because the principles of realism are never frankly faced, and fearlessly and openly adopted. Within a " Democracy " the real things by which wars are won, or anything achieved, are always " under the counter." Even so, it works and the nation survives, when it has a great material preponderance and surplus of latent strength in relation to the task. It will not work when Britain is really up against it and the margin of success is small. The famous " blind eye " of British history is very romantic and it won despite all the deadheads: but two open eyes, in clear and unrestricted command of a given task, would be better still. So we ask for the conscious adoption of the Leadership

170

principle as the executive method in the opening up of Africa on the lines of a planned operation of war.

It is true that " Democracy " in Britain has managed to run even wars to some extent by committees and get away with it, but the fortune described in Chapter II, Part I will not always recur, and it certainly will not always have the same margin in hand for the practical tasks of the future. It is a fact that the " Democracies " won the war despite their only partial super-session of the Committee and Bureaucratic method in favour of the Leadership Principle, which that stress imposed in large degree. But, just consider the margin of strength in relation to their opponents when the combined resources in man power and material of America, Britain, France and Russia are assessed and measured against the resources of the Axis powers. A very short study of the mathematics of the matter would dispel any illusion that the " Democracies " owed victory to the greater efficiency of their system. Despite an overwhelming superiority in natural strength and resources, it was a very close thing. When a fourteen-stone man fights a ten-stone man, and ends a victor by a very narrow margin in a very exhausted condition, he cannot claim that his skill and method are the better. Conversely, when a light man fights a big man it is not enough for him to be better; it is essential for him to be overwhelmingly superior in skill if he is to win.

LEADERSHIP PRINCIPLE

In facing the tasks of peace in the light of the lessons of war, we postulate Creative State Action in place of negative State repression, and the Leadership principle in place of Bureaucracy. A " Democracy " might, of course, choose to employ Bureaucracy in such a project as the development of Africa, instead of the Leadership Principle; such a policy would, at least, provide employment to many who do not normally find that condition easy to attain, even if the results were not so profitable for the Community. But, before the method of the Leadership principle is rejected in such an enterprise, let everyone, at least, be clear as to what it is, and what it is not. The

171

Leadership principle is not the dictatorship of one man: the suggestion is absurd. One man cannot do everything, and, in fact, no man can achieve anything without a host of willing colleagues. His achievement is then in proportion to his ability to evoke the ardour of able men for his ideas.

On the other hand, the Leadership principle does mean that one definite individual is responsible for each task whether it be great or small. Whether the work be the most important or the least important, a person and not a Committee is responsible for it. He is responsible to someone above him, and someone below him is responsible to him. The man at the head of the Government is responsible to the people as a whole. Whether a large or small undertaking be successful or a failure, everyone knows who is responsible for it, and that individual can shelter neither behind a Committee nor any other excuse. The principle is—give a man a job to do and sack him if he fails to do it. That principle goes, whether he is the head of a State, responsible to the whole people and liable to their dismissal, or the man who "sweeps up the dirt" and is responsible to the head cleaner of that particular building. Under the Leadership principle the man who does the job knows where he is, and everyone else knows where he is. There is no ambiguity, and responsibility is always clear: that is the first principle of executive action. In fact, it always has been the first principle of achievement since the world began: that is why institutions like armies, which have to do or die, are never run by committees. For such real purposes the "Leadership principle" has to be employed, and to the extent that this principle replaces the Bureaucratic method success has been secured in war. No one will suggest running an Army by a committee of Civil Servants; war is too serious. In war, too, the leadership principle of responsible individuals tends to replace the bureaucratic method in the direction of industry; it becomes a matter not of choice but of compulsion, when red tape has to be cut in a desperate situation. So, in war, "Democracy" tends to turn to methods of realism, not because it likes them, but because it must. Is it too much to ask that something of this spirit should

172

be shown in a situation of nominal peace, which threatens a condition as serious as war? For such a purpose we suggest that Executive Government should direct the general policy of industry, but not interfere in daily business. The chiefs of industry should be responsible to the Government for the carrying out of general policy. Those engaged in industry would, in turn, be responsible to their industrial chiefs for the detail of the plan. At each stage the chain of individual responsibility would be definite and clear.

This is the Leadership principle which is the opposite of that Bureaucracy which is the creation of Social Democracy. The latter plans just enough to paralyse everything, but never enough to do anything. It controls the producer and leaves free the parasite; so the best go down and the worst come up. Instead of telling an executive individual what is wanted, and holding him responsible for doing it, " Democracy " imposes Committee management and bureaucratic control. Instead of laying down a national plan and holding individual industrialists responsible for carrying out their allotted part of the work, a mass of civil servants are sent to bind them hand and foot in the daily conduct of their businesses. Clear direction is replaced by muddled control; freedom is lost without the gain of efficiency. Under the system we suggest, on the contrary, anyone would be free to manage his own affairs provided he conformed to the national plan. Under the present system, no one is free to manage his own affairs, but no national plan exists to which he can conform.

No more need be written of a controversial character at this stage. Europe can, of course, unite, and can essay to develop Africa with any patchwork muddle of bureaucratic committees, if it wishes: it is always open to great peoples to add another chapter to the tragic comedy of History! But a plea is entered here for a realistic and effective method, before we turn to other aspects of this question.

RELATIONS OF STATE AND PRIVATE ENTERPRISE

Whatever executive method is employed for the development of Africa, it is evident that only State Action, on a great scale, will possess any chance of success. The task is much too big for Private Enterprise, even if it were not required to work under the shadow of current cant, such as the phrase: " for the Colonies, self-government is and always has been the aim," which simply means that the Black will ultimately be permitted to fuddle away what the White has created. We shall return later to the profound realities of the biological problem and the ethical considerations involved. At present it is only necessary to note that the pioneer task is too big for Private Enterprise, even if such enterprise could be attracted to the task by a reversal of the extraordinary values which would rob the European of the fruits of his labours in the attempt to establish a chimerical native self-government. The White Atlas will not attempt to lift the world on his shoulders, if, in the end, his world is to be handed over to someone who merely watched him do it, or was meantime playing with witch doctors in the jungle. In any case, Private Enterprise is not strong enough to play the Atlas role in this matter. A measure of real State Action is, therefore, required, which is as remote from the Labour conception of " Nationalising " obsolete industries at home as it is from Conservative *laissez faire*. But, private enterprise will still have a very vital role to play within the broad boundaries of the whole plan, which will be laid down by the Creative and Directive State.

In principle, it is not difficult to sort out the respective functions of the State and Private Enterprise. The role of the State should be confined to the equivalent of an operation of war, which is the opening up of the new territory. The role of private enterprise is not to participate directly in this process, but to follow it with that infinite diversification of lesser enterprise which builds a complex and desirable civilisation. The pioneer work is too big for private enterprises: but the creation of diverse industries and trading, and the marketing of their products, is much too complex for the State. Properly regarded, the parts of the State and Private Enterprise are complementary and not antithetical. The State can do what Private Enterprise cannot do, and Private Enterprise can do what the State cannot do. The State alone can conduct a big *ad hoc* undertaking, such as the landing in Normandy or the pioneer development of a new Continent. What it cannot do is to manage what should be competitive businesses catering for the subtle variations in human tastes; but this latter is precisely what our doctrinaire Socialists try to make it do by the vicious principle of forcing the people to adapt their tastes to the fads and whims of Civil Servants. This imposes servitude instead of offering service; which should be the attitude of the State to the people. A State is a tyrant which says you must ride in a train instead of a bus, because all transport is in the hands of the State and the Civil Servants have decided that you must. A State is a good servant of the people. if it opens up the resources of a new Continent for the nation by a great measure of creative organisation; instead of only using such methods for the conduct of foolish and unnecessary wars, which leave the country exhausted and impoverished. This is not to say, of course, that the State should refrain from laying down the broad boundaries within which Private Enterprise may be conducted; such indifference leads to the chaos of *laissez faire* in which Finance rules when Government abdicates. The Creative and Directive State must lay down certain limits which may not be transgressed, and, broadly speaking, they must represent the welfare of the country as a whole. Within these wide boundaries of the National well-being, Private Enterprise should be entirely free. While it serves it should be free both in enterprise and profit; when it exploits the strong hand of the Organic and Dynamic State should immediately descend.

THE CONDITIONS OF PRIVATE ENTERPRISE

In the case of African development it would, of course, be very necessary for the State to define in advance the kind of industry which Private Enterprise may develop. The whole purpose of the project would be frustrated if Finance-Capital could come along and develop manufacturing industries in competition with British industries. It would be a nice game for an uncontrolled finance to take advantage of the pioneer work of the State by developing manufacturing industries with cheap, sweated black labour to undersell British goods on the home and world market. That is precisely what would happen, of course, when both Labour and Conservative policies handed back the fruits of white development to the nominal rule of helpless natives, and a swarm of financial racketeers moved in to " develop native industries." That is the kind of thing which always happens under the " humanitarian " principles of the Old Parties; and the process is greatly aided by all the humbug which is talked about native freedom: in practice, it generally amounts to freedom to be thrown into industrial slavery, because government has abdicated the duty of defending those who cannot protect themselves.

More than ever in this sphere will it be necessary for the strong State to save the people from exploitation and the general plan from sabotage. To that end the State must impose two conditions. The first condition will be that only industries may be developed which serve the general plan. The second condition will govern, under rigorous safeguards, the proper standards of native labour. In the first respect the development of no industry will be permitted which is competitive with, rather than complementary to, British industry: this means, in particular, that industrial development will be of a primary character, which is confined to foodstuffs and raw materials. In the second respect, a standard of life for native labour will be laid down on Factory Act lines (*mutatis mutandis*) and rigorously enforced. The standard enjoyed by the native can easily be higher than that he at present possesses under the industrial exploitation which has already begun. On the other hand, it is clear that even a much higher standard than prevails at present will still enable the production of raw materials and foodstuffs, which we cannot produce at home, at a much cheaper rate than any price at which we can now procure them elsewhere. Output and cheapness will be assisted by the operation of much modern machinery, which can be worked by a proportion of enterprising white labour of skilled capacities that will be attracted by the large rewards which the new wealth can afford to offer. White labour will do the skilled work at a higher reward than it can now command: Black labour will do the unskilled work in much better conditions than it now suffers. With the aid of modern machinery, and vast natural resources, both output and cheapness can surpass anything yet known. Modern scientific method can have full scope where no previous restriction of the obsolete exists. The result will be that British exports of manufactured goods will obtain more raw materials and foodstuffs in exchange than they can obtain by the trade of a similar amount of goods in any other market (if they could obtain them at all).

In general, Private Enterprise will thus have unlimited opportunity in developing diverse, but defined, industries of a primary character. The Pioneer State will go in front like a Bulldozer over Forest land; Private Enterprise will follow behind like a plough and cultivator of Agriculture in the culture of varied products when the ground is cleared. In that conception lies the true relationship of State and Private Enterprise. The State will be a Leader who goes in front; not a flea who is carried on the neck; a creative pioneer, not a restrictive bureaucrat.

MACHINERY FOR AFRICAN DEVELOPMENT

It is clear that, apart from current machinery for normal productive purposes, a considerable amount of capital machinery will have to be despatched to Africa for pioneer development. The work of the State will consist largely of railway, road and building construction, and, of course, the provision of power, which can be secured in many areas by the harnessing of water energy, apart from the immense new possibilities in this sphere. This will require the export of capital machinery as distinct from the normal mechanisation of farming culture, which will merely require tractors, etc. The lazy mind will, of course, argue that it is much easier to continue the export of such capital goods to pay for the import of current consumption goods, like the films and tobacco which were purchased with such assets while even our home industries urgently required re-equipment. It is true, also, that the export of such capital goods to Africa will not be so immediately productive in the return of consumption goods as they would if exported to some developed market, which could, at once, send such goods in exchange. By comparison, the development of Africa will yield a deferred, but much greater, result. It may involve, in the first instance, an even sharper effort; a deliberate sacrifice of more immediate comfort to an ultimate economic freedom and wider enjoyment.

Again, the analogy of war arises; a greater temporary privation for a greater end may have to be asked of the people. But this process can be greatly mitigated, if not eliminated, by a wise use of existing assets. Even after the war, Britain still retains abroad considerable capital assets which can be sold for the purchase of such capital goods: a better investment for the remaining external capital of the country could not be found. Various countries, also, owe Great Britain considerable sums which could be paid in acceptable goods: these foreign balances, too, could be used for such a purpose. Finally, Great Britain possesses the remains of the American Loan, and some politicians appear to be looking forward with eager expectation to further assistance from the same quarter. A superficial view might regard any policy of assistance in such a matter as contrary to the interests of America: that fallacy will be studied shortly. First, let us note that, apart from the rigorous policy of reducing current consumption in order to provide capital goods for the development of Africa, Britain possesses two certain sources from which she can derive assistance and another possible provider of powerful aid.

PARTNERSHIP ARRANGEMENTS:
DISPOSSESSION OF INEFFICIENT

It may yet be argued that the development of the immense area of our African Colonies is beyond the unaided strength of Great Britain. Certainly, when we regard the size of the area and the potential of development, it is a formidable task. British possessions in Africa, including the Sudan, but excluding the Union of South Africa and the Mandated Territories, total over 2,600,000 square miles, and exceed by 33 per cent., the whole area of Europe, excluding Russia. Yet, it is my firm opinion that an awakened British people, recapturing the mood and spirit of the greatest moments of their history, could be equal, unaided, to this highest call of Destiny. But, other methods are open to them without losing to any extent their freedom of action or control over their own affairs. A method is available, which is very common in business affairs and is, indeed, preferable to an alternative practice which is sometimes used in commerce, and, at present, is being used in our national affairs: the latter method is recourse to the moneylender. The better course is to bring in a partner, or partners. Britain might be regarded as a man with an expanding business, who seeks to introduce more resources and fresh abilities when he has an idea for some new and big development, which may be beyond his unaided powers. As owner of the business he draws up the conditions of partnership to his liking, and has a free hand to conduct the negotiations as he wishes and to settle on good terms, if his assets are good and his prospects are favourable. If he is a wise man, with some knowledge of human nature and capacity to succeed in large enterprises which require the co-operation of others, he will not seek to drive too hard a bargain with associates, but will admit them to equal partnership on terms which safeguard his own assets and business, but are fair to all. In that manner he obtains the maximum good will and energy in the mutual enterprise, with gain to, rather than a surrender of, his own interests.

In such a vast undertaking it might well pay Great Britain to enter into selected partnerships of that character either in general or *ad hoc* for particular enterprises. In so doing she would promote several good ends. New resources of capital goods production, beyond the now exiguous assets of Great Britain, would be attracted to the enterprise. The recovery of Europe would be assisted by an opportunity to other countries to share in a development which would certainly be greatly accelerated by the participation of others. The Peace of Europe, and the union and cohesion essential to that condition, would be promoted in high degree by a common task and mutual interest,

179

which offered all concerned a " way out " of intolerable troubles by a co-operative effort without parallel in history, either in the magnitude of the undertaking or the results to be obtained. It is for Britain to decide whether she will obtain considerable results in her own territory by her own unaided exertions which, in such case, must be very severe, if a full development is to be obtained within a reasonable time; or whether she will accelerate development and obtain more comprehensive, and greater, results within a shorter time by entering into partnership arrangements. In the interests of her own people and of Europe as a whole, in finding a way out of present troubles and dangers within a narrow margin of time, the latter method presents the greatest possibilities. It is, at any rate, preferable to the present situation of partnership with nothing except chaos, while money is borrowed not even for constructive purposes of capital equipment at home or in the colonies, but for easy spending in the manner of a drunken lout who neglects his land inheritance, which awaits development, and squanders his few remaining cash resources in a little sottish tippling. Let it not be thought for a moment that the suggestion of inviting partnerships on reasonable terms is advanced only in the interests of European Peace and Union, or in the interest of any nation which possesses no territorial opportunity.

Another proposal will now be examined which I suggest should be used for such purposes, without any impairment of one inch of British territory or any partnership arrangement by the British people, if an unaided development of their own African territory appeared possible or desirable in a close survey of the facts. If the principles here advocated were adopted by Great Britain, or anything approaching them, no one would level against this country the charge, or reproach, of failing to develop its territory and wasting its assets. But nations exist which are not free from such a charge, and, indeed are plainly incapable of developing with their own unaided strength the immense territories which bear their colour on the map, but have never yet felt the grip of their constructive hand. We shall begin to consider this matter from the basis of two undeniable premises. The first is that enormous areas of Africa have never been developed by the nations which own them, and, in some cases, are incapable of development by the unassisted power of the countries in question. The second is that no nation has any better right to keep productive land idle, while a whole Continent, or indeed, the whole world, requires food and raw material, than an individual has the right to maintain good farm land in a derelict condition when his whole nation urgently requires food.

The parallel seems exact between a nation which owns African land and refuses to use it, and a man who owns a good farm and refuses to cultivate it. In Great Britain, and in nearly every advanced country, the latter is now very quickly dispossessed by the State. The process has been the subject of much complaint, but it is impossible to deny the justice of the principle if an impartial enquiry is held and judgment is given on a fair ascertainment of the facts, which is quite free from the suggestion either of bureaucratic spite or local jealousy. The principle is that no man has the right to play the dog in the manger while others go in want. He may not sit in idleness, or incompetence, upon the productive asset of good land while good farmers are denied access to land, and the people as a whole are short of the food which such capable husbandmen could produce. It has been found necessary to apply the principle rigorously in most European countries, including Great Britain, and few good farmers can be found to deny the necessity, if the method is fairly applied. Certainly the nation, as the representative of the hungry people, cannot afford to tolerate the neglect of the basic asset of productive land which is vital to the life and well-being of all. If such a principle be now fairly established in the life of individuals, why should it be so remote even from consideration in the life of nations? It is true that the gap between private morality and international morality is still very wide, but it must rapidly be reduced if mankind is to live in new conditions. A principle, which is plain commonsense in the relationship of individuals within a State, can no longer be dismissed as outside discussion in the relationship between States. Once again, life has become too serious; we can no more afford the vanities of diplomats than the obstructions of bureaucrats.

" WHICH TRUSTEESHIP? "

We have heard much about the question of Trusteeship in the administration of African territories. This " principle of Trusteeship " has often been perverted into a principle of idleness, because, as already observed, it has been translated in practice into the principle of keeping jungles fit for negroes to live in. Administration has consisted of a few magistrates; a few hymn books and a good deal of liquor for natives; all applied in the name of " freedom " on the road to a mythical native self-government, which can never be attained except in chaos or a relapse to barbarism. Deliberately I postulate a new and very different principle of Trusteeship in Africa. The Trusteeship is on behalf of White civilisation. The duty is not to preserve jungles for natives, but to develop rich lands for Europeans. We will discuss later the ethics of the matter; whether this great Continent belongs to Europe or to the negroes, whether the Trusteeship is to the highest or the lowest purpose of man. At present it is only necessary to note two things. The first is that the development of African raw materials and foodstuffs has become a matter of vital necessity to Europe. The second is that Africa, in fact, will not be developed if some nations neglect, almost entirely, their large African possessions.

If the excuse be accepted that they are called upon for no action in the development of these resources, because their only duty is to act as custodians of large negro preserves of primitive life, we may say good-bye to all hope of a solution in Africa of the European problem. The latter excuse, in practice, is particularly disingenuous humbug as such nations almost invariably throw open this primeval paradise to the exploitation of Western Finance Capitalism with much profit to political racketeers but execrable effect on the conditions of native life. Here, again we demand a reversal of all existing values. The Trusteeship is on behalf of White civilisation, not on behalf of a nominal stability of Barbarism, which is, in reality, a mask for the racket of financial exploitation. Having established that true principle of Trusteeship, we proceed to the new principle, just discussed, that nations within a new European morality should be subject to something of the same tests as individuals in the concept of morality which prevails within existing States. The efficient will never fear to submit himself to a fair test of efficiency. But nations, like individuals, must acquire some sense of responsibility to the Community as a whole. And, in the last resort, nations should be required to give up territory which they have neglected and were incapable of developing.

Two purposes would be served by this process. In the first instance, rich land would be brought into cultivation. In the second place, vigorous nations, which have had no such opportunity, would be given their chance to make good. Both the wealth and Peace of Europe would benefit from the event. The capable, but land-hungry, nation would replace the incapable and the life weary. Such a policy would not be carried through without friction: but, timely action to give the vigorous an opportunity of outlet and service is always less dangerous, as well as more productive, than to pander to inefficiency until a situation is created in which the able, and frustrated, are compelled to explode or perish. With some experience of human nature, and of the incapacity of some peoples for Colonial development, it is safe to believe that plenty of land would be available in Africa for development by the efficient, if these principles were fairly and fearlessly applied. And why should they not be tried? What is needed to this end? Nothing but the union, for such a purpose, of America, Britain and France. If these three powers decided that Africa should be developed on such principles, no one could gainsay their will in present circumstances. They are presented with a rare opportunity to solve the economic problem of the European Continent and, indeed, to relieve permanently the stress of the world. The interest of Britain and France in the matter is plain; they can solve their present economic troubles and eliminate in advance many of the dangers of the future. But, it would be necessary for them, of course, to set their own house in order and to free themselves from any reproach of neglecting their own African possessions by a vigorous programme of Colonial development. The stimulus of necessity, in setting that example, could have nothing but a good effect on their present fortune and future character.

THE INTEREST OF AMERICA

The interest of America is not, at first sight, so obvious, but it is, none the less, evident. The first question is whether America desires to have Europe living for ever on her charity. If not, what alternative exists to the policy here suggested? Only two other possibilities can be envisaged. The first is that America should continue to supply Europe with food and raw materials for nothing, and should also send her capital goods to equip her competitors' industries; stripped of verbiage, that is what the loan policy means. The second is that Europe should either supply America in exchange with consumption goods, which she does not want, or should compete with her in all export markets with such goods in order to find means of payment for imports from America. Neither method is to the advantage of the American economy. The plain fact is that America neither wants consumption goods from Europe in her home market nor in her export markets. She believes, and rightly, that she can easily supply her home market from her own resources, and she needs any export market she can find for that surplus of production over home requirements, which her present economy makes ultimately inevitable. In fact, if foreign goods either invade her home or export markets successfully, a diminution in outlet for American production must ensue; the nightmare of America will then materialise, which is over-production in relation to existing demand, and a consequent slump both in industry and on Wall Street. That menace threatens even when America is giving away a large part of her production, for which the euphemism is foreign lending. If the capital value of these loans were ever repaid, in the shape of consumption goods sent in exchange to the American home market, or by the process of acquiring means of repayment through successful competition with American goods in export markets, the shock to American economy would clearly amount to a disaster.

So, America has almost reached the strange paradox of only being able to avoid an over-production slump by giving away a large proportion of her current production: the fact that the gift is called a loan makes no difference, and the paradox is underlined by the fact that the loan can never be repaid without a catastrophe. Even so, it is apparent that in terms neither of politics nor economics can Europe live for ever on American charity. Sooner or later Europe must pay for what it receives from the Western Hemisphere, either by sending goods in exchange or by finding the means of payment through selling exports on world markets in competition with American goods. Quite apart from any question of repaying loans, America will then be faced with a contraction of the outlet for her production in one way or the other. When her post-war demand is thoroughly satisfied, and she turns as usual to dispose of her surplus of production over home demand in foreign markets, the position of America will be rendered very serious if a cheaper European labour system is competing in all those markets with the assistance of capital equipment goods which America has been good enough to supply by her loan policy. The wisdom of present world organisation will then be revealed in stark simplicity; and the blessing which it brings to the American people will also be exposed.

The sequence of events, and their disastrous absurdity, is both simple and obvious. First, America sends capital goods to equip European industries for nothing in exchange; this is called the loan policy. Next, American politicians naturally say that loans cannot continue for ever and Europe must begin to pay for what she is receiving. Next, European industries, which have been equipped with American machinery under the loan policy, proceed to export manufactured goods in vigorous competition with America in all world markets, in order to find means to pay her for raw materials and foodstuffs they cannot produce for themselves. Next, America finds that the war-increased productive power of her industry has more than satisfied existing home demand and that she urgently requires to export her surplus production to foreign markets, where she is being undercut by the European industries she has recently equipped. Next, America is confronted by an over-production crisis of a magnitude which dwarfs any pre-war experience. Next, America is driven to avoid the crisis by dumping her own increasing surplus at any price on the markets of the world. Next, as already envisaged, the great power of America wins the game of desperation when she is driven to it, because her strength is so great that she can afford virtually to give away at any price a margin of surplus production, and the European Continent cannot. Next, the Europeans, as a result, again fail to sell sufficient exports to pay for their necessary foodstuffs and raw materials. Next, the European countries begin to go smash again and come back to America for further loans. So, once more, around the mulberry bush, dear boys, once more—and call it Statesmanship!

Will any American argue that this picture is entirely carica-ture? Can any American deny that at least sufficient fact is here stated to warrant the conclusion that it would be an advan-tage to America if Europe were withdrawn from competition with her both in her home market, and in her world export markets, and were concentrating on obtaining both a market and a source of supply in Africa? In fact, the only alternative to such a policy is that mythical expansion of the general " world market," which is discussed by the Socialist doctrinaires of Britain, and is to be obtained by each great nation undertaking only to produce what some international body decides it is best fitted to produce. As already noted, they would have to agree to give up all existing diversification of their industries, with consequent scrapping of many prosperous businesses, and to place their whole productive system at the behest of some international bureaucracy which will operate the theories of the old " Manchester School," that became obsolete in Great Britain toward the middle of the last century. This solitary constructive proposal of the British Labour Government for " the division of labour and the development of specialisation " between nations has about as much chance of acceptance in America as a suggestion to surrender the Atom Bomb to a Committee appointed by the Third International.

It would , indeed, be an exhilarating thought to any American that the development of American industry should be in a state of suspended animation during a few years of international conferences, while Socialist lawyers from Whitehall discussed with American diplomats what American industries would be suitable for continuance, or closing down, under the new plan of specialised production. But, as things are, the choice of America and the world rests between the anarchic smash and grab on world markets described above, and some submission of all industry to the " planning " of some super-bureaucracy in interminable conferences, which is suggested by the British Labour Government. The other way is our suggestion to let Europe develop Africa as a source of supply and exchange for European manufactured goods, and to leave America the Western Hemisphere and the larger part of the other world markets.

THE AMERICAN ECONOMIC PROBLEM

If it be not an impertinence it may, also, be suggested that America, too, would have an opportunity to develop a balanced and relatively stable economy. Such an achievement is, indeed, far easier for America with her vast resources, which are so largely developed already. It would be quite unnecessary for America to adopt that degree of " planning " and Governmental direction which might be necessary to recovery and development in the poorer and war-shattered Continent of Europe. All that is necessary for America is to prevent a recurrence of her great crises in over-production. And that is a problem which really should not be beyond the wit of statesmanship; although, on a lesser scale, it proved beyond the capacity of British Statesmanship for many years between the Wars. All that is necessary in such a case is to preserve some equilibrium between production and demand, and, in the case of an expanding economy of vast natural resources, it could be achieved without any regimentation or bureaucratic control.

The essence of the matter is that market and demand consists in the final analysis of the power of the people to buy. Nowhere has this been more clearly grasped than in the theory of American economists and in the practice, over many years, of dynamic American industry in a high-wage policy. What has been lacking is a national policy and plan to implement the theory of economists and the attempted practices of individual industrialists. All may recognise as individuals that high wages and salaries mean high purchasing power, and that the latter factor alone can provide a large and stable home market with any hope of absorbing American production and freeing it from the vagaries of world demand. But a big gulf lies ahead between the widespread individual recogntion of the facts, and a national plan and policy to meet them. Industrialist A, in a particular trade, may recognise that the interests of his trade, and of American industry as a whole, require high purchasing power. But he cannot implement his belief by pushing up wages in his own business without the fear that Industrialist B, in the same trade, may take advantage of his patriotism and enlightened self-interest. The latter may keep wages as they are while the former raises them, or may even reduce wages within some spheres of American Industry. In that event the man who pays high wages in the interests of his own trade, and of American industry as a whole, is put out of business by the wage under-cutting of a less enlightened rival, and pays for his wisdom and patriotism with bankruptcy. The individual is powerless to implement the inspiration of American belief in a high standard of life in default of State action to protect him in such a policy.

What is required in America is a wages and production policy. Such a wage-production policy, in such conditions, need not imply any degree of control or regimentation. All that is required is some statutory, or agreed, prevention of wage-cutting within specific industries. It would be unnecessary for this purpose that America should go as far as the planned economy of industrial corporations which the writer on other occasions has suggested. All that is required is that American industrialists, within a given trade, should agree not to cut wages below a given standard but to increase them, in accord with a national wage policy, as higher purchasing power was required by increasing productive power. The relative competitive position within an industry would remain the same; if all increase wages and salaries in proportion, the individual's ability to compete remains unaltered. A wage-cutting competition within the country would thus be eliminated, and a progressive increase in standard of living in proportion to an increasing productive power would eliminate a recurrence of over-production crises. The action of the State would be necessary in two respects. The first would be at least to give guidance in co-ordinating the wage policy of various industries in order to secure some national similarity in wage policy and the increase in the standard of life. To this end a national economic organisation in research and advice would possibly be enough in America to support the voluntary organisation of the various industries. The second action of the State would be by high tariff, or exclusion, to prevent under-cutting of that enlarged home market from cheap external competition produced by lower wage standards in other countries. For it must always be remembered that it is not enough to prevent undercutting from without by Tariffs; some organisation must prevent under-cutting from within, if a market adequate to American production is to be built.

A wage policy, which related American internal demand to production by some progressive harmony in the raising of wage standards to meet the ever-increasing productive potential, coupled with the exclusion of under-cutting goods from outside, would solve the American problem. Nearly all raw materials can be produced within America and American possessions. Anything which had to be purchased outside would very easily be acquired by the allocation of a very small proportion of American products in exchange. In fact, America could very easily become almost entirely independent of world markets. She could achieve this condition without any of that wide measure of Government planning and direction necessary to poorer nations. In fact, she could enjoy a complete freedom of private enterprise and competition, provided she eliminated the possibility of over-production by establishing a sound basis of high purchasing power. If American industries conformed in one matter—the raising of wages in proportion to productive power—they could enjoy an absolute non-conformity in everything else. On the sound basis of an agreed high purchasing power, they could erect, if they wished, a superstructure of the happiest individual anarchy of competition, on the fullest traditional lines. In fact, in a new, naturally rich and expanding economy, even this author of many " plans " would agree it is probably the quickest way to get results; and what the world wants to-day are action and results.

But, whether or not America ever decided on such a policy, her interest in the European policy here suggested would remain the same. It is the interest of America to get Europe off her hands, and off her markets. America does not want to keep Europe on the Dole for ever and send abroad the product of American industry for nothing in exchange. America does not wish to equip Europe to compete with her in world markets. Even, therefore, if America retained her existing trade method without any development, or modification, it is her paramount interest to get Europe into Africa. America will need all the existing markets she can obtain, if she goes ahead in the old familiar fashion to the next over-production crisis. Europe is no true and final market for America, because Europe can send her no goods in exchange which she cannot make as well, or better, for herself. In short, Europe to America is economically nothing but a headache; either Europe lives on American charity, or sends goods in exchange which dislocate American economy. Economically, they are better apart as soon as possible, when America has given the primary assistance necessary to set Europe on her feet and on the road to self-help in the African solution. Such measure of assistance is commonsense, because America cannot afford to have a vacuum where Europe was. The subsequent division of the two economies will, ultimately, render easier the union of the two policies.

CHAPTER IV

THE UNION OF EUROPEAN AND AMERICAN POLICIES IN RELATION TO THE WORLD MENACE OF RUSSIAN COMMUNISM

IN contrast to economic affairs, considerations of present security and of final survival require a much closer political union. Apart from all tradition of spiritual and cultural communion, America and Europe have to work together for survival. The reason is that they are faced with the external menace of a fundamentally opposed and very powerful State, which intends the destruction of the civilisation and cultural heritage of the West in favour of that International Communism, which represents the sharp anti-thesis of Oriental values and methods under the challenging leadership of a highly-trained revolutionary Party. To suppose that the Leadership of Russia does not intend this is to presume that they have betrayed everything for which they and their Party have stood during forty years of struggle: a most insulting suggestion that should not be levelled by one war comrade against another. Britain and America should, at least, do the leadership of this war ally the honour of assuming that they are not traitors to their cause. World Revolution, through the force of her own armies and the agitation of various foreign Communist Parties, was and is the aim of Communist Russia. The method is to turn Russia into an army and every opposing country into a mob. To this end the maximum organisation, armament and discipline is required within Russia, and the maximum confusion is created within most other countries. Various Communist Parties in other lands are fostered to secure the latter purpose by ceaseless agitation and the engendering of industrial and social strife. Thus, Russia combines in the drive for world revolution the hitherto disassociated weapons of Imperialist aggression and mob anarchy. The two weapons become formidable, in conjunction, when they are available to the same hand for the first time in history.

191

It is a dangerous and novel technique which is worthy of some comment by those men whose business it has been to study this matter during years, as an essential part of their task in combating Communism in active struggle. To such experience, the ingenuousness of some of Russia's present opponents is always astonishing. Every seeming concession by the Soviet is so eagerly and innocently welcomed at its face value by the anxious liberal spirit in search of that goodwill which vanished some time ago from real affairs. Because they have made their usual mistake of never studying their opponent, they have not the faintest idea of what it is all about. In sport and athletics, the Englishman studies " form " meticulously from the very earliest days of a racehorse or a boxer: in politics, which affect his whole future existence, he seldom gives a moment of serious study to the corresponding " form " of an opponent who may be aiming at his life. If he did, we should not read the fulsome headlines of sentimental congratulations in some Conservative newspapers every time that the Soviet diplomats feel that they have pushed the Americans a little too near a premature war, with the result that they withdraw slightly behind some small concession, which is followed by a back-slapping competition at a vodka and caviare party.

On such an occasion the innocence of the guests must be a source of perennial amusement to the seasoned hosts, who have struggled along a hard and dusty road from Siberia to that festive board, and are not " letting up " now that the world may be within their grasp. Why should they; when a little more patience and cunning, until decisive force can be prepared, may crown the struggle of a lifetime? There is a fire in those bellies which does not permit the happy growth of that paunch of complacency which adorns some Democrats who have " made it." The latter politicians are dealing with a totally different animal to themselves; they have not yet understood that fact, let alone the animal. Difficult as the psychology of such an opponent must be to their comprehension, they yet would acquire some glimmer of understanding if they would even begin to study the principle on which the opposing system is based.

The subject is available to them in writing of considerable clarity and force. For instance, Lenin wrote in the *Infantile Diseases of Communism:* " the strictest devotion to Communist ideas must be coupled with the art of acquiescing in practical compromise, with veering tactics, conciliatory manoeuvres and the semblance of yielding, briefly with every device that could possibly hasten the attainment of political power." Even a knowledge of that single illuminating sentence might bring a short pause in the paean of thanksgiving when Stalin sometimes smiles, and even prompt the suspicious and uncomradely reflection that America has got the Atom Bomb, and he has not—yet! For, this single fact governs the whole situation. Russia has not got the Atom Bomb, or any equivalent weapon. When that fact changes, the situation will change overnight. Let us examine, for a moment, the position of the Russian leadership and assume that they have not betrayed, see no reason to betray, and are unwilling to betray their principles of world revolution and conquest through International Communism. They are obviously not going to force a showdown while they are at a hopeless disadvantage in the matter of weapons: not to mention the necessity to repair some of the damage of the last war before launching the next, and the ever-present possibility that the British or Americans might be coaxed into providing credits which would hurry matters up considerably.

Why, then, the innocent may argue, do they not keep quiet and appear much more complacent and easy-going at International Conferences, in order to lull suspicions while they work secretly to reach equality in armaments? Perhaps, even the measure of goodwill they occasionally show—even their outbursts of ingenuous irritability and unreasonableness—may prove that no such deep and far-reaching designs exist; do they not rather reflect the good and honest character of the simple Slav who finds himself outclassed in diplomatic discussions with the sophisticated British and Americans? So runs the reasoning of the wishful innocent, who is about as competent to take on the Oriental Communist, in the " hell's kitchen " of Modern Europe, as a new-born babe is fit to wrestle with a Boa-constrictor.

Such questioning ignores the whole basis of the technique described above—that duality which consists both of Imperialist aggression and Mob Anarchy. Russia seeks to integrate herself and to disintegrate others. Calm and secrecy might serve the first purpose, but not the second. Russia must not only strengthen herself, but, also, weaken her opponents. A withdrawal into seeming quiescence and secret armament can increase Russian strength, but leaves the strength of other countries unimpaired.

Yet, it is the essence of the dual technique not only to build up Russian power for Imperialist aggression but to weaken the resistance of other countries by promoting mob anarchy within their territories. The latter condition is created by securing their industrial paralysis and military disarmament. To both ends a ceaseless industrial and political agitation is necessary by the conscious, and unconscious, agents and assistants of Russia in other lands. Within their ranks, of course, are many quite innocent idealists who fall for the pseudo-humanitarianism which is one of the many stops in the organ of Communist Revolution. Such mob tactics cannot be inspired and continually fostered without an atmosphere of constant strife and the provision of fresh issues of clash and conflict. It is not enough for the conscious, or unconscious, servants of Russia to seek to paralyse the industries of other countries by inflaming every domestic dispute to the point of protracted and exhausting struggle. It is necessary, also, to mobilise all the completely unconscious dupes in other lands behind issues of pseudo-idealism, which are provided by Russian manoeuvres and mob slogans in international controversy. The other countries must be jockeyed into the position of appearing to oppose disarmament and peace; constant clash and controversy on these lines must be promoted to keep on their toes in domestic debate all the " flats " who have been caught for Communism in other countries.

In industrial disputes they are led to believe that they are fighting for the rights of the workers to higher standards which the " Capitalist " bosses are denying. In political disputes they are led chattering up the garden of international peace, brother-hood, disarmament and universal amity; which, in practice, means that the other countries should surrender their present advantage in armaments to the realists of the Kremlin; who would know better how to use it. Nowhere in politics, has the present grotesque division between appearance and reality been carried so far as in the disparity between the sayings of the dupes, and the plans of the masters, of World Communism. A little reflection, therefore, answers the ingenuous question why Russia does not keep quiet and arm secretly, if she really prepares world war. The answer is that she uses mob tactics without, as well as military tactics within, for the long and careful work of war preparation. While Russia becomes ever more like an army her opponents must be reduced ever more completely to a helpless mob. For this purpose their industrial and social life must be disorganised and their military forces must be disarmed.

To both ends, ceaseless industrial and political agitation is necessary; and Father Russia must give the lead by continually providing fresh issues for controversy. Never previously in history has a political manoeuvre been so successful as to lead thousands of innocent idealists to demand the disarmament of their country in face of an armed enemy, and the surrender to his empty but eager hands of the decisive weapon of world mastery with which a great science has provided their own nation. A man with a riflle is faced by a gorilla; it is suggested by some of the friends and relations of the man with the rifle that he should not merely put it down, but should hand it over to the gorilla together with some instructions in the art of using it. Such is the policy proposed for their own country by many innocents; and by some who are not so innocent. (In passing may I note the contrast with that policy for which I was so much attacked: my policy prior to 1939 combined a demand for Peace with Germany, and the avoidance of European war, with a demand for the powerful re-armament of Britain, for which I struggled in a continual political agitation during seven years before the last war. *Vide* Book—*My Answer.*)

RUSSIA SEEKS DECISIVE WEAPON FOR WORLD MASTERY

It is not strange that this proposal for the disarmament of their countries in face of Russia has not yet commended itself to majority statesmanship in Britain and America, but they are still held captive by the secondary manoeuvre of the Russians. They have not been persuaded by internal political agitation to lay down their arms, and the industries of no great countries have yet been quite paralysed by internal strife. But, they are still kept talking by Russian statesmen at International conferences while Russian militarism is seeking for an equality of weapons. The talks will be kept going, until they have found the weapons; so long, and no longer. Keep on talking—above all, keep on talking—Russia must have time—so, give them the anaesthetic —and it is talk—talk—talk—such is the order to the diplomacy which covers the military tactics of the Kremlin. So America is kept talking until Russia has found the weapon. That is what the Americans would usually describe as falling for a " sucker's punch." But, at the time of writing, some Americans, and more Britons, are opening their guard to it as wide as any Russian could wish.

If it is not the plan of the Russians to keep the Americans and British talking until they can develop decisive weapons, why has Russia refused inspection during months of manoeuvres and bogus concessions which are always retracted when the point of practical application is approached? What reason can be behind the attitude of Russia except the desire to conceal what she is doing? If she is doing nothing to develop such weapons, she has everything to gain and nothing to lose by accepting the American plan of inspection. In terms of power advantage, America would be the loser and Russia the gainer. In fact, the offer of America to expose her secrets, and submit to inspection if other nations will do the same, shows a magnanimity without parallel in the relationship of nations. What other country in history has pursued a policy which even approaches in generosity an offer to surrender the monopoly of a weapon, which might give her the mastery of the world? The Russians would be insane not to accept that proposal unless they hoped in time to secure a weapon which would beat America. What conceivable reason can Russia possess for her attitude other than this ambition, which they are seeking to implement by feverish research and hard work in the field of armaments?

The contortions to which Russia has been driven to cover the obduracy of her policy have provided the most grotesque exhibition known to Diplomatic History. The founders of Internationalism have been reduced to talking about " Sovereign Rights "; while those whom they denounced as Jingoes, " nationalists " and " imperialists " have been offering to renounce them in the interests of Peace. All values are reversed, all policies thrown over, all slogans abandoned in the final harlequinade of self-contradiction with which Russian Communism seeks to conceal the basic fact that it rejects inspection of armaments; because it hopes to find a weapon with which to beat the world. So, the " Sovereign Rights " of Holy Russia are pulled out of old Czarist cupboards and " workers of the world unite " is marked for export only; while scientists work in Russian laboratories for weapons to obliterate working-class homes in every great city of the world. If this is not the reason behind their policy, what is it? Why should they miss such a chance to assuage their old fear of aggression by other countries, concerning which we have heard so much, when the only country strong enough for such an act makes a gesture of such extraordinary generosity that it actually offers to lay down the decisive weapon; if Russia will only refrain from picking it up. No apology and no excuse can cover this long-sustained manoeuvre by Russia.

It can mean only one thing; she seeks world mastery by force of arms and is determined to conceal at all costs her preparations for it. The cost to Russia in political prestige is, of course, considerable, and unaccountable except on the single hypothesis. Even the highly trained and flexible tacticians of Communism will find it requires a long time to extricate themselves from the confusion and ignominy cast upon them by this sudden switch of Communism from " Internationalism " to " Sovereign Rights," from demands for universal disarmament to obvious

197

preparations for war in secret, from the claim to be in the van of progress to becoming all too plainly the rump of reaction, from a world hope to a world fear, from the pose and humbug of being an idealist saviour to the stark reality that they plan to be the assassin of mankind. In fact, World Communism could never have recovered from the blow of that sharp reversal of Russian policy in favour of the new plan of conquest by military force, if their opponents in the politics and press of the Old Parties had not, characteristically, been too inept to follow up this moral rout and turn it into a final political disaster.

RUSSIA'S DUAL TACTIC OF POLICE TERROR AT HOME AND MOB TERROR ABROAD

What now of the military situation? The usual innocents of the West dream world sometimes argue that if Russia does acquire the Atom Bomb, or any equivalent weapon, it will mean no more than a stalemate. Neither side would dare to use it for fear of devastating reprisals: consequently, fear will succeed, where goodwill failed, in inhibiting war. Again, they misunderstand the whole character of their opponent, the very texture of his thought and the whole structure of his system. The world must grasp the basic fact that equality in weapons will give the Soviet superiority in striking power. Equality in Armaments between the " Democracies " and the Soviet cannot mean equality of strength in a balance of power. On this fact rests every calculation of Soviet strategy. Let us see whether their analysis is fallacious. Take first the case of an Atomic war between Britain and the Soviet. The latter can disperse, but the former cannot; the wide open spaces of Russia give a great initial advantage in comparison with an overcrowded industrial island. Russia could, if necessary, evacuate her main cities and disperse their population; a similar measure in Britain would present far greater difficulty. The Soviet can shift her industrial target far farther back, and has probably done so already in the case of all war essential industries. Britain cannot move her industries any substantial distance; she can only put some of them underground.

198

So far we deal with matters which all soldiers can well understand; they could, of course, be much elaborated. But we soon enter a field which the military mind does not easily comprehend—the sphere of mob psychology. What would happen in Great Britain when one great city had been really shattered by Atom bombs and every other great city lay under a similar threat? What would happen in Russia in corresponding circumstances? Within the Soviet system the civil population would either he held at their work by force of a well trained and rehearsed terrorism or would be evacuated in orderly fashion under the cover of machine-guns; anyone who broke ranks in the process or showed any symptoms of beginning a panic would simply be shot out of hand. A highly trained and disciplined police would provide a political-military force, which would act with fanatical devotion to the national Communist cause, and with an utterly ruthless disregard of individual lives, or any human consideration. The civil population would be even more afraid of the machine-guns on the street corners, or lines of march, than they would of the Atom Bomb. They might, with luck, escape the latter, but they would have no chance of escaping the former. They would, therefore, choose possible death rather than certain death. The people of Russia would do precisely what they were told; whether it was to stay at their industrial posts until they died, or to evacuate great cities and move elsewhere in an orderly fashion which would not paralyse military operations or the life of the State.

What would happen in Great Britain when the Atom Bomb came down? It is of no use to cite the experience of the last war and the courage of the population under that degree of bombardment. In this situation, which we envisage, the degree of bombardment would be utterly different and beyond any previous experience or even imagining. All things break under sufficient stress; it is merely a question of degree. Even first-rate troops, in highly trained and disciplined regiments with a great military tradition, have been known to break at a certain point. It is just a question whether the opponent can sustain and intensify his bombardment sufficiently, and thus bring to bear

199

enough pressure upon the human frame to reach that point. Everything breaks in time; all soldiers, with any experience of real war, know that. Again it may be asked whether any civilian population in a " Democracy," even of proved heroism, can sustain atomic bombardment without breaking? If they break— if they leave their industrial posts—if they panic in evacuation— if they lose their order in any operation of daily life on any large scale, the grip of the state is paralysed and the war is lost.

It is the calculation of the Soviet—crystal clear to any mind capable of analytical thought—that the civilian population of the " Democracies " will always break under the shock of modern weapons. It is, also, the calculation of the Soviet that their own civil population will not be permitted to break—will be held by the secret police with utter brutality like stampeding cattle held by barbed wire—at least until after the " Democracies " have broken, and Communism has won the Third World War. Such is the calculation of events by the masters of World Communism; the implementing of the theory depends only upon obtaining a bare equality of weapons. For, equality of weapons means superiority of striking power; that is the basic lesson the Soviet derives from the contrast in terms of war provided by the two political systems.

Is it surprising that the Leaders of Russian Communism, who have travelled the dusty road from Siberia to the Kremlin, may think it worth a few silly banquets to diplomats, and a series of tedious manoeuvres at International Conferences, to gain time for such a consummation? They have learned patience and will never permit a petulant prematurity to forfeit the crown of nearly half a century of struggle. Is their reckoning so very far out? Will any realist affirm that? Is it fantastic to suggest that America and Britain are opening their guard for a " sucker's punch "? We have regarded for a brief moment the possible effect of atomic bombing on the crowded island of Britain. It is true that America has the advantage of space, which would render dispersion easier, though, probably, not so easy as in the case of Russia. But the political disadvantages of America in a war of the primeval savagery which modern science will, paradoxically, provide, should be at least as great as those of Great Britain. Neither of the " Democracies " have either the means or the will to handle their civilian population as the Russians would certainly treat their industrial masses in the event of any tendency to panic. Further, there are not many democrats in Russia, but there are plenty of Communists within the " Democracies." Would even the most fatuous wish-dreamer be sure that all of them would be in favour of a relentless continuation of the struggle when the Atom bombs came down, or would even exert their influence very strongly in the maintaining of that public order and industrial discipline which alone would make possible further resistance to the Soviet Power? At any rate, that would not be the reckoning of the leaders of Russian Communism who have so long and arduously evolved the dual tactics of militarism for Russia and mob riot for their opponents.

ACTION BEFORE IT IS TOO LATE

These matters are, at least, worthy of some reflection by those who demanded immediate action when they saw a Teuton with a cannon but feel quite complacent at the thought of a Slav with an atomic bomb. But, we may set aside all whose fears and passions appear to be dictated more by their political prejudices than by the welfare or survival of their country or Continent. When the weapons of the time were insufficient seriously to touch their own countries, if they minded their own affairs, they clamoured to embroil their nation in any political war that was going on in the remotest corners of the world. When weapons have developed sufficiently to devastate their countries from any distance, they urge on their nations a care-free indifference to the doom which is being prepared for them. Is it still indelicate to ask them on whose side they are? Can it still be dismissed as the question of a " boorish Fascist "? Let us face this problem in the way of serious men who are determined that Europe and the Western World shall live, and are not willing to throw three millenia of great history, together with the brightest prospects mankind has known, on the gaming board of the foolish wish that the Communist has ceased to be a Communist, and the Oriental has been transformed into a Western patriot.

If we face the position in terms of reality, it is necessary to state the plain fact that America has a gun in the hand and that Russia is reaching for a similar gun, but has not yet touched it. In such a situation the only sane action is to command the other man to stand back from that gun; if his fingers have not reached it he has no choice except to obey. In a corresponding situation between individuals the man who held the gun and did not adopt that course would deserve to lose the subsequent shooting match, and, if that were his character, he certainly would lose it. Translated into the terms of International politics this simple realism means that America must enforce inspection now if the world is to be saved from the conquest of Communism. America has the Atom Bomb and Russia has not; that single fact dominates the whole position, but it will not last. If Russia is permitted to play for time, she will, sooner or later, obtain equality of weapons, and that will produce, not a balance of power, but the preponderance of Communist striking power in the showdown of the world. The Leaders of Russia are realists who would certainly give way without a war in face of overwhelming force in the hands of the Western Allies: if they did not give way they would lose, quickly and easily.

At worst, action now might mean a war which we must win. Delay invites a war which we might lose. The best possibility of peace is now to compel inspection of weapons; if necessary, by ultimatum. Not to force this showdown before Russia is ready is sheer insanity; not to remove the incentive to German scientists to work for Russia, and to prevent her attempts to bribe, cajole or force them into the service of Communism is more than imbecility; it is world suicide. This cannot be dismissed as overstatement unless four facts can be denied with certainty. They are: (1) That Russia seeks a decisive weapon; (2) That Russia means war when she has found it; otherwise she would welcome inspection to secure the abolition of such weapons; (3) That Russia lacks the technical ability to produce such weapons without the aid of German scientists; (4) That immense inducements are being offered to German scientists to serve Russia, and, although the best of them still remain true to the West, a terrible strain is being put on their loyalty by the policy of the Western Allies, which, in the end, may drive them to any desperation. The first three facts are a virtual certainty, and the fourth is an observed event.*

GERMANY AND EUROPEAN UNION

The attitude of America, Britain and France to the dismemberment of Germany and the oppression of her ablest sons on the grounds of their political record, is preventing the union of Europe and risking the arming of Russia with weapons and a technical ability which she could acquire from no other source.

The fear of a German revival prevents European union; the lack of that union inhibits the action by which alone Europe can survive. This fear arises from the spirit of negation: both Union and achievement await a new affirmation. As usual in human affairs, fear is self-defeating: in this instance it is producing precisely the situation which it seeks to avoid. The triumphant Allies try to prevent a new challenge to their position by the repression of Germany. But, in so doing, they are providing a new challenger with the means to make his challenge effective. The new Communist Imperialism in Russia emerges in menace to every value of European and American civilisation.

*1. Herr Werner Heisenberg, a top German physicist and winner of the 1932 Nobel Prize, said that Russia had made a standing offer of $6,000 a year to any German atomic scientist who would work for the U.S.S.R.

" I was promised in addition," said Heisenberg, " 50 pounds of fresh meat a month, a ration of 3,500 calories of food a day for each of my six young children, and a comfortable, well-furnished house with many amenities." Heisenberg had declined, but he named others who had not. . . . There are still thousands of cold, hungry scientists in Germany to whom Russia's offer might well appeal. (*Time*, March 3, 1947)

2. " Professor Otto Hahn, the German scientist who in 1939 discovered uranium fission—the process that made the atomic bomb possible—said to-day that two of his assistants had ' disappeared to the East ' while they were on a visit to Berlin." (*Sunday Times*, December 8, 1946)

The new challenger plays for time because he lacks the weapons with which our scientific genius has equipped the West. The Allies use well for him the time which he seeks by driving into his arms the genius which he does not possess. One factor alone might give Russia the means of victory and that factor is German science. It is inconceivable that the Slav can ever challenge, let alone defeat, the West, in a new age which science commands. To have any hope of success he must use the talents which his opponents alone possess, and right well he is aided in that manoeuvre by a self-defeating fear.

A united and active West could afford to ignore in large degree the threat of Russian Communism, provided inspection eliminated the risk of attack by certain weapons. But it cannot be united while German territory and population are under the heel of a tyranny which is saluted by the remainder of the West as an Ally. It cannot be active until negation has changed to affirmation and the whole of Western Europe is engaged in a common task of continental construction. Union and reconstruction are alike inhibited by a mind which fears Germany to such an extent that even the menace of Russian Communism is treated as relatively insignificant. It is unnecessary to repeat any part of the analysis of that fear and dislike of Germany which was a subject of Part I of this book. But it is necessary, in considering the constructive task of Europe, to survey some possibilities which may inhibit any such development by the final destruction of the Continent. Chief among such dangers is the extraordinary paradox that many people in Britain, who most feared and resisted German power, appear to feel little or no apprehension concerning the threat of Russian Communism. Even Conservatives have so long been accustomed to using Russia against Germany that many of them are blind to the new threat: among them habit, of course, often works more potently than the processes of the intellect. In part, too, their attitude is explained by a subconscious feeling that Slavonic civilisation is so inferior that in a clash we can always master it: while they experienced, for good reasons, no such sensation of confident superiority in relation to the Teuton. The network of complexes, which we have already dissected in Part I, render them placid toward a force which they feel they can command, but intensely irritable and suspicious in relation to any power which they feel might be capable of dominating them.

This instinct in relation to the force of Russia would, of course, be perfectly correct if the Soviet could only rely on its own talents for such a struggle. What chance would Russian Communism have in a fight against the whole of Western Europe in union with the strength of America? That question is answered by the recollection that 90 million Germans were able to throw 170 million Russians six hundred miles back, while Germany had one hand tied behind her back through the threat of Anglo-American intervention on the Continent. The present pretensions of the Soviet would appear almost farcical in face of the union of the Western World. It is only the division of the West which brings Russia into the picture of world events, and that schism is perpetuated by Anglo-American policy, with the result that the Soviet is a permanent and ever-increasing threat to world survival. It is the division of Europe which thrusts German talent into Russian service; and it is the genius of German science alone which might possibly give the Soviet world mastery. This is the factor the Old Parties in Britain have forgotten, and which France always forgets: it may be the factor of fatality. In the new age of Science the backward Slav is more than ever helpless against the united power of the West. The worst imbecility of history is to divide the West in order to provide the Barbarian with the decisive talents which he so conspicuously lacks.

What other effect can be produced by the present treatment of Germany? Their country is divided and occupied, and a large proportion of their territory and population is subjected to a power which they have learned by close contact in victory and defeat completely to despise. At the same time that Power offers to any German of talent every inducement, while the Western Powers offer every insult. Men of the highest ability in science and in administration are left to starve in frustration

205

and inhibition by the Anglo-American power on grounds of their political record, while Russia eagerly seeks to bribe and cajole any abilities which may serve her further end. In such circumstances a feeling must inevitably develop among some Germans that in the East, at any rate, they may use their capacities, and the future may bring them many and strange opportunities. The very fact that they do so despise the Russian may lead them to the view that they may serve him for a time in the confidence that finally they might make him serve them. The writer believes any such view to be profoundly mistaken: even a temporary strengthening of Soviet power is liable to result in the complete destruction of civilisation. To place the torch of science in the hands of the Barbarian would now be to ignite the world. And Germans, hoping to seek their lost home in the light of that conflagration, would find only ashes and deep death. But it is a course which, in desperation, high abilities may be gravely tempted to pursue.

What alternative hope is the West now offering to Germany? No hope is being given and, in present circumstances, but one hope can exist—it is the dream that this same science, in a fierce spasm of hard-driven genius, may give Germany alone some weapon of such new and fearful potency that it can be produced, even within the limit of present restriction, and used to give Germany victory over the world. Is that a hope which Democratic statesmanship in Britain and America desires to foster— is that a result it seeks to promote? They may laugh to-day in the arrogance of an easily acquired self-confidence: they laughed once before when glider clubs of young enthusiasts followed the destruction of previous German air power. The English say that necessity is the mother of invention, and the Germans observe, after Schiller, that the glance of necessity is sharp. It is indeed a gamble with dark Fate to impose upon the Teutonic genius but two possibilities of survival: the service of the Barbarian—or a deep plunge into the seething cauldron of secret science to solve the final riddle of world triumph. How hard foolish men sometimes work to produce results precisely the opposite of those they desire. The first lessons of this great age is that all things have become possible: this is both the dread and the fascination of our time.

GERMANY MUST HAVE EQUALITY OF OPPORTUNITY

My constructive suggestion for the German problem is that for the first time Germany should be given equal opportunity both in membership of the European Union and in African development. Such a solution of the German problem is possible as an incident in this European Union, but it would probably appear an incredible risk to present statesmanship: in reality, it is nothing approaching the risk of an inevitably ineffective repression. Realism must recognise that all suppression may at any time be rendered futile by the fresh wind of scientific genius which, more than ever, " bloweth where it listeth." Experience shows that such a degree of talent is very unlikely to be found outside the great nations we have categorised. But the discovery of some new principle may in the present onrush of historic dynamism occur in any one of them; when this happens the face of the world may change almost overnight, and only ruins will mark the place of those who sought to contain the explosion. So, even from the standpoint of " Democracy," any degree of realism would suggest that equality of opportunity for a people of the German potential is a lesser risk than the inculcation of desperation. And, for a great and proud people, any form of dismemberment of territory, and subjection of population to a Barbarian tyranny, is a situation of desperation. Would England rest tranquil while a Mongol horde was bullying and ravishing in Kent and Norfolk; and an assorted mixture of pettifogging bureaucrats was bossing them about in the streets of London with the only result that an attendant menagerie of Oriental racketeers could profit from the chaos which paralysis had engendered. No risk is so great as the continuance in any form of the present treatment of Germany. And, is the risk of equality for Germans within European Union so great even from the point of view of present statesmanship? The Union of Europe must indicate, at any rate, some change in the present concept of national sovereignty. In fact, the more complete the Union, the more effective the attainment of the end desired, which is to prevent the destruction of the Continent by national rivalries armed with new weapons of final ruin. Could anyone have so much reason to fear a German revival when the present alignment of nations had ceased to exist?

My proposals on the structure of Government, within a new Europe, belong to the next chapter; we are here considering, in this connection, the " Democratic " concept. A complete Union of Europe would presumably mean to them a European Parliament. In that event, an equality of opportunity for Germany would mean the right to return members to that Parliament, in some proportion to the numbers of their population. It could not entail the right to develop independent armaments within their national territory; when nationalities, as we know them to-day, had ceased to exist. For example, in 1939 the inhabitants of Middlesex or Würtemberg had no right to develop their own local forces or armaments. Even if Union were not complete, and some Federal solution were adopted, the national right to private armaments would presumably be the first to be surrendered in favour of some super-national authority with an armed force at its disposal. Such abrogation of national power would clearly be accompanied by some rigorous inspection of central authority to prevent the development of local armaments. So, the possibility of secret German re-armament would be no greater than it is to-day, and the incentive would be far less. Democratic statesmanship should, at least, reflect on these things before rejecting outright any suggestion of equality of opportunity for Germans in a new Europe.

The removal, or mitigation, of the fear of Germany is thus incidental to any logical conception of European Union. It is important from every standpoint because the elimination of that phobia in turn removes the chief risk of the destruction of the new Continent through the Western Powers unwittingly providing the barbarian with his means to that end. If the Union of Europe be necessary in any case, it is a rare fortune that a solution of the German problem can be regarded as a normal incident in the attainment of that policy, and as a logical part of a larger whole.

It has been charged against the writer, as a reproach, that he is pro-German. I reply that anyone who wants either to save Europe from destruction or to get things done in a new Europe must be pro-German; because, if Germany is not brought into European Union, the West will be divided and the East will triumph. But Germany can only be brought finally and securely into European Union as a united and satisfied people in full possession of their own land. Beyond the question of meeting the present menace and ensuring the future safety of our Continent, the further question of development within the new Union is no less important in the longer vistas of Statesmanship. The reasons for my attitude are simple and clear. All my life I have striven to do something in my time to improve the lot of man and raise his fortune: my life has, at least, proved a certain dynamism. In the Germans I see a people with an energy and capacity which can contribute greatly to large construction and high design. Whether the world likes it or not, they are a force for good or evil—for construction or destruction: like all great elemental forces they will either find an outlet or explode, they will either greatly serve mankind, or, in the end wreck the world in the bitterness of their frustration. The spirit of the Doer, in eternal opposition to that of the Denier, reaches out to Germany the hand of a comrade in high endeavour. What inhibits that understanding with the German people, which can bring union to Europe in the winning of present security—and in the building of a future civilisation beyond the weak imaginative grasp of that loose idealism which has denounced us builders for our " ruthless " realism?

The Interests of France

Let us first consider the objections of a people for whom the writer has always felt a great affection—the people of France. That great nation was considered by many in the past to suffer from some kind of anxiety neurosis in relation to Germany. May we enquire whether her feeling was so unreasonable in the light of history, before we consider whether any justification for that sentiment still exists. France has good historic reason for believing that after any successful clash with Germany her allies would extricate themselves as soon as possible, and leave her once more alone to face the far larger man-power of her traditional enemy. The dual fear that she would be deserted by her allies, and again outnumbered by Germany, dominated the whole policy of France. Her answer to this apprehension was invariably the attempt to hold Germany down by force and thus to prevent the latter developing the full resources of her latent strength. In practice, this policy failed, because it could only be achieved by wrecking the economy of Europe, and, in the end, the majority are always driven to oppose a destruction which affects their own lives. Further, a nation, as strong and vital as Germany, cannot finally be held down by any force, and, certainly, not by the power of a country which is numerically weaker. The will of Europe as a whole, inspired by a tardy sense of self-interest, has thus, always, combined in the last resort with the natural energy of Germany to frustrate the policy by which France strove to save herself from the repetition of a tragic experience.

In the final test of reality, France's policy was not strong enough to prevent the fatal recurrence, but only effective enough to provoke it in a yet fiercer form. No repercussion is so disastrous as that of an attempted repression, which fails. In examining any attempt to apply a traditional policy to a new situation, the first question to ask is whether the premises still exist on which it was based: the enquiry becomes yet more necessary when the policy has previously failed. The answer must be that neither of the premises of that policy any longer prevail. In the first instance, France's allies cannot leave Europe, because their own lives are inextricably interwoven with the fate of that Continent. As evidence of that compulsion accumulates, France will, therefore, be reassured that she will not again be deserted by her late allies in face of a stronger opponent. In the second instance, the numerical and, previously decisive, preponderance of Germany no longer exists in effective terms of power reality. This statement does not mean that attempts to dismember Germany, and to strip her of population and resources, will succeed; they are only likely to produce exactly the opposite result of that intended. Something very different to such old world calculations is inherent in this new consideration.

What matters now in terms of power reality are not the numbers of a country's population but the decisive weapons which it possesses. In all spheres quality will be nearly everything and quantity almost nothing. If a country can produce, or become possessed of, the decisive weapons it will be all-powerful in face of a far more numerous enemy force, which does not possess these weapons. The old fear of France that she will be outnumbered has, therefore, no relevance at all to the new situation. In any clash between France and Germany the vital question will be not relative numbers but relative weapons. Therefore, both premises of past French policy appear to have no bearing upon any realist policy of the future. France's old allies cannot leave Europe and the superior numbers of Germany mean nothing at all. All that matters, in terms of power, is the ability of a nation to produce decisive weapons and the incentive to produce them. It is, of course, a matter of opinion, but experience suggests that the incentive to produce decisive weapons is likely to be a greater factor than the initial facility to do so. Whatever systems of inspection are devised, such decisive weapons will probably be produced by some new principle or method of science, if the incentive to produce them is sufficient. The greatest incentive, of course, would be the perpetuation of intolerable conditions of life for a great and proud people. If all their energies and abilities are frustrated and left with but one hope—the production of a decisive weapon—the lessons of nature and history indicate that such a weapon will finally be produced. Other countries besides France should bear in mind that probability in the treatment of Germany.

For France, in the particular light of her traditional policy, the question is whether the risk of driving Germany to such desperation is greater than the risk of bringing her into equal partnership, within a new Europe. The answer should be assisted by the fact that all countries within such a new union of Europe will voluntarily subject themselves to armament inspection. Whatever safeguards can be provided will thus be secured. But, if incentive is sufficient, all safeguards in the end can be overcome by desperation. France, therefore, would lose no safeguard in bringing Germany into a new European partnership, and would gain the security that the main incentive to a German explosion would, thereby, be removed. If the safeguard of inspection is the same, whether the policy be partnership or an attempted repression, the removal of incentive to destruction is all gain and no loss. In view of a completely new situation which removes both premises of her previous policy, and of the equal physical safeguards provided by a new approach, is it too much to hope that the genius of France will contribute to a constructive solution in which the crystal clarity of the Latin mind is particularly required?

Old animosities will never be overcome by a mere negation: only the mutual effort to succeed in a constructive task can bring a new harmony. In fact, the dynamism of achievement is as essential to the winning of peace as to the finding of an economic solution for current chaos. The age-long conflict between Gaul and Teuton may at length be subdued by the necessity to find a new way of life, when the only alternative is Continental death. At least, all are confronted with the need to think again in the light of a new situation; that is the moment to ask whether the premises, on which old hostilities were based, have any longer any validity. The answer is plainly, no, when we survey the historic causes, and present facts, of the main rift of our Continent, which is the traditional antagonism between Germany and France.

THE JEWISH PROBLEM

What are the other causes of European division which tend to prevent union and thus to inhibit peace, security and an economic solution? The other factors of bitterness, psychological rather than tangible, appear to be rooted in those dark, atavistic memories of the European mind, which, in recent times, have found a partial and unilateral formulation under the general heading of " Atrocities." It is necessary to probe and to cauterise in analysis of fearless realism this sepsis of the European spirit. We will turn next to the general theme, but, in the first instance, it is necessary to deal with a subject, which, in the mind of many Anglo-Americans, forms a part of that general discussion. This view is incorrect because the Jewish problem, of course, has a deeper significance than any contemporary tumult concerning events in the recent war.

It is always difficult, and especially at the present time, to secure any rational discussion of that problem. But, the purpose of this book is invariably to attempt a constructive solution of all problems. The writer is all too well aware from personal experience, as well as from a study of history, that the constructive solutions of reason are seldom permitted to operate in real life. It is, so far, only rarely that the mind and will of mankind work in that way. Nevertheless, in my opinion, it is always our high duty and our wisest course to begin by offering the constructive solutions of reason. No one will accuse me of shrinking from the politics of passion when the unreason of men, or the overweening arrogance of an over-confident opponent, force them upon me: my record frees me from that suggestion. But, it has always been my way, in the first instance, to seek reason: if my opponents insist on passion, I am always ready. In this age-old problem I offer, once again, the solution of reason. For over two thousand years the Jews have asked for a national home, and sought again to become a nation. I adhere to the suggestion that they should be given a national home and the opportunity to become a nation. Will any of them be found to denounce as persecution the granting of something for which they have asked for over two thousand years?: if so, let us hear the reasons.

The Jews, of course, like the rest of us, cannot have it both ways. They cannot ask to be members of their own nation, but to retain membership of every other nation. The favour of dual nationality is rarely accorded to anyone, and the current tendency seems to curtail rather than to extend that principle. But we may surely assume from this long and very legitimate demand for a national home, and the dignity of nationhood, that they will face the facts as well as claim the advantages of their choice. A constructive statesmanship, in the next phase, will seek the constitution of that national home with the minimum friction and the maximum prospect of final and stable solution.

To this end I propose the partition of Palestine and the placing of Jerusalem under a super-national authority which will afford Christian, Arab and Jew impartial access to their Holy Places. It is plain that even the whole of Palestine would not afford an adequate home to the Jewish population, even if it all were available without outrage of justice in the treatment of the Arabs. Such statesmanship would, therefore, in any case, be confronted with the problem of finding additional living room for the Jews. It is, naturally, desirable to provide such accommodation as near as possible to the Home Land of Palestine. But, this consideration is not now so pressing in view of the rapid facilities for travel provided by modern transport. After all, the limbs of British Empire are a long way from the heart, and that was so even in the days when some of the journeys involved might occupy very long periods. Distance did not even then sever the ties or affection of relationship; still less should this happen in an age when science annihilates distance. No insuperable difficulty should be encountered, therefore, even if the main bulk of the Jewish population had to live at some distance from the traditional national home. Palestine would remain a home to them in the same sense that the Dominions regard England as home. But it should be possible to find an outlet for Jews in the constructive work of nationhood much nearer to the National Home.

The reader will recall the suggestion that nations could not expect to remain in possession of African territory which they were unable fully to develop; and the further proposal that even strong and efficient nations might find it desirable to take other peoples into partnership for development purposes, if the full and rapid cultivation of their colonial resources was beyond the powers of their own population. The opinion has been very vigorously stated in recent times that Abyssinia was capable of managing properly her own territory, and that Italian Fascism was quite wrong to suggest a contrary view. But, few people would argue that all the great potentialities of that country could be rapidly developed with the unaided resources of the local population. It would be very improper, in the light of principles outlined in this book, to suggest any dispossession of the Abyssinians in favour of some other people, without that full and impartial enquiry into the facts of each case which the suggested principles demand. Setting aside any such possibility, which would not even be discussed in the absence of proved facts, it may yet here be suggested that it might be an advantage to Abyssinia to adopt the second course, advocated in our plan, and to take another people into partnership, on proper terms.

It might be greatly to the advantage of both Abyssinians and Jews to enter into such a partnership for the development of Abyssinia, and it would certainly be to the advantage of the chief European powers to give all the encouragement they could to a solution which would promote both world harmony and economic development. The Jews might thus find an outlet for their national energies in a territory very near to their National Home. If this solution, in this particular territory, be unacceptable, it should not be beyond the limits of ingenuity and modern opportunity to find an alternative which could provide living room for Jewish Population in reasonable proximity to the National Home, under conditions of modern travel. The National Home is, and always has been, the final solution of the problem. We cannot blame nations for failing to solve the problem in that way, if they had no outside territory to their disposition: that charge, at least, cannot be laid at their door. But, in this great shake-up of the world, and the re-disposal of many lands which it must entail, it would be a tragedy for lack of energy and realist principles to miss so great an opportunity for the settlement of an age-old problem. It is a matter, too, which could be settled by consent if we accept as true and continuing the immemorial desire of the Jews to become again a nation. Failure to find a solution will mean the perpetuation of many troubles and evils. It has,

already, been observed in this book that the attempt to mix like
with unlike, and to blend incompatibles in unnatural political
or economic union, can bring nothing but the breakdown and
disaster which History has recorded so perennially in
such events. The main biological principles which influence
these affairs will be regarded in general during the next
chapter.

We have now reached a point in the study of these matters
where some observed deductions may surely be suggested. It can
be treated as a subject of science without relevance to prejudice
or passion. But, in the political considerations now under
discussion, we need only note the lesson of History that the
attempt to bind together those who differ considerably does not
succeed. In apparent, but comprehensible paradox, the contiguity
of peoples, who differ not considerably but completely, is easier
to sustain without friction; British success in Colonial administration has often proved this. It is the union of peoples who
possess some things in common, but differ fundamentally in
certain decisive respects, which always produces the maximum of
friction. When all is said and done, this is not a matter of
theorising but of proved practice in the Jewish case. The trouble
has gone on for a very long time among many different nations
and in many different climes. In that actual practice, with which
practical politics are primarily concerned, the trouble, in one
form or another, has nearly always recurred; and it is, therefore,
necessary to seek a solution which humanity, as a whole, will
approve. The differences which have caused the trouble, have
been greatly stressed by Jewish thinkers. Few scientists would
go so far as the Jewish leader of the Conservative Party, Mr.
Disraeli, who observed, " race, all is race." What validity
attaches to that conclusion will be discussed in the next chapter.
For the moment we are facing a practical question, how to
stop the disturbance of European harmony by the row about
the Jews. A solution of reason is here suggested which gives
the Jews the National Home they have always asked, and gives
to Europe freedom from that problem, and the healing of an
old and open wound.

" ATROCITIES "

THE UNION OF EUROPE AND THE MORAL QUESTION

It is necessary now to consider the general subject of " Atrocities," as they are compendiously described. It is essential to face this question, because a great and abiding bitterness can inhibit both European Union and something more important than any economic solution—the new way of life which may come from a new and wider opportunity. Let us begin by a most unpopular process; let us free our minds from cant. We will ignore for the moment, the darker phases of more ancient history and regard only the story of the great nations over the brief span of the last generation. In the course even of the last thirty years, the great countries, or various political elements within them, have accused each other of almost every crime in the calendar. Nearly all nations have been accused of these things by their opponents. But, we cannot accept the verdict of a contemporary enemy as history, even if he provides both accusation and judgment with the most differential pomp. Just look at the charges which have been flying about in periods of political passion in the last thirty years: we will return later to the specific matter of the last war.

Americans have been accused in reports published by leading British Daily Newspapers of the following actions: burning opponents alive at the stake; shooting men and women; flogging and other methods of torture; deportation of men from their homes; imprisonment under *ex-post facto* laws; deprivation of food and water; herding prisoners like sardines; and racial persecution.

Britons have been accused in reports published by leading British Daily Newspapers of the following actions: murder; rape; robbery; flogging and other torture; looting; arson; outrages on women; deliberate starvation of villagers; flogging of innocent schoolboys; kidnapping of children; brutal ill-treatment of prisoners; and racial persecution.

Frenchmen have been accused in reports published by leading British Daily Newspapers of the following actions: murder;

217

rape and other outrages against women and children; deportation of civilians from their homes; harsh and indecent conditions of imprisonment.

Among the smaller countries, citizens of one or more of the following nations: Hungary; Finland; Rumania; Turkey; have been accused in reports published by leading British Daily Newspapers of one or more of the following actions: deportation and massacre of men, women and children; brutal flogging of both sexes; imprisonment under insanitary conditions, producing typhus and wholesale deaths; plundering of hospitals of milk, etc., thus causing deaths of babies; murder; rape; and racial persecution.

Finally, Russians have been accused by reports published in leading British Daily Newspapers of wholesale murder; mutilation; torture of the most revolting description; rape and other outrages on women; herding in prisons under overcrowded and insanitary conditions; religious persecution.

Soviet Russia has also been indicted by their wartime comrade-in-arms, Mr. Winston Churchill, in the following terms: —

" Bolshevism, wherever it manifests itself openly and in concrete form, means war of the most ruthless character, the slaughter of men, women and children, the burning of homes, and the inviting in of tyranny, pestilence and famine.

" All the harm and misery in Russia have arisen out of the wickedness and folly of the Bolshevists, and there will be no recovery of any kind in Russia, or in Eastern Europe, while these wicked men, this vile group of cosmopolitan fanatics, hold the Russian nation by the hair of its head and tyrannise over its great population."

Germans have been accused by a Court and Judges constituted by the Allies at Nuremberg in terms too recent, familiar and voluminous to require, or permit, any repetition here. Germans will eventually have the opportunity to argue before History whether, or not, the " horror " conditions in their war concentration camps were largely produced by Allied bombing and consequent epidemics. History will consider such questions in relation to the morality and chivalry of hanging young girls who happened to be placed in official positions in such camps at such a time. Here, we are necessarily concerned for the moment more with what is conveniently forgotten than with the subject of continual reminder from politics and press, From the foregoing catalogue only one fact emerges: if the verdict of opponents were accepted as final, nearly everyone would be guilty of the most revolting crimes in greater or lesser degree. Further, if all these charges were subject to impartial examination by a neutral court, it is possible, and probable, that no nation would be entirely free from any charge which would, in varying degree, be the subject of shame under any high code of morality. What now of this question of degree? Does it enter seriously the question of morality? Without casuistry, is it legitimate to enquire whether a man is any less a murderer if he has committed only half a dozen murders than if he has committed a thousand; once a crime has been committed the repetition appears more a matter of additional temptation, or opportunity, than a question of further immorality. But, it is unnecessary at this stage to be drawn into any speculative realm of ethics or philosophy.

THE MORAL QUESTION IN NATIONS FACED WITH DEFEAT

Let us all agree that such crimes cannot be excused, and that the most that can be urged in favour of the accused is a plea in mitigation. (We assume for the moment that the charges have been proved in a neutral court, which is not the fact in any case to date: neither the charges against Germany, nor any other nation, have yet been examined in a neutral court, and History will not accept them as true until they are). Now, if we agree that no defence for such crimes exists, but only a plea in mitigation, what factors should weigh in such a plea? Is it wrong to suggest that the only factor which can weigh is national necessity? It is not a defence but a plea in mitigation. Let us take an extreme hypothetical case, which illustrates the point. If the life of British Empire had depended in the recent war on the killing in cold blood of one prisoner, it would have been murder to kill him; but the plea in mitigation would have been that the lives of millions had thereby been saved, a mighty structure of civilisation had been preserved, and one thousand years of great history could reach out again to future glories. To take another case, the killing of a man by Lions in the arena of Ancient Rome to make a crowd laugh would, in terms of fundamental morality, have been precisely the same crime; but the plea in mitigation would have been far less, in fact, non-existent. If we agree at all on these premises of the argument, which seem ineluctable, the preliminary conclusion appears to be inevitable. To murder one man is the same crime as to murder many; no defence exists for such a crime, but only a plea in mitigation; the only plea which appears at all tenable is the higher necessity of the survival of the nation or a great cause.

If, at this point of the argument, some slight psychological resistance is developing in some reader who happens to be a worthy Conservative Churchwarden, or a Socialist Nonconformist lay preacher, because he scents some danger in the path along which he is being led by easy stages, let me ask him one question. Supposing in 1940, it had been put to him, as a matter of fact, that the life of British Empire depended on the shooting of one man—the writer of these pages—would the fact that this writer could not even be charged with any offence against any law have deterred him from voting in favour of the shooting? Can he put his hand to his heart and swear that in such circumstances he would not have committed a crime which in any law, or under any system of accepted morality, would have been murder? Further, would the memory of his decisive vote in favour of shooting me even have ruffled his smooth complacency as he carried the offertory bag down the aisle of his church next Sunday? A little enquiry into the subject of motes and beams might well prelude this discussion. For, once our Churchman has accepted the (to me) lamentable fact that, in these circumstances of national necessity and desperation, he would have been guilty of a technical murder, he has lost the whole argument. The excuse that he could advance for his action is precisely the excuse by which his opponents could cover every action of which he accuses them.

No such situation of desperation arose in Britain to provoke any such action. Invasion was a possibility for a short period, but the life or death of the 1,500 British subjects, whom the Government held in their prisons without trial, was entirely irrelevant to the issue, even if those persons had been ill-disposed instead of proved patriots from the Air Force and trenches of the previous war. But the situation of Germany, reeling back in defeat in 1945, was very different. Men were short, food was short, disorder raged as all supply services broke down under incessant bombing. They held in prisons or camps a considerable disaffected population, some German, but most alien, who were requiring guards and good food supplies that were wanted elsewhere to the point of urgency and desperation. They were faced in a harsh and very practical form with the very hypothetical question stated above.

We must stress again that, in point of crime, it makes no difference whether the killing is of one man or of many: in practice the dilemma only arises when it affects many. In such a situation would any great nation have lost the last war, because of a moral scruple in its conduct? It is useless to say that the war was begun for moral reasons; they all say that, and anyhow, it has nothing to do with the point. The question is quite different—would any great nation lose a war, and suffer national destruction, rather than treat some minority in a brutal and immoral way? We all know the answer; if we have ever been in a minority in a moment of passion. Everyone knows the answer: no nation would be wiped out, rather than behave in this way. There is nothing which every great nation will not do, rather than accept defeat. Only those, who, faced by the test of fact, have accepted defeat rather than violate a moral principle, can throw a stone at others.

Modern war is the end of morality. Those, who are responsible for beginning war, are, also, responsible for ending morality. Can our Churchwarden then continue to rend the soul of Europe with eternal animosities against the German people because their leaders, now dead, followed a principle, which, in similar circumstances of a losing fight, he would have found it very difficult himself to deny. The argument here stated is no sterile dialectic; it will, no doubt, be very unpopular—the destruction of humbug always is—but it goes to the root of the matter in terms of that morality which comes so lightly from so many thoughtless lips. There are times when self-deception and hypocrisy do not matter; these things are old and amiable idiosyncrasies of many of our people. But such humbug to-day is a world menace; because it strangles the soul of Europe.

Let us carry the argument forward to a point where the smug gentleman of our imagining must face further vistas of the horror that sometimes confronts men in real and terrible things. If he found a prisoner in a cell who held a secret on which the life of his country, or at least the lives of many of his comrades, depended, would he watch with gentle equanimity the derision of that prisoner at his ineffective efforts to obtain that information; if he had overwhelming force, and brutality, at his disposal? That is a situation which seldom confronts Churchwardens, but is often met, in varying degree, by military police in an occupied country, where resistance is being organised on a large scale. Did all the Black and Tans emerge quite so spotless from the same test in much the same situation in Ireland, as the Church-warden would have liked to think in Church on Sunday, just after he had voted for the Coalition Government which used them in the attempt to break the spirit of the Irish by terror? Let us remember that Britain was not fighting for her life at the time the Government employed the Black and Tans in Ireland, but that every country, which occupied another country in the late war, was, at that stage, fighting for its existence. It is not pleasant to face facts, but even the most complacent must be made to face them at last, if fresh air and sunlight are to be let into the dark places of the European soul as harbingers of that new Springtime which shall follow a winter of oblivion.

FINAL MORAL QUESTION

Let us not shrink from carrying the argument to that final question which has embarrassed in fine dialectic and deep moral searching some of the noblest minds of Europe ever since the zenith of Sparta first exposed to the enquiry of mankind an utterly ruthless method in the service of a higher purpose. The classic world discussed much the right to kill for the purpose of preserving, or fostering the emergence of, some species which was held by the prevailing sentiment to be worthy of much care. Does the best modern thought throw any light on that subject? The reader must settle for himself; at this point I do not seek to interpret such thought, but only direct attention to it for purposes of enquiry. Take a passage from the favourite Sage of our age in a writing which he, himself, selected as the finest, and furthest reaching, exposition of his thought. He is not only a superb intellect: he is also one of the kindest and most generous men that any of us, in any creed or party, have ever known. The passage runs as follows: —

ACIS (*to the She-Ancient*) Is she all right, do you think?

The She-Ancient looks at the Newly Born critically; feels her bumps, like a phrenologist; grips her muscles and shakes her limbs; examines her teeth; looks into her eyes for a moment; and finally relinquishes her with an air of having finished her job.

THE SHE-ANCIENT. She will do. She may live.

They all wave their wands and shout for joy.

THE NEWLY BORN (*indignant*). I may live! Suppose there had been anything wrong with me?

THE SHE-ANCIENT. Children with anything wrong do not live here, my child. Life is not cheap with us. But you would not have felt anything.

THE NEWLY BORN. You mean that you would have murdered me!

THE SHE-ANCIENT. That is one of the funny words the newly born bring with them out of the past. You will forget it tomorrow.*

Is it still necessary to say to our Churchwarden in the language of this same Sage, " Think child, think." Turn to the teaching of a moral philosopher who has long been accepted by many very serious and moral thinkers as pre-eminent in moral theory: " As for doing evil that good may come, it is really a meaningless

*Bernard Shaw: *Back to Methuselah.*

223

phrase: because if good comes of it, and it was done with that intention, it cannot be evil." Considerable qualification and development follows which the reader should study for himself, but the conclusion appears more or less to be: " From the point of view of practical decision, the end does always justify the means, in the sense that the course of action which will produce a balance of good results in the circumstances should be the one adopted."* These are principles which have been laid down by leading thinkers in very different spheres, who have long and rightly been greatly honoured in Great Britain.

I will not attempt to apply these principles to the cases we have discussed, or to pronounce any verdict upon such actions in the light of those opinions. Each reader must work out such problems for himself with the assistance of the best minds which the contemporary world can offer. These principles are here quoted for one reason: it is necessary for many people to realise that these deep matters of theory, and hard facts of reality, are not quite so simple as they wish to believe. It is time, in fact, that they stopped chattering and started thinking.

THE CRIME OF SUBSTITUTING TERROR FOR POLICY

For my part, I return to the point where I began. My position is that such crimes, as we previously discussed, cannot be defended, and all that we can do in this respect is to listen to pleas of mitigation. The only possible criterion of such excuses appears to be national necessity which rests on the degree of danger to the life of a great nation, which would have arisen if the crime had not been committed. In such a light I should certainly judge events within my own experience. For instance, it would appear by this test that certain actions of British Government in India were less reprehensible than in Ireland. Personally, I opposed in Parliament and outside both the policy which employed the Black and Tans, and the policy which utilised similar measures in India. In both cases, incompetent and frightened Governments were, in my view, substituting brutality for efficiency. Their failure either to present a policy

*G. C. Field: *Moral Theory.*

or to grip the situation was covered by an ineffective terrorism. They were characteristic of the epigram of a wise old man upon a well-known Conservative family: " they can never come to a decision until they have lost their temper." Such Governments fumbled and hesitated in paralysed indecision until the situation frightened them, and, then, turned weakly to the brutality of passion.

Neither terrorism had even the excuse of necessity. But the plea in mitigation in the case of India would obviously be the greater. The reason is not that any more justification can exist for mal-treating Indians than Irishmen. The reason is rather that in India a tiny White population was surrounded by a vast sea of hostility in which it would be rapidly submerged if the situation got out of hand, even for a very brief period. Terrorism, therefore, was employed both as a substitute for a policy and for a sufficiency of efficient force. In Ireland, no such plea in mitigation could be argued. The home island was adjacent and possessed over-whelming force; the use of Black and Tan terrorism had no vestige of reason except that it was a dirty little under-the-counter substitute for an open and effective repression by regular troops from which the Government shrank because of its effect on American and world opinion. In the first instance a Govern-ment had at least the excuse of being frightened into brutality: in the second case terrorism was part of a squalid intrigue which masked dishonesty and hypocrisy.

The extreme of extenuation can be urged in the case where the whole life, history and future of a great people is at stake: the minimum of mitigation may be pleaded in a case where bewildered old men seek to cover the bankruptcy of their policy and the squalor of their souls, in some dispute which has no vital significance, by a little sly terrorism and back parlour sadism. I regret that it is necessary to refer to these old policies of vile memory, which are very much within my personal experience, because, with a small band of companions, I began the Parlia-mentary fight against them, which ultimately succeeded in checking brutality if not in securing a constructive policy. Brutality and terrorism, born of fear, laziness and incompetence, have always seemed to me as contemptible as they were unforgivable. If anything rough has to be done in a dark, fierce world which, on occasion, compels the facing of such reality, by men hardened to a higher purpose and called to the steel test of great events, it should be done openly in the full light of day, and explained in terms of such high necessity that men may understand and God forgive. Such things cannot be defended: but mercy can hear a plea in mitigation, and it has been said that to understand all is to forgive all.

These memories are here revived for one purpose only: it is necessary to redress the balance of Europe. Even so, let it not be thought that only the past can be cited to restore an equilibrium to the moral position, which will enable Europeans to live together. It is unnecessary to refer to the occupation of Germany after the previous war, concerning which we have already cited some facts alleged from responsible British sources at the time. We have, also, already, referred to some events of the present occupation of Germany, and observed that many Englishmen can extend to the Germans in this respect a sympathetic understanding because some of the " Britons " now occupying Germany have already occupied us. I will go further in the determination to restore some balance to an argument which has too long been one-sided: because, whatever offence is now given, the attainment of a new equilibrium is necessary to the future harmony of Europe. Therefore, I now reprint in this book a brief article which I wrote at the time of Nuremberg and the beginning of the post-war starvation of Germany: —

NUREMBERG AND AFTER

" With courts, judges and gaolers we are not concerned. They loyally and faithfully execute the laws which political forces lay down; they can do no other. These words are addressed to some of those political forces, and to some only among them.

" Are you yet satisfied? Or will you now permit the slow murder of a whole people by mass starvation? Even the finer spirits among the war leaders revolt against that; only the

small—the incredibly small—demand still further vengeance.
The large of mind and spirit have more than had enough; is it
not now enough even for the lesser?

"The principle of retroactive law has been firmly established
in Europe. By that principle an opponent can, at any time, be
eliminated by a new retrospective law made to fit his particular
case. Do you not yet feel safe? You have not merely killed
political opponents in cold blood: that was a commonplace at
certain periods of history—we thought they were past. You have
also killed brave soldiers who obeyed orders. You have made a
zoo and a peep-show of your victims for the gloating joy of
everything that is lowest in human or beast. You have mocked
and derided the sufferings of the women who loved these men.
You have done things not often known in the millenia of Western
history—why?—Modern science has taught us the answer, even
if the history of brave men had not already told us that such
things are only found in those who fear.

"What else can it all mean?—the long, slow ordeal of ' trial '
and killing to assure yourself that they are really dead, and that
it is just; the frenzy of indignation because they were permitted
last words, and you fear that even from the scaffold they will
say something you cannot answer; the scattering of the ashes in
an unknown place so that even their bodies may not rally the
souls of men and prove them in the end stronger in death than
you are in life. (Study the psychological works on Totem
killings, and subsequent Totem fears, if you are interested to
follow further the ' rational ' processes of the ' Democractic '
mind.) Then the desire to debase by every means, and, above
all, to prevent any dignity in death: the manacling of the victims,
the terror of suicide. Why not pemit it—if you were determined
they must die—it was the habit of a finer civilisation in the
Hellenic world than you have yet known.

"To try to prevent suicide, and to fail, was to enshrine Goering
for ever, in the mind of every German, within the lustre of that
immortal line from Goethe's *Achilleus,* when the hero is
ready to ' take from the hand of despair the glorious crown of
unfading victory.' You incurred that reverse because you could

227

not bear the thought of a suicide that might rob you of your ritual of debasement.

" What can all this signify in terms of the psychologist, except a deep sense of personal inferiority in your subconscious measurement of yourself against the victim? But we need no such learning to teach us that. For a man—a real man—in victory has but one thought—to prevent the necessity of further strife. The elimination of the opponent is enough—preferably not by death if he is a brave and manly figure. Can we conceive a real man—in victory dancing round a manacled enemy— shrieking insults in the face of death—laughing at the suffering of the women—frightened of his victim's last words—frightened even of his ashes—terrified of his ' legend '? What strange, dark spirit of some remote underworld has possessed our virile England?

" Even now is it not enough? Must you also destroy the million masses of ordinary people? Surely it is only the outstanding whom your natural character, for reasons obvious to any psychologist, leads you to hate. Cannot you spare the ordinary, the poor, the humble, the suffering? Is vengeance not yet slaked? Can you not even now leave the past to history? Or do you fear, too, the cold contempt in the eyes of posterity?

" It was well said within our time that the ' grass grows green over the battlefields, but over the scaffold, never.' This grass will not grow green. Revenge will follow vengeance until some generation is found great enough to disrupt the circle of fatality, and to break this ' Bondage of the Gods.' "

Look Forward

The last sentence of this article provides the reason for my present striving. Europe must forget and forgive, if the Continent is to live, in which resides our history, and on which rests the hope of Mankind. Can any great nation look back on the story of even the last generation without some sense of *mea culpa?* The answer is clearly, no; but few are sufficiently influenced by the creed which they profess, to be any less interested in the throwing of stones. Is it too much to hope that a New Europe will grow away from the memory and influence of such events, as British Empire and French civilisation have developed far beyond many of the impulses and occurences which marked their origin? Who would condemn the present structure of British Empire by reason of the brutal and bloody incidents which occurred in the establishment of some Colonial outpost, or in the Indian Mutiny? Who would blame the fine flower of twentieth century French culture for the dark fertility of blood with which the Revolution soaked those deep roots? If National Socialist and Fascist civilisation had reached a maturity which was a glory of constructive achievement, would any philosopher of the future have troubled more about events discussed in Nuremberg than the birth pangs of any other civilisation? Can any serious thinker condemn a man of thirty, because there was a mess in the bedroom when he was born? To adopt this attitude is to show a lack both of the historic sense and of any realistic appreciation of the way of nature and of life.

The greater good cannot always be achieved without the lesser evil. Will that be denied by those who justified the dropping of an Atom Bomb on civilian populations with the plea that the war would be shortened and the lives of soldiers would be saved? That argument could only mean that it was more important to save the lives of British and American soldiers, which would have been lost in the invasion of Japan, than the lives of the relatively few Japanese children who perished in the agony of Hiroshima. The argument that the end justifies the means, that national necessity overrides the suffering of individuals, and that the few must be sacrificed to the many, could scarcely be pushed to a further extreme of moral dubiety. It is not for us here to judge these things, and no attempt is made to do so. The purpose of this writing is rather to eliminate an hypocrisy which poisons the soul of the world. In the light of recent history a little humility is not amiss in judging others: not even in those who profess the creed which makes humility the chief virtue, but refuse with insensate arrogance even to contemplate the possibility that they have constantly committed the crimes of which they accuse others. Such types in daily life are merely laughable: in the

229

seats of power they are a world fatality. The wounds of Europe must be healed before the work of construction can begin. They are wounds of the spirit, and they are kept open by these animosities and memories of atavistic savagery. These old things have no interest to the creative mind, but they impede our work. That is why we ask Europe not to look back, but to stride forward. In these pages I have attempted to describe some possibilities which beckon us onward in the march of the European spirit. They are worth that effort of the living mind and will, which forgets the past and, thus, achieves the future. Division is death, but Union is life.

CHAPTER V.

THE SYSTEM OF GOVERNMENT:
ILLUSION AND REALITY

THE more complicated life becomes the more difficult will it be to sustain a system of the State which rests on the theory that everyone understands everything. This is the basic assumption of the idea which is now called " Democracy "; and, already, it has become a manifest absurdity. In theory, the opinion of everyone is given equal weight once in five years, or less, to settle every question of national affairs from the intricacies of currency management to the mathematics and strategy of the new scientific warfare. Between the hours of 8 a.m. and 9 p.m., on the appointed day, the whole adult population leaves factory, bench, office desk or public house to give their deeply considered verdict, which will govern all those questions for the next five years. In the interval of their daily work, they are supposed to have found time to follow all these matters with sufficient application and intelligence, not only to give a general verdict on the question whether the results of Government are good or bad—but, through their parliamentary representatives in detailed debate, to give precise instruction in their work to all experts in all these affairs. That is the basic assumption on which the whole system rests. Everyone is supposed to understand everything in a period when it is becoming truer to say that nobody understands anything. The more complicated everything becomes, the more completely ignorant people are brought in to settle the question. When the complexity of the problem is obviously beyond the grasp of the existing electorate, the only popular remedy is to extend the franchise. As things develop, and the electorate finds all questions difficult to the point of the impossible, the logical reduction to absurdity of the existing principle will be to give the vote from birth.

This is not to argue that the people should not have power over their own destiny and that of their country. On the con-

231

trary, I suggest that this right should be restored to them: they are now deprived of it by an elaborate swindle. It is necessary to create a system by which the will of the people can be carried out and the people can be served by Statesmanship. If we define Democracy as service of the people, I claim that the view expressed in these pages is the only true Democracy. My point is that the people cannot be served by the form which is now called " Democracy," because that form inhibits the action by which alone the will of the people can be implemented. As usual in this system the divorce between principle and practice has become complete. The people are supposed to govern everything and so govern nothing. Instead of confining their power to a sphere they can control, their nominal power is extended to regions they plainly cannot control; so they lose control of everything. This suits very well those who desire power to reside elsewhere; in the hands of the financial speculators.

They are naturally the most assiduous in flattering " Democracy " into taking on tasks for which it is quite unfitted, so that all government is paralysed and only chaos reigns. In such conditions the producer alone is " controlled," and the financial parasite is entirely free to speculate, in the larger sphere, among the fluctuations of prices, and, in humbler regions, to draw his reward in the black market, which is engendered by universal shortage. When the police force has been made well and truly drunk, the burglar community reaps a good harvest. In this instance, the force of the people's power has been made drunk with the heady wine of that flattery which is the main beverage of the day. Tell the people that they are omnipotent and possess sovereign power: if they believe it, you can then filch from them the effective power they might possess, and get on with the swindle. Tell them that they are the " Image of God " and quite perfect in every way: if they believe it, they will develop that fatuous and pathetic complacency, even in the most wretched conditions, which will remove from them all energy and driving will to improve either their surroundings or themselves, and, in so doing, to upset that most profitable racket which you now conduct at their expense. So, flatter the people, dope the people—is the order of the day—let the politicians black their boots, while the financiers pick their pockets. Flatter them and make them silly: Tell them they run the world, and, then, give them the films, the " dogs " and the Press to stop them thinking about anything. It all runs as smoothly as the oldest confidence trick on earth: tell the " mug " he is the " hell of a fellow," give him lots of drink—and—then—go through his pockets. This is " Democracy."

THE POLITICAL SUBCONSCIOUS

At this point the intelligent reader may shrink back in suspicion of that over-statement, which the higher modern education has taught him to regard as a far worse failing than a well-developed technique of self-deception in face of unpleasant facts. Let us, however, at once, agree that many worthy and able men support " Democracy " without any sense of being racketeers who delude the people in order to rob them. We have, already, observed at an earlier stage of this book some of those subconscious movements of mind and motive, conditioned by innumerable experiences and pressures of class, heredity, education and national circumstance, which form the complex substratum of a simple political belief, honestly and loyally held. We have, further, agreed that it is impossible to avoid falling a victim to such forces and being almost exclusively animated by them, until long study of a new science, and reflection on personal position, has enabled us to sort them out in ourselves and to distinguish between the interested and the disinterested in our own thought and motives. Such a long and arduous process will be a normal part in the training of the Statesmen of the Future; it plays no part in the training of Statesmen to-day, unless a provident society has thrown them for a long time into a political prison with access to modern thought and science, and they happen to possess an energetic and enquiring intelligence.

In short, it is very true to say of the political mind that it resembles the iceberg with only a fraction showing above the water line of the conscious, whilst the vast bulk is immersed in icy depths of atavistic memories, selfish class interests, and

233

primeval pack instincts. Our statement, therefore, appears crude to the intelligent reader, not because it is untrue, but because it draws into the light of the conscious what normally reposes in the depths of the subconscious: that was, also, the factor which antagonised many "intellectuals" in much of our pre-war political propaganda, which they denounced for the violence of its black and white "extremism" that contrasted with the monochrome grey of "balanced judgment." If our intellectuals would move, just a little further, into the realm of the intellect they might understand some tendencies and methods which they have hitherto misunderstood. In the sphere of Art they begin to understand the Surrealist concept of portraying what is occurring in the underlying reality of the subconscious. They do not yet understand the equal, indeed more urgent, necessity in politics to reveal to the light of day those dark processes which animate political actions behind the smooth facade of the most respectable and benign appearance.

We do not blame the men whose motives we expose: they have not even learnt enough as yet to have the slightest idea of what they are doing, and why. But, if the world is to be saved from the recurrent disaster occasioned by their chronic self-deception, they must be made to regard not only the results of their actions but the reasons which really inspired them. It is a painful process, but "know thyself" may check many crimes on that road which is paved with good intentions. In the meantime, we cannot expect many people yet to analyse the motives which maintain "Democracy." In fact, so much nonsense has been talked about the system, which is now sanctified into a complete neo-religious mumbo-jumbo, that it is almost impossible to secure any serious thought or discussion concerning its merits or demerits. To posterity, the basic assumption that everyone understands everything will probably appear the most ridiculous and inexplicable aberration which ever possessed the human mind. At present it is accepted as an axiomatic fact; and, in voting to settle the future of Government, the opinion of the leading scientist of the age carries no more weight than the latest success of a "special" school, whom great care and skill has just saved from being a permanent " burden on the rates " in the local asylum. A system, which is so divorced from reality, can only be maintained by much deception. And, once deception becomes a commonplace, the extension of the principle knows no end.

THE INEVITABILITY OF CHARLATANISM UNDER " DEMOCRACY "

It is clear that the more complex the facts of the age become, the less can everyone understand or even discuss them. But, as the people have to believe that they discuss and settle everything, they are, in fact, given things to discuss which have no relation, whatever, to the matter which is really settled. Therefore, as national and world affairs become steadily more complicated, the things which are discussed at election times become progressively simpler and sillier and more and more remote from actuality. Political slogans have less and less bearing on reality as the gulf between what has to be decided and what the people can understand becomes ever wider. A new class of public entertainers must, then, be brought into existence to keep the people amused by catch-cries and acrobatics which have no relation to reality, while other men get on with the serious work of Government. In these conditions, the first class has come to be known as the Politicians and the second class as the Civil Service. The Politicians keep the people amused, and the Bureaucrats do the job; at least, to their own satisfaction.

We will return shortly to the present phenomenon of Bureaucracy, which boasts, and correctly, that it is the real Government of Britain. Let us first dispose of an argument which is urged in extenuation of " Democracy." It is, sometimes, admitted by intellectual defenders of the system that it is obvious the people cannot, and do not, understand most of the subjects which comprise the intricacies of modern government. But, they argue, the results of Government are at least felt, and, therefore, broadly understood; while, in the election of Parliamentary representatives, they, in fact, delegate the real work of Government to those who understand it. The last assumption is very doubtful;

235

but, to the extent that the argument has any validity, does it amount to anything more or less than the claim that the absurdities of " Democracy " no longer matter, because, in reality, the system has been unobtrusively transposed into Fascism? If it were true that the people merely gave their verdict on the results of Government, which they can observe and feel, and that they delegated all the serious thought and work upon the real problems of Government to trained experts, that system would be much nearer to the plebiscite of Fascism, than it is to Democracy. But, is it true that this happens? Is it correct that Government is left to experts who are trained, selected and directed by people who are well qualified to judge their capacities and command and co-ordinate their labours? Obviously, nothing of the kind occurs.

In practice, the present compromise, which must occur in order to circumvent the blatant absurdity in the theory of present " Democracy," combines the worst possible features of both systems. The people have no effective control over the practical affairs of Government, but these affairs are not conducted by experts, or any serious persons, but by charlatans. This must occur by reason of the manner in which the rulers are selected. If the intellectual argument, just mentioned, is driven to concede that the people cannot understand the present complexities of Government, it is also forced to admit that they have no criteria by which to exercise their present function of judging and directly electing those who are charged with understanding the problems, and controlling and selecting the management of these grave affairs. It is no use even speaking of Members of Parliament, in the manner of the " Left," as Delegates of the people, when they have ceased to be " representatives," because no intelligible opinion any longer exists to represent. A Delegate cannot function honestly and effectively unless the Delegator has some understanding of the problem to which he is a delegate. In practice, that election candidate becomes a Member of Parliament who is most adept at inventing specious absurdities, and spinning plausible promises which have no relation, whatever, to reality: not to mention his concern with the traditional labour of baby kissing and Bazaar opening, which would rapidly exhaust and vitiate any competent intellect in the course of a few years indulgence, even if such an intelligence would tolerate such work for a longer period than a racehorse could sustain the labours of a coster's donkey.

In fact, the greater the divorce between the realities of Government and the understanding of the people, the greater becomes the degree of Charlatanism in the character of the people's " representatives " or " delegates." Just as the growing complexity of all problems requires a more profound and thoughtful type in Government, the fundamental weakness of the system must produce a more frivolous and dishonest type in politics. This is the inevitable result of the basic lie that everyone understands everything, on which the system rests. The more difficult it becomes to understand anything, and the less the people understand of real problems, the greater becomes the degree of chicanery which is necessary to secure their votes. In short, at the moment that historic evolution requires Statesmen with the serious character of creative philosophers, scientifically educated, this system inevitably produces the apotheosis of the Clown. When Destiny calls for a cohort of Caesars, who have been trained beyond personal ambition in a Platonic Academy, " Democracy " inevitably provides a gaggle of Grocks.

This tendency was very apparent in previous Democracies, notably in the rapid decline of the Athenian State to defeat and collapse under the progressive deterioration in the governing character which this system always produces. But, nothing approaching the present momentum to disaster was present in the classic scene. Man could both understand far better what he was doing and had far less means with which to wreak his self-destruction. A small class of citizens, endowed with leisure and opportunity for culture by slave labour, debated in great detail problems which any relatively intelligent man could understand. Even so, that very special definition of the system of Democracy reaped the results of increasing ignorance in Government in terms of contemporary parody, which have become immortal, and in a State disaster which became permanent. How much greater is the potential of tragedy in the present situation when everyone decides everything without the opportunity to think about anything, and the result may be not the downfall of a City State, however exquisite, but the explosion in irreparable ruins of a world. We have added to the natural tendencies to decadence, inherent in a Democracy, the complexities of the modern Age, which render more than ever absurd the very premise of the initial theory. The attempt to surmount the basic weakness of the system results not in the delegation of Government to wiser types, which the intellectual apologists claim, but an ever-increasing competition in silliness for the winning of votes, which are given with no reference at all to the problems they are supposed to decide. The greater the divorce between the reality of Government and the pretences of politics, the greater the excesses of charlatanism and chicanery in those who win the people's votes, but represent nothing but the conflicting vested interests which support them.

IT IS IMPOSSIBLE FOR THE PEOPLE TO LEARN THE TRUTH: BUT EVERYONE UNDERSTANDS POLITICS

Only one thing is more mistaken than to support this system; it is to blame the people for it. How can they know what is going on? How can they judge anything except by results?; and, in the latter process, they are distracted in the exercise of their faculties by the great excuse and diversion machine, which is blaring through the organs of propaganda the rival slogans of the two sets of mobsters; even if all such instruments are not attuned to a raucous harmony of hatred for some foreign scapegoat, when things are getting too hot to hold much longer the communal racket by which the whole ruling gang thrive. (Again, reflect—wilting reader—that it is necessary to drag into a harsh daylight the subconscious motive which underlies governing technique.) Let us ask ourselves the serious question how any person of ordinary intelligence and employment can distinguish between these conflicting noises sufficiently to hear even a note of truth. How could anyone possessing the greatest intelligence arrive at any appreciation of the facts in a scene of such confusion, unless his whole time and energy were available to study them?

At this point we encounter another grotesque illusion of the present system, it is that no time, specialised training or knowledge is required to understand politics. Anyone is held competent to walk away from an exhausting day's work and get a grip of any political question in a few minutes' talk over a glass of beer. - The voter is led to believe this is quite natural; but, in his capacity of craftsman, his indignation would break into a forcibly expressed irony if some politician wandered into his factory and started to give him instruction in some technical process which it had taken him a lifetime to master. In daily life no person is more ridiculous than he who affects to understand a complicated matter to the study of which he has given no time or attention. But this is precisely the position into which the electorate has to be flattered and manoeuvred under "Democracy." If they were permitted, for one moment, to realise they did not understand everything, they might start "making enquiries," and that might be awkward for their rulers. But the process has to be carried further than this. They are taught to believe in public life that it is utterly unworthy of them to ask, or receive, directions about anything. To give anyone the power to do something serious for them, which they cannot understand for themselves, is held to be the constitution of a dictatorship.

To keep up this great fiction of the "Democratic" racket every inferiority complex, latent in the mass, is assiduously nurtured. It does not give me any sense of inferiority, or set up any complex of resentment, to go up to a policeman on the corner and ask him the road to my destination. He knows the way and I do not; his help is very valuable and much appreciated. But, if my mind moved in private life as the true "Democratic" mind has been conditioned to work in public life, great rage would rend me at the thought of being "bossed about" by that policeman, even if, in fact, he was performing to me a considerable service in pointing out something which I did not know. How curious it would be to experience such sensation in normal life when taking advantage of someone else's specialised knowledge. Yet, in the most comprehensively complex question the world has known—the art and science of Government in the modern age—the mass of the people are taught to believe that to accept direction from specialised knowledge is the hall-mark of slavery. So, to the initial fallacy that everyone understands everything is added the final error that the more complex a subject is, the easier it is to understand. When, at length, we reach the most complicated of all subjects we, at last, attain the blessed and unique condition of being able to understand without effort. Further, if anyone draws attention to the mistake in this assumption, he is an arrogant bully who desires to be dictator. Such is the heady wine of fallacy and flattery with which the natural vanity of man is inflamed to that condition of exalted idiocy which alone makes tolerable to his wretched conditions the great racket of a small ruling clique, who are very far from being the " chosen " of the people.

BUREAUCRACY—BRITISH AND SOVIET

The result is, of course, rule by Bureaucracy. When the theory of Government is so impracticable as to be quite unworkable, practical power must reside elsewhere. The general direction of Government rests with the great vested interests, Finance and Trade Union, while daily administration is left to the Bureaucracy; in a condition of increasing chaos the latter power of administration tends more and more to become the only real force. Bureaucratic rule is the worst system in the world, because it rests on the principle of power without responsibility. The least admirable type in Government is the man who loves power but fears responsibility; he is the perfect bureaucrat. The lust for petty power, and small persecutions in some types, can be satisfied by the Bureaucrat behind a smoke screen of anonymity. In his little way he can indulge the worst instincts of humanity to play the tyrant and escape the consequences. Provided Bureaucracy does not push opportunity to excess it can become a miniature despotism, which is not merely untempered

by fear of assassination but is even unshadowed by the apprehension of losing pay, or pension right, for grotesque inefficiency
or callous inhumanity. All crimes are permitted to a Bureaucracy, provided they are not great. Everything is forgiven to
these beatific creatures, on condition that they create nothing,
either good or evil. Lethargy is their security and indifference
their interest: every rule of nature and of real life is reversed
within the sheltered portals of a Government building. Such is
the stage of Bureaucratic Government which is being reached
in Britain.

In the Soviet Union, on the other hand, a further stage in
Bureaucratic dictatorship has been attained which evokes a
bolder type in the Civil Service who approximates to a pure
racketeer. What else can happen in a system which permits no
production to remain in private hands, but encourages differential rewards, which are determined by Bureaucracy, and allows
the investment of the proceeds in 5% State Loans, which
may be left to private families in a hereditary caste system. This
is the system which now prevails in the Soviet Union, according
to the almost unanimous testimony of Press Correspondents
returning from a long sojourn in Moscow at the 1947 Conference: some among them have been noted for conspicuous friendship to the Soviet Union, rather than the reverse. It is not
necessary here to recite their account of the results which were
available to all in the large Daily Newspapers. They were pained
and astounded by the glaring contrasts between wealth and poverty,
privilege and slavery, which transcended anything they had seen
in capitalist societies. The privileged classes, who are described
as " preferential categories," could eat, drink and ride in large
cars between sumptuous offices and luxury apartments, in a
degree now unknown to the wealthy in Britain; while the poorest
lived, slaved and starved in hovels which were worse than those
prevailing just after the Russian Revolution. We are not concerned here to paint the horror picture; that has been done very
competently by brushes which have, hitherto, depicted society in
Red and Pink shades. We are concerned rather to analyse the
causes which underly, and the system which produces, these

extraordinary disparities in condition between privileged and oppressed that add up to a racket of astral dimensions.

Whatever the origin of the Russian Revolution, and the forces which inspired it, the present method of Government is plainly Bureaucracy on a gigantic scale. It is of particular interest to Britain, because this is the direction in which this country is pointing, although, obviously, nothing approaching this perfection of the technique has yet been reached, or will be without a further and considerable victory of the " Left." Let us, therefore, consider briefly this picture of Soviet life, according to the virtually unanimous testimony of these diverse Press Correspondents. The basic facts are that production is not in private hands, but rewards are differential. The key question is, who determines the reward which is given by the State in the form of salary and wages. As no private enterprise exists, all reward is plainly determined by the Bureacracy: further, as no private enterprise exists, all higher posts must clearly be occupied by Bureaucrats. Here, in fact, we confront the final apotheosis of the Bureaucrat; his ultimate heaven. Great rewards can only be allocated by Bureaucrats and the only persons who can receive great rewards are Bureaucrats. The system, in fact, is mutual " back scratching " on a gigantic scale. Nepotism is sanctified into a principle of Government: " you raise Willy's salary and I will raise Billy's," (or do the equivalent by fixing the " category " of his job which determines his salary) becomes inevitably the only principle on which reward can be based, unless and until human nature suddenly sprouts angel's wings. And, it is not surprising to learn that the former rather than the latter condition is actually occurring. Everywhere are the marks of overweening privilege and grotesque inefficiency, which are reflected in abundance of luxury goods for the ultra-weathy, but miserable shortage for the mass of the poor.

When all production is removed from private hands to the Bureaucracy, all test of efficiency in production or service of the community is eliminated. A man is not rewarded because his skill in production, or ingenuity in service, commands a market which others cannot secure. He is rewarded because a fellow-bureaucrat can "work him a job," and what he produces, and how he serves, has little or no relation to the matter. The only check on his efficiency arises if the abuse of privilege brings about such a breakdown in some sphere of the national economy that a popular scandal arises: then an occasional shooting of someone who has "dropped the catch" satisfies public indignation. But the system goes further than substituting reward determined by fellow-bureaucrats for reward secured by the efficient sale of goods in a competitive market with a free choice for the people. When his colleagues have awarded some popular figure in official circles a reward that gives him an excess spending power even above his requirements in luxury goods, whose prices are far beyond the reach of the masses, he is permitted to invest the surplus in 5% Government Loans and leave the results of his "labours" to his children.

So is created not only a privileged class, but a hereditary caste to which is added many prizes beyond the financial, in the shape of special opportunities for children of bureaucrats in education and life, which, in comparison, reduce to triviality the favoured position of rich children in England after the successive operations of present death duties. This system was reported in the following words by the *Daily Herald* correspondent: —"Equality of opportunity is also out of fashion. ' Suppose,' I asked, ' a boy thinks he would like to be a doctor? ' " " If his parents can afford it he will go to a secondary school " was the reply of Russian Bureaucracy, to the Socialist Journalist! Such is the Soviet system, which has been called the " Workers' Paradise." It interests us at this point of our argument from one aspect only; it is the supreme example of rule by Bureaucracy. As Government breaks down in the complexity of modern conditions under the fundamental absurdity of the " Democratic " theory, Bureaucracy tends more and more to become the real Government, subject only to the general desires of the stronger vested interests, such as Finance and the Trade Unions. Few will be disposed to deny that this is the tendency in Britain to-day. We are, at least, on the road to the " preferential category." No wonder that many of our present rulers, who have long ceased to be either "servants" of the people or "civil" to their subjects in the present reversal of positions, see something in the Soviet Union which attracts them as much as a "Workers' Paradise" would repel them—they see the final Valhalla of Whitehall.

GOVERNMENT AND REALITY: TRANSITIONAL SYSTEM

We have reached a point where the pretence that the people govern has yielded to the reality of an administration by Bureaucracy under the general government of vested interest. The old Oedipus-Puritan complex forbids the government of Britain by a Lion, but it has replaced the suspect figure by many a thousand jackals. The results, in terms of liberty for the people, are much the same as the anarchic rule of the mediaeval barons, which preceded the rise of a strong centralised Government under the Tudors. Monopoly and Bureaucrat replace Brigand and Noble in holding up the small man to ransom and subjecting him to petty persecution. Insult is added to the injury by telling him he is perfectly free to refuse to buy essential goods from monopoly, which he cannot obtain elsewhere, and, anyway, he has no complaint because he is the sovereign lord of all in the exercise of that vote, which has never yet made the slightest difference to his material condition or brought any vital change in the Government of the country. So, the question is how to restore liberty to the people and meaning to the vote, which expresses their will. To do this we have first to relate the system of Government to reality and truth. Let us begin by enquiring what power the people can exercise without being betrayed into the belief that they are controlling a situation in which effective power resides elsewhere. May we postulate that the people can exercise real power in two respects. In general, they can give an effective verdict upon the results of Government which they can observe in terms of their daily lives. In particular, they can judge the work and conditions of their industrial life with the specialised knowledge which, alone, makes judgment effective. If, therefore, we are to relate the system of Government to truth, and eliminate deception of the people, we must build our system of government upon these two facts.

This must mean in practice that the people should be invited at regular intervals to vote " yes " or " no " on the question whether a Government should continue, which they can judge by the results it has secured. In the event of a negative verdict, the Crown in Great Britain, or an appropriate judicial and dispassionate instrument elsewhere, should be charged with the task of selecting an alternative Government. The new administration would then be subjected to a fresh vote of the people for confirmation or refusal. It is unnecessary to discuss the detail of this plan which I described in another book (recently reprinted in *My Answer*). It contains that essential simplicity, which is the core of all effective executive action. It is unnecessary, also, to discuss the concomitant view of freedom in speech and Press, which rests on the novel assumption that the papers should be required only to print the ascertained truth to the best of their ability; the details of this system are described in the same book, and these principles are equally capable of being adopted, modified or extended to meet the requirements of the present day. In not repeating that detail in this book, where new subjects press for space, I trust I shall not be exposed to the familiar charge after making a speech, " you did not mention so and so and, therefore, have no policy on the subject," and be reduced to the stock reply of saying that, in one speech or one book, you cannot deal in detail with every subject on which you have an opinion.

The same observation applies to the industrial organisations, which I described in considerable detail in the same book. In brief, the Industrial Organisations not only provide opportunity for the expression of opinion by the people, but constantly invite their opinion in the sphere of their daily work, which they best understand, and in which they are most interested. The whole system rests on a principle which is very strange to the present day: every subject should be discussed, but only by those who understand it. Outside a subject which we understand discussion becomes meaningless for any of us, and our opinion carries no weight; if our verdict be given on such matters it merely brings confusion. In spheres outside our own knowledge we cannot effectively shape events; we can only give our verdict upon the results achieved by others who possess specialised knowledge.

The role of the individual is, therefore, dual. As a producer, or expert, on some subject, he states his opinion while events are still in the making; and so takes his part in shaping a development which he is competent to judge and form. As a citizen he gives his verdict on the general results of Government, which he can grasp by the practical effect on his daily life. In the first instance, he gives his opinion before the result has occurred and, therefore, takes effective action in determining that result. In the second instance, he only gives his verdict after the result has occurred and, therefore, does not form the event, but judges the work of others by its practical effect. What other system can operate the simple principle of reality that men should only discuss and settle what they understand, and, in matters they do not understand, can only judge the work of others pragmatically. If I am a mechanic, I can take some part in making the engine go; as I am not a mechanic, I can only judge the mechanics by the result of their work, which depends on the question whether the engine goes or not. This limitation, imposed by my ignorance, gives me no sense of angry inferiority; because I can play my part in other affairs which I know more about and, consequently, interest me more. The moment that we depart from this basic principle of life and reality we enter the miasma of self-deception, leading to that morass of charlatanism and chicanery by which the present system of government cheats the people for the benefit of Bureaucracy and vested interests. Let us, at last, face the bare fact that a man should only discuss and settle a matter which he understands; in matters beyond his own knowledge he can only judge by results. This way lies truth and sanity: the rest is madness— and it rules to-day. But, as ever, there is method, even if subconscious, in the great racketeers; if you would steal their real power away from the people you must first make them drunk with the wine of flattery, which makes them believe they can understand everything, and, in the final delirium tremens of deception, even believe they control everything.

THE MACHINERY OF GOVERNMENT

Let us return to the basic principle of service to the people. The way to serve the people is to carry out their will: and the way to carry out their will is to improve their conditions. This can only be done by creating a machinery of Government which is capable of action. To these ultimate simplicities the controversy of our day can be reduced. It is not so much a matter of finding economic solutions, which are now so endlessly discussed. In each epoch, more than one economic solution has usually existed which might have met the situation. Very often several economic plans of diverse character have been suggested, any one of which might have brought alleviation, if not final remedy, in the event of actual application. The chief difficulty has never been to find an economic solution: the best brains of our period have suggested them by the dozen, and most of them were more or less workable. The real trouble has been to get anything done: man has not lacked ingenuity, but the will to act. The whole situation has been characteristic of an intellectual society in decline: the engine of intellect has been active enough, but the chassis of will has not been strong enough to get it anywhere. The first essential is, therefore, the will to action in Government, and the creation of an executive machine for government which is capable of action.

Once again we postulate dynamism as a necessity: in the present world we cannot stand still. To fulfil this purpose I have suggested three principles: — (1) Executive Government which has absolute power of action, subject to the right of the people to dismiss it by direct vote; (2) Industrial organisations, by which the opinion and will of the people can be constantly expressed, through the media of their own trades which they so well understand. As I wrote elsewhere, " the people must always know what the Government are doing, and the Government must always know what the people are thinking." The industrial organisations will be both the means to this end, and the continuous method by which the people can work out their own daily problems in their own trades without Bureaucratic interference, and subject only to the overriding interest of the whole nation, as determined by elected Government; (3) The Leadership principle in executive action and administration. The latter method is covered in Chapter I, Part II of this book, and the first two principles were described in considerable detail in the book which has already been mentioned and is reprinted in my recent book, *My Answer*. It comes to this: Executive Government for design, plan and action, elected by the people and subject to dismissal by their vote: the voice of the people in the industrial organisations, to give constant advice to Government on large issues with which they are acquainted, and to command their own daily lives through a machinery of continual discussion and consequent co-operation between employer and worker; individual responsibility in executive action and administration: these three principles in conjunction will provide the machine of action to win from chaos a new civilisation.

If the reader is interested in the details of these proposals I must really ask him to study my other writings: as most remaining space is here required, not for repetition of past thought, but for the formulation of new thought in relation to the permanent system which must lie beyond any period of transition from chaos to a new civilisation. In these old writings, for example, he will find suggestions for the relating of purchasing capacity to productive power and thus eliminating the recurring cycle of crises. He will find, also, suggestions not only for the progressive increase of the purchasing power of the people through higher wages and salaries, as science increases the power to produce, but proposals for co-ordinating these processes with the wider interests of the national economy in provision for reserve and fresh capital equipment. A system is suggested for an equitable allocation of national production between wage, salary, profit for the producer, and new capital equipment: all subject to the dominating fact that the people can protect their interests by the control of Government through the direct vote. This machinery and economic method are still very relevant, and will press for application when post-war boom (if such it can be called) passes into another economic crisis. But, except for the new proposals relating to new sources of raw materials and new markets in Part II, Chapter III of this book, which, at the present time, hold the field, as they present an alternative economic system and the Old World suggest nothing, I am not here concerned with the economic problems that I have discussed so extensively in the past, and for which I have suggested solutions with a fecundity which no doubt the people find tedious until ruin stimulates interest.

As already suggested, many and diverse economic solutions have often existed in the past. Our difficulty was not the absence of plan but the force of inertia: that old opponent, the spirit of denial. What is lacking is not so much invention as the will to act. This fact is vividly illustrated in war, when Science, which represents the ingenuity of man, is released by Politics, which, at last, represents the will of man to act. In times of Peace, Science, as invention, is inhibited by Politics which, then, represents not a positive but a negative. The means can always be found if the will to act exists. My proposals, therefore, prior to this book, have combined economic policies with the more important suggestions for rapid executive action by which a new civilisation may be brought from chaos, in accord with the people's will to find an escape from conditions which become intolerable. The purpose of the rest of the book is not to discuss again the executive methods of transition, but to consider only the principles of that new civilisation towards which the minds of men are turning in search and longing. But certain other matters, which relate, in part, to the period of transition, should first be discussed.

LIBERTY

It is the fear of many that any executive system of Government might entail a destruction of liberty. This view is a complete *non-sequitur:* it arises very largely from war experiences in which liberty is torn to shreds by any system of

249

Government for reasons already analysed in this book. It is quite unnecessary for executive Government to destroy liberty: but a new concept of life inevitably brings changes in the law. Freedom is not destroyed if an alteration is made in the law with the consent of the people, because they have been persuaded to change their view of the basic principles of life. This premise will be denied by many who seek so to emphasise the rights of minorities that they rob the majority of their rights by depriving them of any means to implement their will to better things. The logical end of that habit of thought is to forbid a whole nation to save itself because one man has a conscientious objection to national life. Majorities, also, have their rights, and we state as another premise that the right of the majority is greater than that of the minority. If, therefore, a majority decides to alter the law in accord with a new view of life, that action is not a denial of freedom.

Only those can traverse this principle, who assert, in effect, that the right of the minority is greater than that of the majority. Even they will admit that an open and avowed change in the law is preferable to the vile system of *Lettre de cachet* which Democracy copies in time of war from the French exemplars of the Bastille system in the eighteenth century. When the law is changed, everyone knows where he is; if he breaks the law, he does so with his eyes open, and must be prepared for the consequences. Under Regulation 18B, which was the modern equivalent of the Bastille system and the *lettre de cachet*, no one can know where he is. A man can be thrown into gaol without trial, and without even being told the real reason of his arrest, on account of something he may have done years before at a time when such action was perfectly legal. Every kind of abuse is possible once law and trial yield to the arbitrary power to arrest opponents and hold them without even the suggestion of a charge that they may have broken any law. Long before I suffered from such experience, I pledged myself, for those reasons, never to be associated with the establishment of any system of Government in Great Britain which included imprisonment without trial. I stand by this pledge and can see no difficulty in translating into

250

clear law the principles in which I believe, when a majority of the people agrees with them.

There is no principle which cannot be stated in clear terms of law: the *lettre de cachet* system is quite unnecessary to executive action, however convenient it may be to an incompetent and spiteful bureaucracy. For instance, it would be perfectly easy to enact in law that a man should only discuss in public, matters which he understood, by securing that he should do so through the medium of the appropriate organisation for which he could produce adequate and specified qualifications. Less extreme applications of this rational principle, which studied the English dislike of the ultra-rational, would be even easier to define in law. It would, also, be possible to state in legal terms the doctrine that penalities should attach to the deliberate statement of an untruth in an organ of public opinion: to determine whether the action was deliberate or not would be a matter of fact and evidence, direct and circumstantial, which would present no greater difficulties than are daily considered by the courts at present: while it would be easy to embody the provision that in the event of an inadvertent statement of a proved untruth equal space should immediately be devoted to the correction. It is, in fact, just clumsy cowardice to filch sly powers in " democratic " fashion in order to shut the mouths of opponents and suppress newspapers. It is clumsy because it is unnecessary and a dirty job: it is cowardly because it is doing something " under the counter " which should be done, if it must be done, openly and in full light of day, and should be justified before the whole people in clear statement and argument upon the necessity. Even from the point of view of opponents this method is preferable: it is not then necessary for whispered lies to be circulated about them as an excuse and camouflage for the simple fact that you had to shut their mouths because you could not answer them. In fact, any such powers are much less needed in emergency by a Government whose energy in action is sufficient to command the enthusiastic support of the people, and whose spokesmen are competent to defend a policy which is defensible.

At the same time it is, of course, obvious that we shall get nowhere in the real and great affairs of a dynamic age if we all chatter at once about things we know nothing about. When an army is on the march to a decisive battle every private in every unit is not shouting directions at the higher command and relapsing into hysteria if his individual whims are not instantly served and his vanity constantly flattered. Such luxuries can only be reserved for the early days of decline in a Democracy, which has inherited great resources from a previous system and from very different men, before it has had time to fritter them away. When things get serious, fantasies must give place to facts. Great changes in the law will be necessary to permit executive action and to implement the coming will of the European peoples to win a new civilisation. But, let law be published and declared in the open, manly fashion. Let Europe on the march leave behind retrospective law, and all the vile trickery whereby sly rogues can do in the dark things they dare not do in the cleansing sunlight.

SYSTEM OF LAW AND CLASSIC THOUGHT

It must be clear that a new civilisation requires a new system of law: and it should rest within the power of the declared will of a majority of the people to secure what system of law they desire. The corollary of the principles we have here suggested is clearly some change in the system of law, which would not be a deviation from the European tradition of law, but a correction of the present perversions. Few things are more paradoxical to the student of history than the almost complete reversal of values which the practices of a modern " Democracy " have introduced to the original Greek concept of the basis of Justice; and we must remember " Democracy " continually boasts that the whole system of law is derived from the Graeco-Roman sources of the classic world. But the idea of " Justice " meant to the Greeks something nearer to our idea of " function " than the present democratic concept of " equality before the law," which is a humbug as blatant as the pretence that everyone has an equal freedom every night in the choice whether to dine at the Ritz or sleep on the Embankment. Men are only " equal " before the " Democratic " law if their purses are " equal " to those of their opponents and " equal " to the strain of taking their suit from the first trial to the House of Lords.

Such " equality " before the law has little relation to the classic conception of Justice in that Greek thought from which modern " Democracy " claims, in an extraordinary distortion of the truth, to have derived its idea of law. Without attempting to give my own interpretation of the original, it is possible to prove this point conclusively from authorities who are very far from agreeing with my view of modern politics. In the most-acclaimed definition of Greek thought in recent years we find the idea of justice was the " completion " with which every section of the community " expresses its peculiar virtue in it and fulfils its specific function."* In the writing of a former authority who secured sixteen editions in Great Britain in addition to much scholarly appreciation, we find a definition of " Justice " as " the maintenance among them of their proper relation, each moving in its own place and doing its appropriate work."** Quotations from diverse authorities, and from the original, could be multiplied to establish with conclusive evidence that the idea of justice in the Greek mind was much nearer to our word " function " than to " equality before the law," which, in practice, cannot exist in present society. It must further be admitted that this idea of justice was by no means confined to Plato, whose terminology has often the exactly opposite meaning to that employed by those who used to quote him most for current political purposes. For instance, his idea of " virtue " is much more an appropriate participation in a natural order and harmony than the current definition which is, of course, supplied by neo-Puritan repression. On the question of equality before the law, Aristotle goes so far as to observe that nothing is more unjust than to " treat unequals as equals."

However, the clash between Greek thought and modern " democratic " ideas need not be laboured here, because a most

*Werner Jaeger: *Paideia* Volume II.
**Lowes Dickenson: *The Greek View of Life.*

curious and entertaining event has recently occurred. The intellectual world of "Democracy," which, for years, claimed to be based on the sublimity of the Greek mind, has recently rushed with erudite and impassioned treatise to present our contrary opinion with most that is worth having in Greek thought. We are not, at the moment, speaking of the market place, but of the intellectual background of the "Democratic" mind, which is familiar to all who follow the trends of Neo-Hellenism. An analysis of the reasons for this strange metamorphosis, and complete reversal of previous pretensions, should be the topic of another work devoted to that subject. The contemporary hatred of outstanding men, and of exalted thought, seems to have gone so far that even the great figures of the classic world, to whose knees "Democracy" previously clung in reverence without much appreciation of what went on in their heads, must now be branded as "Fascists" and hastily driven over to our camp—a most welcome present and a strong reinforcement. So, no more need be said than to acclaim the present tendency to admit that classic Greek thought was much nearer to our present thought than to present "Democratic" ideology, and to receive with high honour those distinguished recruits whom we should have claimed in any case. (The world may be indifferent to the exchange of a Roland for an Oliver, but who would not swop a Popper for a Plato?)

We must be ready, however, to meet the storm of abuse which always follows a "Democratic" transition from love to hatred, and will now, no doubt, be directed by lesser scholarship, and more vehement propaganda, against that Hellenism which used, mistakenly, as it now seems, to be worshipped by the sentimental humanists. The simple answer to the coming attack that Greek life was based on slavery is that in modern life the machines can do the work of slaves, and modern science has, therefore, rendered any such question entirely obsolete: if "Democracy" could only be induced to adopt a system of State which abolished the present "wage slavery" which, in many respects, is worse than the nominal slavery prevailing in the ancient world, because neither employer nor community has complete responsibility for the well-being of the man or woman who has given a lifetime of work and service. In this respect " Democracy " might learn much from the " Labour Charters " of those States it has recently destroyed in the name of Freedom. These Laws, at least, removed the " chattel " concept of Labour, which " Democratic " practice, if not theory, still retains. But, our contact with Greek thought serves only one purpose at this stage: it establishes that in conceiving " justice " more in terms of " function " we are as much in harmony with the true European tradition as with the laws of nature.

FUNCTION AND DIFFERENTIATION

The idea of " function " does not traverse any cherished belief of Religion and the State on which the modern world is founded. If it be true that " God created men equal," and that they are " equal in his sight," it is at least very evident that he equipped them very differently for the only discernable purpose of performing different functions. The leading physicist of the age is differently equipped by nature to a negro boxing champion: the former is better in the laboratory and the latter in the boxing ring. They are equipped by God, or the nature which serves his purpose, for different functions: that is the long and short of it. To argue that the principle—God made men equal, and they are all equal in his sight—means that all men are equal and the same in equipment for function, is plainly at variance with the facts. If anyone denies this, let him put the negro boxer in the laboratory and the scientist in the boxing ring: in the latter event, at least, he would understand what was happening, and he would find his theory entirely shattered (as well as the scientist). The plain and obvious fact is that men are not equal or the same in respect of natural endowment and capacity for function. Different men can do different things. Therefore, function, whether we like it or not, is inevitable, because it expresses a fact. The physicist must be accepted as an authority on physics and the negro boxer as an authority on boxing. Perhaps one day the world will go so far as to say that a Statesman, who has been trained (not " groomed ") during a lifetime for the purpose of politics, should, also, be accepted as some authority on that subject: or, must we persist in the illusion that only the most complicated matter is the subject that everyone can understand?

To recognise the necessity for differentation in function is merely to recognise the facts of life and the laws of nature, which are the only empiric evidence, as opposed to *a priori* concept, of the purpose of God in the world. Certainly, every attempt to contravene them has, so far, entailed the grotesque tragedy towards which present " Democracy " appears to be pointing; grotesque, because the rules of conduct have no relation to observed facts, and tragic, because this error may bring an irremediable disaster. If we are to recognise fact, we must admit that differences exist between diverse men and diverse races, which suggest that they must perform different functions in life. We can set aside the sterile argument whether one function is " higher " and another " lower "; it is enough to establish that they are different. In terms of pure morality, or in the " sight of God," the work of sweeping a street may be no lower or higher than that of running a State; in fact, a certain flat uniformity in the two tasks might well be present to a vision which was sufficiently exalted.

FUNCTION AND RACE

It is a waste of time to argue how these differences have arisen or which functions are the greater: it is enough to recognise the essential differences which are now denied. For instance, much time has been wasted in the past in argument whether an " Aryan " race exists, and whether it derives from the Northern regions of Europe, the Persian Plateau, the lost Atlantis, or Heaven knows where. The attempt to define things too obscure in origin for exact definition must count among the weaknesses of the Teutonic mind, and expose it to the time-wasting dialectics of an opposing science which had nothing constructive at all to offer. In this sphere, there was some truth in the brilliant and brutal epigram of an English writer that " The Germans always dive deeper and come up muddier than any other people." The failure conclusively to establish in scientific terms things which did not really matter brought some discredit on the plain and observable fact that some races, in their present and proved forms, can do certain things and others cannot: just as some men can do certain things and others cannot. To make a physicist do the work of a negro boxer and *vice versa* is a stupidity: to make a European race do the work of a negro race and *vice versa* is an even greater stupidity, although not so readily recognised.

An argument on the observed data of commensense is on stronger ground than the search for a theory which has no practical relevance. But it may be objected that to prove the remote origin, and trace the whole development, of the various races is essential in order to preserve their purity and thus increase their power in function: if that were true, the work, of course, would be vitally important. But, as a practical man in such matters, who was brought up with a prize-winning Shorthorn herd, and has a long hereditary and personal interest in the breeding of cattle in which he is now engaged, I deny that origin, in so remote a sense, can either be established with certainty or have any relevance to practical purposes. The life of our British Shorthorn breed is about 150 years, or about 40 generations. We know enough now, with skilled management, to transform the productive capacity of a herd out of all recognition in three or four generations. I am, therefore, not interested to trace back the ancestry of a Shorthorn to some particular herd of Buffalo. It is enough to study the special characteristics of our breed, acquired over the forty odd generations of its differentiation, and to take advantage of them for further development. We do not study the various types of wild cattle which roamed the plains of Northern Europe centuries ago, giving a milk yield of a pint or two a day! We examine the rival merits of Shorthorns, Friesians, Ayrshires, etc., and all the various breeds of cattle which have acquired a comparatively recent differentiation.

But, even a tyro in the business does not fall into the error of expecting these highly developed and specialised animals to perform the functions of goats or donkeys, still less do we attempt to cross them with such strains in breeding, if that were possible. These egregious errors are left to the statesmen of humanity with results which can be observed in many quarters of the world. We get our results by "holding the line," which means, broadly, that we seek to intensify rather than dilute a good stock when we find it, and only vary it with closely comparable strains which possess characteristics highly suitable for the purpose we require. We say, "here is a good strain, keep it, hold it, build on it, develop it, intensify it, but beware of over-specialisation and refinement." To avoid the latter danger and to acquire other desirable characteristics an occasional "out-cross" may be valuable, but it should not go outside very similar strains. To render the subject of animal breeding easily intelligible by taking a human parallel, it would not be desirable to go much further, in selecting an "outcross" with the English type, than a kind as close as the French, German or Scandinavian; or the further Latin types for special purposes. At this point in animal breeding we begin to reach a practical science; it is a more fruitful occupation than examining nearly prehistoric skeletons to find the original Buffalo that was nearest to a Shorthorn or a Friesian.

Turning now to human affairs, I am opposed for analagous reasons to all attempts to confuse the issue of the European species by trying to trace it to Atlantis or the Mountains of the Moon. It is sufficient that the great breed or "kind" should have existed for thousands of years with characteristics which are now so plainly differentiated that it can easily be recognised, protected and developed. We are favoured by the inestimable blessing of a European race, which is based on millenia of differential development, and possesses the treasure of a unique culture: even the duration of the latter reaches a hundred generations. There is a colossal fact, which transcends all theory: there is a fact beyond all theory on which to build the future. So, let us take known history, it is more than enough! The sterile opponents who attempted to laugh off the effort of serious German thinkers to found a deeper theory with trite absurdities, such as the observation that negroes had white palms to their hands, etc., cannot evade the comparison between the culture and achievement of the European and that of other races. Here we are on the firm ground of fact which none can deny. Our breed, in the modern world, is sufficiently differentiated for anyone to recognise it as a fact, and, also, to know what it has achieved, and to sense what it is capable of achieving. It is as useless to argue that all races are equally gifted, as it is to argue that all men are equal in mind, muscle or in character.

The moment that great fact is accepted, as it must be if we do not spurn the obvious truth, a differentiation of function is as essential for different races as it is for different men. Setting aside cultural comparisons, which some find too painful, it is clear that Europeans are better at inventing and organising, and negroes are better at manual labour in those tropical conditions where the untapped raw materials of the world can still be found. To argue that the European has no permanent right in Africa means that these resources will not be developed, and that Africa must relapse to jungle when he retires in favour of native " self-government." We do not suggest that the negroes should be exterminated and, thus, suffer the fate of most Red Indians: this task would require a " Christian spirit " as strong as that of the Puritan Fathers, which we do not aspire to possess. We make only the moderate suggestion that in Africa, as elsewhere, the rule of reason and of nature should persist, and that the life and work of men should be organised on a functional basis. Let each man contribute according to his abilities, but let us recognise that the abilities of men vary widely. To claim that everyone can do everything is as foolish as to pretend that everyone knows everything.

CHAPTER VI

STRUCTURE OF GOVERNMENT IN PERMANENT SYSTEM

THE HIGHER SYNTHESIS

A PERIOD of transition must always precede the permanent system of a new civilisation. Enough has been written and said about that epoch, in this book and on other occasions. It is, of necessity, painful, and is bound to be the subject of violent controversy. To invite men to move, and to move rapidly, is always unpopular, even when the house is on fire. But, can we not secure a wider measure of agreement on the principles of a new structure of civilisation, if present society should prove to fail, as I am certain it will? Most of this book has had direct bearing on this subject, but we have not yet discussed the actual method of Government in a permanent as opposed to a transient system. The same postulate of the effective will of the people must, of course, apply: by direct vote at regular intervals they must retain the right to approve the work of Government or dismiss it. But we have no reason to apprehend that the system of Government will be subject to the instability of any violent fluctuations if it secures the relatively rapid improvement in the conditions of the people, which modern scientific method makes possible, and can explain what is happening through existing media of information with the requisite degree of political skill. Therefore, let us consider the principles of such a system with some assurance that, once established, it will endure.

Our first question is whether it is possible to find some synthesis at a higher level of the opposing forces in the chief conflict of our age. Is it possible to reconcile the theory of liberty with the thesis of achievement, and the desirability of discussion with the necessity of action. We will set aside for the moment the argument that the reality of liberty for the average man is economic and not political: the concept that, if he obtains a good standard of material existence, with opportunity for leisure and the higher culture, he will be quite indifferent to a " political liberty " which has proved in practice to be a tedious process of time-wasting deception. Without entering again into that controversial field, let us see to what extent these proposals for the conduct of a permanent system can reconcile, at least, the sincere antagonists of our epoch. We begin with the postulate that it is desirable for all things to be discussed; and time will permit this in the more spacious period of a permanent system which will differ from the present period in much the same manner as the conditions and methods of peace may vary from methods which are necessary in the conditions of war. But we postulate, also, that it is only desirable for a subject to be discussed by those who understand it: the opposite principle is not only a waste of time but brings more confusion rather than greater clarity.

Within the category of those who understand a subject, however, exist several types of mind. All have their contribution to make, but should find their appropriate function; otherwise, again, confusion is increased, as it always is when a real force is wrongly used or frustrated. Let us, therefore, begin by trying to sort out the types of mind which are capable of making an effective contribution to discussion. My definition of categories may be improved, and many subdivisions will occur, but I will attempt certain broad differentiations from observed facts. Let me delineate four initial categories and give them, in the first instance, their appropriate terminology. (1) The Proposer. In this category I would include all, a priori, creative thinkers; imaginative writers, system thinkers; all who are capable of the more speculative flights of grand design. (2) The Critic. This is the mind which can always analyse but seldom create: it is invaluable for purposes of dissection and exposing the unworkable, the pretentious, the meretricious, and the impracticable. In this category I should include the mind of most Barristers and many of that higher type of permanent Civil Servant whose sincere and serious efforts to grapple with the problems of a great age place them beyond all strictures upon the lesser fry of a time-serving, sterile, restrictive and repressive Bureaucracy. (3) The Assessor. This mind is invaluable for the sifting of evidence and the elucidation of facts. It is neither particularly creative nor critical; it is essentially judicial, and its hall-mark, and value, is the love of truth. (4) The Executive. Here is the dynamic man who gets things done: here is the force which turns the wheels of the world. Here, too, is often that weakness which jumps to conclusions before facts are clarified, and may wreck all by a precipitancy which is occasioned by a well-justified fury against obtuseness, obstruction and lethargy. Harness these four minds in the service of the peoples, and let the peoples judge them by the results of that service: if we can do that by any system of creative thought, we shall have gone far to unravel the tangled skein of human affairs and to weave it again into a new harmony of almost infinite potential.

THE SYNTHESIS OF DISCUSSION AND OF ACTION

Combine the mind of the " Proposer " with the mind and will of the " Executive " in one person; add to these qualities a natural harmony of nature, and balance of character, acquired by long and special training, which must include knowledge not only of the main facts but of the method and approach of modern science—we begin then to envisage the qualities of the Thought-Deed man who will be capable of high service to the people in the conception and execution of great design. But, before we consider the type which the future will demand in Government, and must produce, let us follow to some conclusion the working of the executive machine. We start from the premise that all things should be discussed, but only by those who understand them, and from the further premise that it is desirable so to frame discussion that the individual mind can make its most effective contribution. In practice, this will mean that any new departure in the policy of Government should be subjected to a triple process. The Proposer should state the case for the proposed action: the Critic should state the case against it: the Assessor should then sift the evidence and present it to the Executive with a report in accord with the balance of the evidence. Final decision and clear-cut responsibility must always be left to the Executive in any workable system; but every fact, and all critical analysis of facts, will be available to inform and to assist that decision. This procedure should be followed either in central discussion of the larger problems of Government, or in the delegation of lesser matters to instruments, either permanent or *ad hoc,* which possess a limited authority, and are responsible to the central executive in that clear chain of responsibility which is a *sine qua non* of the proposed system.

In every organ of national life, whether governmental or industrial, the same procedure would be followed: discussion would precede action, but it would be serious and informed consideration of the subject. To secure this character, it would appear essential that discussion should be in private and that the only audience should be expert in the subject. This is the only way to obtain serious and expert deliberation of a matter, and to avoid that " playing to the gallery " which leads back to the congenital silliness of the present system. That absurdity is produced initially by the debate of a subject before an audience which does not understand it. Smartness must then replace thought, and a slap-stick, back-chatting comedy inevitably ousts that earnest search for the truth, which is appropriate to a situation of pending tragedy. Such is human nature that an audience will get clowning even from the most serious performers, if it can only appreciate and applaud a clown. Our circumstances are too grave for the circus: we need an altogether different method in our discussions. When a general holds a conference with his staff officers before a great battle, the atmosphere is necessarily that of a serious search for fact and truth, with each man pooling his knowledge in a mutual effort of the mind. At such a moment, and in such a work, no man would seek to draw attention to himself, or hope to acquire promotion, by giving a pert and silly answer to a serious enquiry (*e.g.,* when that hero of the Conservative Party, Mr. Disraeli, went to Oxford during the controversy which followed the publication of Darwin's great contribution to Science, he observed, " they are discussing whether man is descended from an angel or an ape; I am on the side of the angels." He had not even the excuse of speaking before an ignorant audience; but he possessed the requisite slick silliness to cover his ignorance of, and indifference to, serious matters, and thus to become the " Chosen " spokesman of the Conservative Party).

Reality, in fact, creates an atmosphere, and imposes a method, utterly different to the ways of " democratic debate." When we face the final battle of man with fate, is it too much to ask for a corresponding seriousness in outlook and reality in method? In such an age all discussion must be transposed from the way of " debate " to the spirit of a mutual search for truth. This can only be done by confining discussion to those who understand the subject, and the audience to serious men who dedicate their lives to the discovery of truth in their particular sphere of knowledge. At all costs, in a situation of this gravity, we must avoid ignorance and frivolity, which are the hall-mark of present debate, and arise inevitably if the audience does not understand the subject. When you cannot understand what Hamlet is saying your eyes, of course, wander to the grave-diggers: but that is an error if your fate is bound up with that of Hamlet, and, in this case, it is your grave that is being dug.

DIFFERENCE WITH PRESENT METHOD

The objection may be made to these proposals that some such process already occurs in discussions between Ministers and Civil Service before a Bill reaches Parliament. This could not be honestly stated by anyone who has ever been present at such deliberations, but that will not prevent the point being argued. To the extent that anything of the kind were true, it would, of course, merely confirm my contention that the country is at present governed not by Members of Parliament who are supposed to be responsible to their constituents, but by a Civil Service, which is elected by none and responsible to nothing, and finds no difficulty in manipulating as it wishes, through the expert field of administrators, those nominal ministerial chiefs whose weakness and ignorance of real matters are the inevitable product of the " Democratic " school which we have already analysed. But, in fact, nothing of the kind occurs. What happens in practice is that the Minister proposes something to implement his Party programme, and the Civil Service produces " conclusive " reasons to show that it cannot be done; and that is the end of that! Even this slight breath of vitality—from the ministerial ranks—pre-supposes the rare occurrence of a Minister who believes at all in the Party programme, which won the votes of the electors. We are, of course, here discussing the doing of serious things, not the buying of obsolete industries at the taxpayers' expense, and their transfer to State management. Bureaucrats cannot be expected very strongly to oppose a proposal to provide further and more lucrative employment for Bureaucrats at relatively simple routine tasks in which the hard work of establishing the industry was done long ago by others. But, even if the theory of ministerial deliberations with Civil Servants had any relation to the practice, it is clear the present system bears no comparison with that proposed.

At best, the present system provides a one-sided discussion between an ignoramus, who has never learnt to do anything but talk, and highly-skilled obstructionists who, at least, are experts in their particular subject. It requires a statesman of extraordinary capacity and will-power to break down the force of inertia in the Civil Service; it can be done, and it has been done by diverse men on a number of occasions, but statesmen of the requisite power of mind and will are very rare in present politics for reasons already considered. In general, the deliberations of Ministers and Civil Servants are an ever unequal and hopeless fight between a politician who may possibly want to do something and Civil Servants who are determined not to do it. It is safer and easier for them to keep things as they are : new departures mean new risks for them, but no new rewards; and their reaction to this prospect is " human, all too human." If anything is to be done we must transfer action to a very different sphere. We must shift the scene from this back-scene Bull-ring, in which the honest politician plays the Bull and the Civil Servants the matadors, to a high court in which all are not only expert but charged with a sense of mission. The latter essential belongs to the yet more important regions in which we consider not the production of a system but the production of men. First, let us mark the difference in the machinery which is here suggested. The Proposer of our system will, to some extent, be in the position of the honest politician. He will be full of general suggestions for improvements, and of a higher and more imaginative kind than are ever now suggested, because he will be differently trained, and selected for qualities of the Study rather than the Circus. But he will not be at the mercy of the critics, because he will be assisted by the Assessor in much the same way that an unskilled witness is now protected from the barrister in the Law Court by an impartial judge. The parallel is very far from being exact, because, as was observed above, the Proposer will be the highest type of creative and imaginative intelligence which the period can produce. But this analogy is taken as an illustration of the serious character of the discussion and of the method of eliminating mere debating skill with the object of eliciting truth. We contemplate something very different to anything now existing if we envisage the initiation of policy on the proposal of the highest type of imaginative intelligence, which meets an open and avowed critical analysis, but is sifted for truth and finally adjudged by an expert intelligence which is, also, judicial and dispassionate.

A PERSISTING DYNAMISM

It is clear, however, that the mind and character of the Assessor must contain an additional ingredient, which is not always present in judges. All these men must be imbued with a sense of the necessity for dynamism as with the force of a religion. We must return later to this governing subject, but it is right here to indicate that such men must hold as a religion the idea of continuing progress in the evolution of ever higher forms on earth. In other words, the judicial mind must change in root instinct from being a defender of the Static to a promoter of the great " Becoming." Before their eyes must ever be the eternal words of Aristotle: " The process of evolution is for

267

the sake of the thing finally evolved and not for the sake of the Process."

We touch here, admittedly, the hardest part of our task; it is so much easier to make systems than to make men. But, even the hardest things must be essayed if the final tragedy is to be averted: that disaster is the ossification of a revolution of thought into a new Bureaucracy. For instance, in all great movements of the human mind and will circumstances produce the original men. In our system of ideas a Leader is appointed, not by a Committee, as in " Democracy," but by the test of nature, which is his capacity to attract a following and to achieve! But, after the passing of that generation, arises the, hitherto, unsolved problem how to obtain a persisting dynamism toward ever higher forms. After the Caesar generation of supreme creative urge and action, how is mankind to avoid a Bureaucracy or a Nero? The only answer is by the training of a new type of men who possess with the fiery force of a religion the faith of continuing progress to higher forms. It is necessary to instil such a spirit not only into the executive type but, also into the judicial mind. For, the selection of the future executives must rest with the Assessors or some such body of specially trained men. We must, at all costs, avoid the selection of Bureaucracts with the inevitable result that everything, in which the dynamic founders of a new way of life really believed, will be reversed by the customary technique of a subsequent and static officialdom, or priestcraft, which ever uses the names of the creators to stifle their creations. This means that the Assessors must acquire qualities so high that they are capable not merely of judging the merits of executive proposals, but of selecting the future generation of Executives. To reach this rare degree of mind and spirit they must combine the judicial with an appreciation of the dynamic. This is the most unusual of all mental and spiritual combinations, which can probably only be acquired as a permanent attribute if the idea of continuing progress toward higher forms on earth grips the minds of men h the force of a religion of the State. Yet, the judicial mind ts not only the law but the spirit of the times, and a change

268

in both will work great changes in the minds of all prominent men.

AUTHORITY AND RESPONSIBILITY: THE SELECTION OF SUCCESSORS

The figure of the Assessor must become a keystone of our structure and it is necessary to define his relationship to the Executive.

It is evident that in any practical method of Government which implements this system of thought, the Executive must be supreme: authority must never be divided and responsibility must always be clear. The Executive, therefore, should be subject only to the will of the people as expressed by direct vote. So long as he retains their confidence his decision is final in all matters, which must be remitted to him after the process already described. His decision is final, too, if he forwards a proposal on his own initiative to the Assessor for examination and report. He must submit any initiative he undertakes in policy to that process, but has complete power to persist in face of an adverse finding if he thinks fit. But, in so doing, he must, of course, shoulder his clear and heavy responsibility for proceeding despite the apparent balance of evidence. Only by such method can the principle of undivided authority and responsibility be maintained, which is the only principle by which effective action can be secured and able, fearless, and honest types obtained for the purposes of Government.

In all spheres of policy, therefore, the Assessor is in every respect subordinate to the Executive. The task of the former is merely to sift evidence and to report for the decision of the latter. The purpose of this work is to save time, to discover facts, and to present them without bias. But the task of the Assessors is dual in that in the event of the death, or defeat by popular vote, of an Executive, it would be their duty to select the Successor; or, in the case of the British Constitution, to advise the Crown on the subject. They would be particularly equipped by practical experience for that task in that during the course of their work they would have heard frequently all the ablest men argue various cases in front of them, and would have had unique opportunity to watch their performances when charged with executive tasks. For, it should be clear that a certain flexibility is envisaged which involves some interchange between the four categories we have described: an undue rigidity of function is to be avoided, particularly in the early stages of an able man's career. It should, therefore, be possible to pass from one category to another: in fact, the higher the degree of talent the wider should be the experience and the greater the possibility that the capacity for several functions could be united in one person. It has already been suggested that, at least, categories (1) and (4) should be combined in a supreme Executive type, and an ultimate Executive should, if possible, undergo every major experience which the State has to offer. In observing the work of such men the Assessors will, therefore, have every opportunity to form a comprehensive judgment of their qualities and capacities as chief Executives.

It is possible at this point of the discussion that some reader may be " popping " with erudite indignation in the belief that he recognises in the Assessors the suspect figures of the " Elders " of the " Republic." He may relax, because, while admitting that I have been so unfashionable as to learn something from the philosophers, I must make the yet more serious confession that I have learnt even more from life. After hard and practical experience in the affairs of men, can anyone devise another system for the selection of supreme executives which fulfils the simple principle that the selector should know what he is doing? Who can know what he is doing in such a matter if he has not observed the work and character of the candidates in intimate detail over a long period of time? What is the alternative? A selection board which " likes his face " at the first time of meeting, and exercises that intuition which the fairies gave them at their lucky christening: a party caucus in which the decision works out in favour of the most pliable on a rough estimate of " who gets the jobs ": the familiar farce by which the Press dresses up some monkey who is ready to climb on to their barrel organ and so prove himself to be fit for nothing else: the slap-stick harlequinade of " popular debate " which must tend more and more to turn the leading clown into the outstanding states-man as the subjects to be discussed pass further beyond the comprehension of the audience: or the " voice of the people " which is being influenced by very interested parties towards the belief that the loudest hiccup in the noisiest public-house alone can indicate the necessary qualifications for the high decisions of statemanship in the age of Nuclear Physics. If we do not adopt some such principle, as is here suggested, when and where is the nonsense to end and sanity to begin? It is not essential to rely on the old philosophers for guidance, although it is no disadvan-tage to have studied great doctrines, " which have slumbered for more than two thousand years in the ear of mankind," in an age which at last compels high thought, not merely as a matter of intellectual interest but as an affair of life and death urgency. But, it is vitally necessary to rely on our own hard sense and observation of life in practical affairs in an age which presents the alternative of crashing, burning death—or new civilisation.

THE IMPORTANCE OF POLITICAL SKILL

It has, already, been observed that it is not enough to change the system of selecting men: any new system must fail unless we can produce new men. There is at present no alternative to some kind of politician for the work of Government: it must, of course, be understood that the work of government in this context means, at present, managing the people, and the exercise of political skill, not governing in the executive sense of doing something really constructive. The reason is that power, or even the semblance of authority, attracts the strongest types—for good or ill. They may be drawn in rare case by the prospect, or hope, of constructive achievement and high service to humanity; they may be pulled to politics by the fact that such power gives opportunity for the biggest rackets in contemporary life, or they may merely be lured by that sterile vanity which is so large a factor in the mental and spiritual make-up of life's permanent adolescents. Whatever the motive, the fact remains that the

271

strongest types are drawn to the skill-game of politics, and this is proved whenever they are matched in such clash of mind or will against other products of the present system. Neither business-man nor Civil Servant has yet been able to measure up to the politician when they have entered the political arena: the soldier just cannot begin to compete. Political skill is a very real fact, and the prize of power has attracted to this match of some reality the most vigorous intellects and most energetic characters of this kind in the present world. Nor, does any reason exist to suppose that the scientists of the present time can step into the ring of politics and succeed where business-man, Civil Servant and soldier have so completely failed. On the contrary, their past education and present pre-occupations would generally place them at a more hopeless disadvantage in comparison with the politician than any of the former types whose training has been to some extent in the world of political affairs.

In fact, the scientists of the present period can only function effectively in politics in conjunction with political types who understand them and whom they can understand, if any exist whose view of life is acceptable to them. Isolated scientists in the political arena, who only possessed scientific training and experience, would be as helpless as new born babes in combat with powerful and experienced serpents. The infant Hercules of Science, who is adequate to that task, is not yet born. The time may come, and we must do all we can to hasten it, when Statesman and Scientist will be combined in one form. Until then the World requires a union between Statesmen who understand enough of science, and Scientists who understand enough of politics, to make their co-operation effective in this strife with chaos to win a new world order. In the first stages we shall need the Thought-Deed men of politics working in close co-operation with colleagues from the world of science, who not only form the link between technical achievement and political possibility, but begin to develop the essential character which is part statesman and part scientist. But we must defer for a little the study of these types, whose evolution is essential to the world of the near future.

THE NEW ADMINISTRATION—HIERARCHICAL SYNTHESIS

In our survey of the outline of a new system we have, hitherto, chiefly considered the initiation of new policy: the essential work of constructive Government. It is necessary, also, to consider the changes in administration which are necessary to any system of achievement. The method I suggest can conveniently and compendiously be described as Hierarchical Synthesis. The idea rests on two premises: the first that it is always necessary to allocate administrative responsibility to a definite individual: the second, that it is vitally necessary to synthesise the many branches of national life and activity which are now uncoordinated. Everything in the present system is run by Committees for which no individual is responsible, with the consequence that blame can attach to no one in the event of failure, and the corollary that no means, therefore, exist to make an effective change. At the same time these Committees do not perform the function which should be the one merit of a multitude—namely, the co-ordination of various and diverse activities. Everyone of any administrative experience has been confronted constantly with the extraordinary situation of innumerable administrative organs working in vacuo without any contact with adjacent bodies, and, often, even traversing the same field without ever meeting. This is not only the case in the Civil Service where the unfortunate enquirer is shuttled round the departments for ever in futile search for the person responsible for the subject in which he is interested; only to find in the end that half a dozen departments are concerned with different bits of it, but no one is in a position at any point to grip the whole matter and give a decision. Outside the Civil Service in the great professions, we often find parallel lines of research which never meet, although co-ordination, or synthesis, would plainly bring the possibility of a great forward spring in knowledge.

The writer has long been absent from the sphere of ministerial administration and direct access to such information; further, it is always hazardous to quote a particular instance in an expert field. But I will venture the enquiry how much co-ordination exists in Science at the present time between Physicists and Biologists. And even in the narrower sphere of medicine, is any responsible body attempting any complete synthesis between the experiments of analytical psychology and those engaged in research into the endochrynol system? The necessity for some close co-ordination in the latter field should be clear even to those who often cannot " see the wood for the trees "; while in the former and larger sphere of science it must soon occur, even to workers in very diverse departments, that it will become at some point necessary to study closely the type or species which is necessary to survival in the age of Nuclear Physics; and how his evolution may be assisted, and to what end? At that point, such abstract and remote persons as Philosophers, Educationists, Social Workers, and even religious teachers, might enter the picture. What co-ordination, let alone effective synthesis of effort toward a clear-cut objective, to-day exists, among such diverse workers and seekers of the truth? Instances could be multiplied over the whole field of national life and would not only be suggested by the familiar paradoxes of the Civil Service.

What, then, is the remedy? I suggest an administration of national life with the structure of a pyramid. At the base in every region would be the ultra-specialists engaged on work of greatly diversified detail. At the next tier of our pyramid would be a number of individuals who would each be capable of understanding, co-ordinating and representing the highly detailed work of several of these specialists at the ground level immediately below them. At this new stage a more general knowledge would be required, but the responsible administrators must yet retain sufficient detailed knowledge to understand enough of the work, in their allotted sphere of responsibility in the tier below them, to co-ordinate and represent it. Each individual at this level would have contact and regular meetings with all other administrators in this same tier who directly, or indirectly, were connected at any point with the work with which he was concerned. In the next tier above would be other individuals who would each be responsible for a section of the above-mentioned administrators in the tier immediately below them, and charged

in similar fashion with co-ordinating their work at a higher level.
So we should proceed, tier upon tier, toward the summit of our
pyramid with the work of the nation co-ordinated and synthesised
at each level. The knowledge of the responsible individuals
would become less detailed and more general at each stage as we
approached the apex of the pyramid; but, through the successive
stages, detailed knowledge would be synthesised at each level
into an organic and executive whole. The work of directing that
whole from the summit of the pyramid must be in the hands of
men with the widest possible general intelligence and diversity
of training and experience, which would be deliberately conceived and formulated to secure the union of reflective
intelligence and active will in a new harmony, but, also, in a
continuing dynamism.

However, before we consider the new character on which all
must ultimately depend, it is necessary to define the relationship
of the Civil Service to such an organisation of the State. In the
first instance, it would be very much reduced in size. A great
many of the duties which it now performs would be delegated to
industrial self government. Other tasks would be devolved to
the various professional bodies of the kind just suggested. Above
all, the work of devising and initiating new policy would be
transferred to the executive machine which we recently described.
A deflated Civil Service would, therefore, be left in a sphere
very similar to that it used to occupy before it was so greatly
extended to cover unnatural tasks which it was quite unfitted to
perform. It would be confined to the strictly administrative
duties which no body other than the Government can perform.
In that sphere it would not initiate policy, but would carry out
instructions: that and that alone. When, and where, the Civil
Service operated, it would be conducted not by Committees but
by the system of individual responsibility described above, and
promotion would be by selection of merit on the decision of a
special authority, who would be delegated power for the purpose
by the Chief Executive.

The outstanding types of devoted public servants, whom the
Civil Service often produces, would have their outlet and

prospect of promotion to any position of national service in the various institutions constituted by Government, either executive or administrative, which we have already described. But they would have to win their place like everyone else by the test of achievement. The Civil Service would automatically receive their training for wider opportunity. For, at each stage of their work they would be dovetailed into our pyramid structure, and would there be related to the appropriate region of national life as a functioning part of the Hierarchical Synthesis. They would not be remote from the life of the people, in lofty disconnection with ordinary existence, but woven into the very fabric of the nation in a system which integrated its whole being into an organic system. Such, in broad outline is my proposal for a new way of administration. No man, any longer, can " take all knowledge for his province "; but we must organise to make the whole province of a far greater knowledge still available to man. It cannot be left to the haphazard, or the methods of chance: life has become too big and too serious.

THE QUESTION OF POWER

It is clear that even this permanent system of the State would leave in the hands of certain men very great power. The chief executive would, in fact, possess complete power, subject only to the right of the people to dismiss him by direct vote. Apart from the wider argument concerning the accord to any individual of great power, which we will shortly consider, two stock objections are raised to any such procedure. The first is that the Government would not go in the event of an adverse vote. The answer to this is that technically any Government with a majority in Parliament can vote itself perpetual life at the present time, without any regard for the feelings of the people outside, and subject only to the constitutional right of the Crown to dismiss it: the life of the War Parliament, which was returned on a peace programme, was thus extended. The technical power of the suggested Government to prolong its life in the face of popular opinion would be no more than this: in some respects less, because the vote of the people at regular intervals would be a constitutional necessity. In actual practice, of course, no such power exists in either case, because great peoples cannot be governed against their will.

It will still be objected by those who pay no attention to the evidence that Germany was so governed. Without entering into this sterile controversy with enquiry why it was then just to impose such severe retribution on the German people, it is possible to meet that foolish suggestion with a simple illustration. When the Nazi Party was in power in Germany, a vote was held in the Saar and the secrecy of the ballot was preserved by British troops. That German population voted in the same way as their relatives across the border, with whose conditions they were thoroughly familiar, despite a storm of propaganda to do the contrary. It will not be suggested either by politician or simpleton that this vote was a fake. In fact, neither the Germans, nor any other great people, can be governed in modern conditions against the will of the majority. The second stock objection to any such system is that without the propaganda and counter-propaganda of Party warfare the public have no means of making up their minds. I have dealt, elsewhere, with this remarkable insult to the intelligence of the people, which suggests that they are too stupid and inert to come to any decision on the observed facts and conditions of their daily life without a host of little politicians bawling nonsense and counter-nonsense into their ears during a three weeks' honeymoon of mutual abuse, which has no relation whatever to the real issues the people have to settle. The mass of the people are quite capable of making up their own mind whether a Government is good or bad by the effect of its measures on the national life, and their own lives, without any such " help."

If any advice is needed, let it be given by people who understand the subject: if the suggestion is not too bizarre for the " Democratic " mind. For instance, at a time of the direct vote of the people, it would be quite possible to enact that the Assessors should have the right to publish a measured criticism of the Executive, and that the latter should have the right to reply. Once appointed, it is clear that the Assessors should hold their appointments until death or a fixed age, so they would be moved neither by fear nor favour. It is possible, of course, to devise many other checks or limitations on executive power within the same main structure of the State which we have suggested. All these things can be discussed and settled in the light which many minds might bring to bear upon them. The predilection of the writer is frankly in favour of the maximum possible measure of power in the hands of the Executive, because that is the way to get things done. In proportion to any diminution in the urgent necessity for action the power of the Executive could be decreased. But, in general, what is required is not to reduce the power of Executives but to increase their capacity and fitness for exercising power.

THE ARGUMENT THAT " ALL POWER CORRUPTS "

When a man argues in favour of granting any power to any individual the easiest way to get him down is to shout that he wants this power for himself. It is a device so simple and effective for frustrating all action that it readily occurs even to the most limited intelligence in the ranks of the obstructionists. If you want to stop a new house being built, the easiest method is to say that anyone who suggests building it is in no way interested in the future occupants of the house but is only concerned with getting the job of building it. If this habit of mind spread from political to ordinary life very few new houses would be built. But, we must look beyond the corner boys of controversy to those sincere and earnest minds who believe that the granting of power to any individual is among the most serious evils that can occur. The old cliche is ever on their lips: " All power corrupts, and absolute power corrupts absolutely." To this the first answer is—if power corrupts a great man, how much more will it corrupt a small man. If a Statesman, carrying open responsibility for power, is corrupted by it, how much more will a Civil Servant, who evades all overt responsibility, be corrupted by power? The plain fact is that, in a complicated society, executive, or at least administrative, power must reside somewhere: things do not just run themselves; at any rate, they will not much longer. We have really only three choices: *Laissez faire,* which obviously will work no longer, because life is too complex and too much has to be done: Secret Power, which is wielded by Civil Servant, or Financier, and is responsible to nothing but private and hidden interests: Open Power, publicly exercised by selected Statesmen who are responsible to the whole people. It is not really a choice between Power and No Power: it is a choice between open power and secret power.

What is the alternative to this decision? It is simply to let matters take their course; to permit blind forces of materialism to operate in ultra-marxian determinism. In that event, they will take their course to complete collapse and destruction. If the spirit of man abdicates, chaos will reign: if the fields are not cultivated the wilderness will return above the graves of humanity. Even if this analysis of the result of *Laissez faire* in the new conditions were incorrect, other forces exist which will not permit matters to "take their course." For the pure doctrine of Marxian determinism is always, in practice, disregarded by Communism in the light of that experience which is described in Trotsky's *Lessons of October.* If the Marxian analysis were valid, to the extent that collapse and revolution would come in any case purely by force of economic determinism without any intervention from the will and energy of man, what would be the point of being a Communist? Why not have a quiet and happy life until economic determinism had finished the job? But, in practice, if chaos came not quick enough, eager hands would be available to help it on the way. A static *Laissez faire* can never long impede a vigorous will to destruction for further ends, such as exists in organised Communism. Even if present civilisation were so stable that it required no direction from executive government, it would be overthrown by the active challenger. So the choice, on all counts, is not between *Laissez faire* and Power Action: it is between Open Power in the hands of men who have risen to a high place in the full light of day by reason of their high intelligence and tested character, and Secret Power, welded in the dark by little

279

men who have crept to their hidden vantage points with the assistance of influences still more obscure. We have, already, discussed sufficiently the ingenuous contention that Ministers appointed by Parliament are the *de facto* rulers, which many people now recognise for an absurdity, except in a period of such great crisis that even " Democracy " must permit a real man to rule for a brief period.

PLATO—THE POWER-PROBLEM—THE PSYCHOLOGISTS

We are faced with the fact that we cannot do without power: the only remedy, therefore, is to make men fit for power. What was desirable in the time of Plato, becomes a necessity in our time. It will, no doubt, soon be unfashionable to refer to that great intellect since he has been virtually dubbed a Fascist by the new thought of " Democracy." It is interesting, however, to note in passing that he was a strong opponent of power in unworthy hands, but the leading protagonist of power in the hands of men who had been selected, trained, and even bred, for that highest function. His denunciation of " Tyranny," which was exercised by a drunken and licentious lout, led the lighter minds in " Democracy " at one time to proclaim him their champion. Until recently they failed to notice that he advocated giving powers to his chosen type of " Philosopher-Kings " far in excess of any authority he ever denounced in a Tyrant. In ultimate analysis, the difference can be reduced to simplicity: the former was fit for power and the latter was not. Plato was not against power, as the second thoughts of " Democracy " have now observed: he was preoccupied with finding methods to make men fit for power.

This problem occurs again, in a far more acute form, in an age which will turn the question of survival, or destruction, on the fitness of men for power. We should possess means for such purposes, however, which were not present to the time of Plato. In the first instance, the advantages conferred by the new Science of the mind should be great, if it is not diverted from the methodology of Science. This recent sphere of knowledge, or rather study, for, as a Science, it is yet in the stage of infancy, began with the handicap of that exaggerated materialism of outlook, whose origin may be traced to Marxian influence in the subconscious of our psychologists, if such impiety may be permitted! Sexual determinism is not so very different in essence from economic determinism. But this tendency was steadily corrected by the most outstanding and comprehensive intellect which the new science has yet produced, even to the extent of admitting the spiritual urge which inspired as a motive force those illuminated minds that have indicated the path of humanity to new heights. It matters not that the weight of years and pressure of current circumstances later dimmed that great contribution: the correction was made, and the higher motive rose again as a rational possibility above the slime of the materialist pit. But, a second disadvantage emmeshed the early life of the new science which accounts in large measure for the intellectual aberrations of some of the lesser exponents. The study was concerned in the first instance with disease and had little opportunity to analyse the normal; still less the supernormal. The attempt, therefore, to base an anlysis of the supernormal on a knowledge which was largely confined to the subnormal, soon became an absurdity as well as an impertinence.

Even within the ranks of the psychologists, the great mind— to which we refer—discovered some occasion for irony in contemplating the smart little people who set out to " analyse " the " Christ case " or " the Nietzsche case." The ridicule deserved by such pretensions was self-evident. But, it may still be necessary to point out to some of these protagonists that they may be fair judges of the neurotics who pass through their consulting rooms, but very poor judges of Statesmen whom they have not even seen. Their experience has been concerned with disease, not with the problems of abounding vitality. It is surely evident to plain sense and observation that the reactions of the strong and healthy mind are as different from the reactions of the weak and unhealthy mind as the resistance of a strong and healthy body varies from the non-resistance of a weak and unhealthy body. A powerful and vital man receives a heavy blow, and it leaves, at worst, a bruise: the strong body resists, and works its own cure in throwing off the effects. A weak body, which is predisposed to disease, may receive the same blow and succumb to it: if the shock does not kill outright it may leave behind some tumour, abscess or cancer. In the case of the weak body such a blow may lead to the surgeon's operating table: in the case of the weak mind some early adverse circumstance may lead to the psychologist's consulting room. The strong mind throws off such an event as easily as the strong body rids itself of the effects of a punch. The powerful intellect and spirit is, of course, much assisted in such a process by acquiring some knowledge of the new psychology; bruises of the mind vanish quicker if we know how they have occurred.

NEW SCIENCE OR OLD WITCHCRAFT

If these conclusions have any validity, and they are surely a matter of plain sense, psychologists in general are not yet equipped to judge, let alone train, statesmen, because such types are right outside their experience. So far, they have had ample opportunity to study the diseased, but not the healthy and the extra-vital; the latter work belongs to the future, not the present, of their science. Is it unfair, therefore, to dismiss as pretentious nonsense some tendencies to analyse outstanding men? It is not, if we adhere to the justice of our principle that important matters should only be discussed by those who have first-hand knowledge of them. That is surely a principle which should, at least, be acceptable to scientists. In a quite different context, any attempts of mere propaganda journalism to enter this sphere of science must, of course, be watched with some care. In that region the discussion of what you do not understand has occasionally been erected into a first principle. And it is interesting to observe how a technique may be developed, in the sphere of psychology, which serves well the propaganda purposes of those who are concerned to preserve the *status quo*. Certain catch-words can be purloined which, in science, denote various well-known manias: they can then be applied in a general broadside of loose terminology to anyone whom a particular set of political interests happens to dislike. The broad category of their displeasure, of course, includes anyone who wants, for any reason, to change things as they now exist: as observed earlier in this book, the present situation is still acceptable to the ruling class as a whole.

In general, the power elite of the moment are always against all real reformers: and they are beginning to invent a new species of witch-doctors to smell them out. Propaganda can be " dolled up " in scientific jargon, like a native taboo man decked out in fearsome and mysterious ornaments, to hypnotise " the general " with the new mysteries, and set the mob on all disturbers of things as they are. Any man who wants to change anything, or get things done, can be described as " maladjusted "; to what? we enquire—and the truthful answer would be " to the existing racket." If he is not perfectly content with all the performances of the present Heaven-sent order of things during the last twenty or thirty years, he must be suffering from all kinds of persecution manias and resentments against society, which can be given an impressive variety of highsounding names, usually wrenched from different contexts and connotations in scientific terminology for the purpose of stirring to an ecstasy of pseudo-intellectual emotion the middle-brow readers of " high-brow " weeklies, whose knowledge of the science is usually confined to a few short articles by some petulant little " Lefty " who has mugged it up the week-end before in order to have a crack at so-and-so! The whole process can become a simple and beautifully conceived expedient to prevent anything being changed.

It could have been used against all the great teachers and Doers of History from Christ to Mahomet, and from Caesar to Napoleon. Even Mr. Gladstone was obviously " maladjusted " when he upset Landlord society by wanting settlement instead of shooting in Ireland; Lord Shaftesbury was a sad " misfit " when he checked the criminal sadism of the treatment of child labour in the early Victorian age. If such men had not been " maladjusted " they would have been quite content to let the grouse follow the London season in the usual social ritual of their class and epoch. By such a line of argument it would be possible to shout down any man who wants any reform: if he does not like the smell of your cess pit, it is clear evidence that he requires an operation on his nose: if that does not cure him, he must be insane!

A small instance of such tendencies arose from the experiences of the writer in Brixton Prison, under the notorious regulation 18B. A fellow-prisoner, who had no connection with my political beliefs, engaged me in a long conversation. At the end he expressed his astonishment at finding I was not mad, and was good enough to say that he was convinced I was very sane. An enquiry as to the reason of his previous conclusion elicited the strange reply " Well, you are a rich man and all the policies you have always advocated have been in the interest of the people and generally against your own interest; it seemed to me that any man who advocated something which might injure himself must be mad." It was, of course, easy to point out what Marx and the psychological exponents of materialism had done for him. He had been reduced to thinking that no man in public life could possibly serve any interest except his own. He had even been persuaded to believe that any man must be insane who set his conception of the national interest, and that of the people as a whole, above the immediate profit of his own pocket. In fact, not to be a scoundrel was to be insane! Such was the *reductio ad absurdum* not only of an old school of psychology but of a long-established and flourishing political movement. No trained psychologist, of course, ever went quite so far as to suggest anything of this kind. But, what a racket science can become in the hands of propagandists. And, what a blessing science might be in the hands of trained scientists who could reach out to touch the hands of Constructive Statesmanship. In the end such grave matters will be entrusted to Scientists who are trained like Statesmen and Statesmen who are trained like Scientists.

Union of Mind and Will in a Higher Type

The Thought-Deed men of the Future must be part Statesman and part Scientist: until then we must get along with

Statesmen who understand enough of the methods and results
of science, and scientists who understand enough of the art of
politics, to make their co-operation effective and fruitful. The
problem is not how to abolish power; that becomes less and
less possible as life becomes more complicated: the problem is
how to make men fit for power. We want more great men: and
greater. This fact is much resisted at present, but the necessity
will soon be proved by the rule of the small. A study, which is
concerned with the permanent system of the future, should,
therefore, pursue to some conclusion the problem of producing
in greater number a higher type of man.

It was observed by a British Statesman, who enjoyed the
unique distinction of having won the Derby and having been
Prime Minister: —

"Heredity counts for much, far more than we reckon in
these matters. We breed horses and cattle with careful study
on that principle: the prize bull and the Derby winner are
the result. With mankind we heed it little or not at all."*
As he also possessed the disadvantage of great distinction of
intellect he did not last long in the rapid development of " Democracy." But, his words remain as a most suggestive possibility.
Such things can only come, of course, as a voluntary movement,
born of a new social consciousness. When they come their effect
can be relatively rapid and decisive. An enterprise promoted by
an elected Government, which is, however, purely a movement
of volition, can hardly be denounced in the name of freedom.
Yet, those who chose to participate would raise their species to a
higher type, according to existing evidence, while those who
preferred present methods would probably not remain as they
are, but, as a species, would deteriorate very quickly in the
usual manner of a declining civilisation. The normal " Death
instincts " and " Lethal tendencies " in these elements of denial
from the old " Democracy " would operate quite quickly in face
of all efforts to save them by persuasion, which would, of course,
preserve too great a regard for the " principles of freedom " to
insist on their rescue against their will: we are, indeed, remote

*Rosebery's *Life of Chatham.*

from the tyrannical spirit of the Mediaeval Christian Inquisitors who imposed with great brutality a compulsory salvation on dissentient and quite uninteresting types.

We have already touched on the extraordinary results achieved in the animal world by modern scientific methods. They are secured, in broad definition, by breeding, selection and environment. To these three factors a voluntary movement to evolve a higher human species would add the great fourth factor of training, or education, which, for all practical purposes, is not present to the animal sphere. If we add training to breeding, selection and environment, an extraordinary acceleration could almost certainly be secured in a Science which is, already, beginning to be proved by results. It may be true that it would need many millenia to produce an entirely new species: but it needs in terms of history a very short period so to improve our existing species that the practical effect is equivalent to the production of a new type. We are well on the way to proving this: and most people, who are actively engaged in animal breeding, would claim that it is already proved. It is an expert study and belongs to other and more technical occasions. For the purposes of a practical survey of the politics of the future, we have rather first to enquire what it is we wish to produce.

To this question I give the initial answer that we require the union of intellect and will. The main trouble in the contemporary scene is the divorce between intellect and will. How familiar is both the man of intellect without energy, or will to act, and the man of action without the intellect or vision to act rightly. The rare combination of intellect and will in one nature can be, and has been, a turning point in history. The genius of Greek civilisation consciously sought that balance and harmony between mind and body, which is the essential basis for the union of intellect and will. We must give robustness to the intellect and reflection to the will. To revert, in this context, to a simile we have already employed, we must build a chassis of the will strong enough to lend effective purpose to the engine of the intellect. How often we observe the busy, mental engine of the intellectual, knocking to pieces the weak chassis of an almost physically defective will power directly the flimsy machine is taken out on the rough road of action. How often we see a chassis of physical will strong enough to drop over a precipice without much hurt, but motived only by an engine of the intellect just strong enough to convey it to the edge of the nearest cliff! Our images are crude, but they will convey our meaning. In contemporary life, the union of discerning intellect and effective will is the rarest occurrence. To enable the emergence of a sufficiency of such Thought-Deed men is to transform the world. And it is not a case merely of improving the world, but of ensuring its continued existence.

To this end it is necessary to produce enough men who are beyond childish things: who are adult, in the true sense of the word. This necessity has preoccupied some of the leading minds of the age on both sides of the Atlantic. Our domestic Sage has suggested that men must live for several centuries in order to become mentally adult. But, no way has yet been found to open this path even to those natures who are harmonious enough to affirm this new and most interesting version of the " eternal recurrence." On the other hand, Science is rapidly providing knowledge by which an existing species can be greatly improved by following the line which gives best results. To this practical end it is necessary to study the best types for our purpose which History has yet revealed, and to use every means, which science and persuasion can place at our disposal, to build on our experience of such characters, and multiply their type in the future in ever-higher forms. To live for ever is a dream: to evolve a higher type has become a practical aim. Once again we postulate that the prime necessity of our age is to accelerate evolution. This generation must play the midwife to Destiny in hastening a new birth.

Chapter VII

GOVERNMENT AND PURPOSE.
GOVERNMENT IN RELATION TO THE PURPOSE OF MAN AND THE MEANING OF EXISTENCE

The Three Types of Will

THE future is the Thought-Deed man; because, without him, the future will not be. He is the hope of the peoples and of the world. His form already emerges from this thought, in an idea which has been derived from both theory and practice. In the long years of prison or arrest, opportunity was given to read what the psychologists have to say: and the leading minds of the subject have expressed themselves with great lucidity either in German or in English. In an earlier period I had opportunity to study most leading Statesmen of the world at first hand: which is an advantage lacking to the psychologists and most other men of science. My conclusion, on this matter, is that the leading political characters of history can usually be defined in two broad categories; and that the future of mankind depends on the rapid evolution in sufficient numbers, and in ever-higher form, of a third type, which we describe. A terminology may be given to each of the three categories: the Will to Comfort, the Will to Power, and the Will to Achievement. The conduct of the first type of " Will to Comfort " politician has been analysed in sufficient detail in Chapter I. He belongs to a power elite which has attained power, or has been born to it in stable and agreeable conditions. His commanding motive is to stay there: his love is the *status quo:* his hatred the disturber of things as they are. His technique is toleration and a general aura of pleasant good-fellowship.

The long-sheltered condition of the British Isles has provided the natural seed-bed for this type in politics, and that gentle clime produced a fine profusion of choice blooms which were more decorative than useful. Their easy-going psychology, and the graceful ability to yield before any dispute came to a real clash, was the ideal instrument for disarming and stifling the incipient Spartacism of the "Left" masses behind the Labour Party, so long as British conditions were tolerably comfortable and the state of the Nation was still reasonably safe. On the other hand, this same instinct, and deep-rooted technique, became as disastrous to the country and themselves as it had previously been successful, directly the situation changed from the static to the dynamic. The "Will to Comfort" was never an admirable type: but, in a certain sense, it was all right for a fine day. When the barometer changes from fair to stormy, it becomes, at once, an anachronism, an absurdity and a tragedy. They stand in the gale of our age bereft of every garment which previously impressed and deceived, covered only by the very inadequate fig-leaf of their engaging manners. True to type, they revert in panic to the qualities which, in normal theory, they most deplore. When they are frightened, the high priests of toleration lead the cult of intolerance, and their "pietistic" atrocities rival, and often surpass, in squalid brutality any deed committed by the open advocates of violence. When humbug has to be discarded under the shock of reality, the will to comfort becomes the will to sadism, and the smug hypocrite of yesterday is *capable de tout* to-day. At that moment the neo-Puritan tradition runs true to form in a reversal of every value in which it professes to believe, and celebrates its complete sterility of constructive thought or effort in an orgy of sly savagery, which is born of a long repression of all normal and healthy instincts and can no longer be concealed beneath the white robes of cant. The end of the type is as vile as the beginning is futile: it is familiar in the politics of "Democracy."

The "will to power" type is, at any rate, preferable to the fundamentally despicable character with which we have just been concerned. It is a limited and adolescent type, but it is a more open character and, while ruthless in action, is usually kinder in deep instinct and private inclination, because it is not afraid. An analysis of the desire to dominate, which is found in all human beings, has been the foundation of a whole school of psychology and need not, here, be repeated. A certain confusion in terms has occurred in this sphere, because the psychologists employed the language of philosophy to mean something very different. But, in either case, we can agree that the type is inadequate because, in the lower sense, it implies merely the crude desire to get on top, and, in philosophy, it is confined largely to a desire for self-emancipation and development without any clear connotation of creative purpose in terms of high achievement. It is clearly a cavalier treatment of this subject to pass over in a few sentences the work of one of the three main schools of psychology and the whole philosophy of Nietzsche. But, it is only necessary to mention either the psychological theory or the very different philosophical thesis to mark the divergence between any such concept and our third type.

The " Will to Power " man of psychology is fundamentally a person without a purpose. To dominate, is to him an end in itself. If he were a keeper in a Zoo he would fulfil the instinct to dominate if he went into the Monkey House with a whip and made the inmates obey him. No matter if he despised the material with which he was dealing, and had no hope of obtaining any results from his contact with them, or, indeed, of implementing any constructive purpose to secure any higher form of life, he would yet be satisfying the desire to dominate. The philosophical use of the term, in the sense rather of individual emancipation from existing values and self-fulfilment at another level of life is, of course, a very different definition. But, either concept differs completely from my idea of the third type, who is a man imbued with a constructive purpose, which can only be expressed in the will to achievement. The great interests of lethargy, for the customary reasons of obstruction and maintaining the *status quo*, have ever striven to confuse in the public mind the types which we describe as the Will to Power and the Will to Achievement. The categories are fundamentally different, because the first had no constructive purpose, at least, in terms of contact with other people, and the second is all purpose in whole nature and being. The idea of the Will to Power, in so far as it relates to other people at all, is merely to dominate the inadequate, and so, in ultimate analysis, merely to use more effective means to preserve things as they are than the Will to Comfort.

WILL TO ACHIEVEMENT: THE HIGHEST TYPE

The Will to Achievement could never be content merely to control and preserve an insufficiency and, therefore, to frustrate its dynamic purpose toward fundamental improvement and the attainment of a higher level of existence for humanity. Will to Achievement must clearly use Power, but only, and always, as a means to an end. We must attempt now, finally, to define the character of this third " Will to Achievement " type on whose presence, in sufficient numbers and power, not only the future of mankind but, possibly, the very existence of this Globe may depend. Nearly enough has been said to delineate the outline of this nature. This is essentially the character of the creative artist: he does because he must. He is beyond money; that means nothing to such natures, and never has meant anything. He is even beyond power, which only means to him what brush and chisel mean to the artist in the plastic arts. Power is the instrument for the great doing: not the deed itself. Such men are " Daemonic " in the profound sense of Goethe. The normal man is made to strive by pressure of circumstance, or even by the blows of Fate. The Will to Achievement man is moved by the fire within, which will lift him to great striving from a bed of roses as surely as from a couch of thorns. Material circumstance, environment of hardship or luxury, count for nothing in balance with the power of the spirit. In this nature the motive force passes far beyond the material to derive all strength from the realm of the indefinable, the incommunicable—in short, the spiritual. This is the type before which even the greatest exponent of an originally materialist psychology stood, at last, in baffled and reverent recognition of something beyond science. In the highest type of being the spiritual controls and directs the course of humanity as surely as the great cataclysms of nature still disturb and compel the rearrangement of man's material designs. But, at this stage, we must stop short of any sphere of metaphysics.

In terms of the severely practical, the Will to Achievement man, whose recognisable type we desire to foster and multiply, combines certain characteristics which are usually dissociated but must be harmonised for the fulfilment of higher purposes. Such a character unites mind and will, and combines the executive and imaginative qualities. Robustness of physique and will is joined to the sensitive and perceptive qualities of high intellectual attainment. The lost force of the intellect finds again life's purpose in the acquisition of effective will. The final and most difficult of all syntheses is at length achieved, and harmony and dynamism are combined in one nature. For an individual to win harmony with himself, and the world, and yet to retain the striving will toward ever greater purposes and higher forms —to unite harmony and dynamism—is not only to become a near perfect man, but also to be the near perfect instrument of Destiny in high achievement. This was the great vision of Goethe in the prophetic rapture of his Faust. The harmony of Greece—that sublime at oneness with self and nature, which needed no beyond in the ecstasy of a genius for life-fulfilment— was married to the eternally aspiring and heaven-reaching Gothic of eternal dynamism, which can know no final fulfilment in the ever new becoming of ever higher forms. This reflection of the Infinite has been seen in the highest natures that have yet appeared on earth, which are but the first shadows of the thing to come. These are the men who do because they must : the supreme artists of action and of life : the instruments of Destiny, and the servants of any people who willed high things. If Europe requires great service in great new purposes, this Continent must devote some attention to hastening the evolution of more such men.

THE INTEREST OF THE PEOPLE

A reader, who has failed to grasp the whole argument, may exclaim at this point, " What is the interest of the People in your Thought-Deed Man and all this scientific, yet mystic, nonsense? " The answer is that the interest of the people is to find men fit to serve them. On that discovery depends the future of the peoples of the world. No one but a fool, or a charlatan, can pretend that the whole of the people can themselves conduct the detail of their Government. If that fact is accepted, it is clearly necessary for the people to find men who can serve them in Government and carry out their will to better things. This is the first purpose of our present enquiry—to find men who are fit to serve the people; and, in so doing, to save the world for their enjoyment. The people should not be opposed to such a search unless they are perfectly content with the present order of things. The few among the people in any country, who enjoy any satisfaction with the present conditions, is likely to diminish rapidly as the situation develops. All present methods of government have broken in the hands of the peoples: they have failed, and this fact becomes increasingly evident. Is it mistaken, then, to suggest that the people should do in public life precisely what they would do in similar circumstances in private life? If the tool of a workman breaks in his hands because it is not up to the job, he looks for a better instrument to serve his purpose. This is the situation which has arisen in politics and, if the people show the same sense in public life as in private life, they will do the same thing. They will seek a new instrument to carry out their will to improve their conditions and their lives: and the instrument can only be a new and higher type of man.

In circumstances which become ever more extraordinary they must find instruments beyond the ordinary. The attempt to reduce everything to the ordinary, or below it, has failed. We must go beyond the ordinary or succumb. To this end this book has not merely attempted the description of a new economic system and a new structure of Government; but has suggested the necessity for a new type of man in Government. Machines are nothing without men to work them. If mind and will is lacking to energise and direct, mere mechanism becomes a lump of cold steel. It is important that a new machinery of Government should replace the obsolete and outworn in order that the will of the people may be carried out. But this will avail the people nothing until they can change the character of those who govern: Mind and Soul must prevail over Mob and Money. The change of the spirit must ever precede the change of material things: the attempt to reverse this natural order is responsible for many present failures and troubles. So, an attempt to apply the material remedies of this book, without a corresponding change in the character and spirit of Statesmen, will not work for any length of time; although such measures might bring temporary alleviation which would give time for longer developments. Some of the proposals in this book for a new system of civilisation may seem fantastic to the contemporary mind, but not so fantastic as the new facts, which Science has recently introduced to the world, would have appeared if they had been described in advance to the current opinion of ten years ago. It would then have seemed grotesque to ask the mass to think in terms of Nuclear Physics: it should not seem so strange to ask them now to think in terms of the logical consequence of such developments. The shrinkage of the world compels the Union of Europe: and that will bring, in time, the union of the best, whose division has made possible the triumph of the worst. The dust and ashes left by the tragedy of that division will drive the European to the development of Africa in a common task and mutual mission which alone can overcome the memory of present folly and past savagery. The attainment of greater ends, and the fulfilment of higher purposes, will entail a new system of Government; and the system, here described, can be applied to a nation, a Continent, or a greater area as the mind of man develops to grasp greater possibilities, and his eyes hold further visions.

THE LIMITATIONS OF PERFECTIONISM

All things are possible: that is the fascination of this great age. But " all things " comprise the best and the worst. We strive ever for the former, but must be ready to meet the latter. The reason is that we have not only read our history, but have taken some part in great events and seen the actual working of present human nature. Such experiences do not lead to an easy optimism. Great things are never easy: they seldom, if ever, come in the best and easiest way that mind can devise. The higher purpose, which governs earthly things, has a different method for reasons which may not be impossible to discern. A great new birth of the spirit comes usually like a new birth of nature, with long pain and deep striving. So, while in these pages I have described the most perfect way which I can conceive for the peoples to follow to a new way of life, I am by no means convinced that they will pursue it in time. I have read too much of history, lived too much in the field of action, and seen too much of human nature to believe in an easy perfectionism. Our idealism toward that which shall come must ever be tempered by a certain cynicism in relation to that which is. A high idealism in relation to posterity is perfectly compatible with a measure of cynicism in regard to much contemporary humanity. Our attitude to the fully developed is naturally different from our feeling regarding the undeveloped: we expect much of the former but little of the latter.

It is clear that the present world can save itself from further agonies, but it is by no means sure that it will. We may point out to them a smooth path to the future; but it is more than possible they will stumble blindly to the rough passage of further pain before they reach the same goal. Nevertheless, if they are left to themselves, I firmly believe the peoples of the West will follow the paths we have described, because their ultimate good sense will lead them to see the necessity, when the present system fails and drifts to disaster with ever gathering momentum. As already observed, the Constitutions of such countries as America and Britain will permit them to change rapidly and peacefully to a new order of things by vote of the people once the peoples are convinced of the danger and the necessity: our duty is to persuade them to move in time. But, will they be left to themselves, and will they have time? This is the tragic question which is presented by considerations that were discussed earlier in this book in relation to Russia. Our policy is to persuade the people to save themselves by their vote and, so, to bring peacefully the changes which are necessary. But, would Russia ultimately permit Peace under any circumstances? Does she not seek to impose by violence the change on which she is determined: the change which, for reasons already analysed, the peoples of the West would never accept without compulsion?

RUSSIA AND THE DEMOCRACIES

My answer is that Russia plans to impose Communism on the rest of the world by force, if she is given the time to prepare it. That is the situation—the worst—which we must be ready to meet. Let us strive for the best, which is the peaceful acceptance of a new way of life by the declared will of the peoples of the West, who will in time seek an alternative to disaster that is compatible with their culture, history and tradition. But let us be ready to meet the worst, which is the attempt of the East to impose by violence on the West the alien creed of Oriental Communism. My reasons for believing in this plan have already been given in this book, and need not be repeated. Despite the traditional deceptive and evasive tactics of Communist manoeuvre, they should soon be evident to anyone with eyes to see. In summary, the Soviet plays for time in the hope that Russia can acquire the Atom Bomb with the conscripted assistance of German Physicists. They believe that an equality of weapons will give them a superiority in striking power, because, in addition, they will have Police terrorism to keep order at home and mob terrorism to create disorder in other countries. In pursuit of this strategy they seek to militarise Russia and reduce every other land to an impotent mob. Meantime, Russian diplomacy keeps the world talking about nothing until the dual weapon of Russian militarism and Communist mobs is ready.

The plan of Russia is plain: and the answer is clear. The reply should be an ultimatum to impose the American plan for Atomic inspection before Russia is ready to strike. If the showdown were forced before Russia had an equality of weapons she must either give way or be easily defeated. The realists of the Kremlin, in accord with the traditional policy of Lenin, will always yield rather than suffer a disaster. A firm decision of the peoples of the West would thus secure Peace without War. But, will any nettle ever be grasped in time by Governments of the " Democratic " system? We have to face the fact that it is more than possible they will continue to hesitate. We have to face the further fact that war will then be probable. In view of this contingency, I thought it my duty earlier in this book to give some warning by surveying the lesson of the last war; in the coming struggle Europe may be given no time to wake up either by the previous limitation of science or the old mistakes of the opponent. The cold, clear eyes of realism must even regard without flinching the further possibility that the West might be defeated, if action is not taken until it is too late. Everything we have must be given to avert this disaster: no matter what the system of Government may be, the peoples of the West must unite in a European patriotism to throw back the red death that will come from the East. All argument and all dispute about the future system of Government would have to wait until that is over. We will do our best for our country and for Europe.

COULD EUROPE RISE AGAIN?

But, the question must yet be asked, what will happen if " Democracy " vacillates so long that Russia can acquire weapons, which, in conjunction with mob terrorism, may bring her victory over Europe and America? It is not a question that would personally concern the writer, as, by then, he would almost certainly be dead. But it is a question that may have to be faced by our Continent. My answer to this question is the absolute certainty that Europe will rise again, and that America will rise, too, with the sister Continent. For a time, it is clear, everything that mattered in Europe would have to go underground. Culture, Science, the beginning of a new organisation of Government, would all be secret from the Barbarian conqueror. All that is vital in the life of Europe would have to be conducted by a secret order, dedicated to rebirth. But

298

the reader may enquire—how could any resurgence occur?—
because, if Russia were victorious, she would obviously do what
the Western Powers should now do, and would prevent any
building of Atomic plant, etc, which was outside her own control, by a system of rigorous inspection.

My answer is given without any scientific information or
concrete evidence, which I do not possess, but it is given with
complete conviction, born of historic experience and some
knowledge of the ways of nature and of life. The lower could
never permanently hold down the higher in such conditions of
execrable degradation and abasement to an alien and inferior
Power. Ways and means would be found, and desperation
would show new paths to science and to politics. In this great
unfolding of the scientific genius many new principles must be
very near: strange and fantastic possibilities are in the very
air we breathe. The sharp glance of necessity would awake in
the genius of the West overwhelming response. Does any reason
exist to suppose that decisive weapons will always require such
immense industrial apparatus to produce them? Talent and
invention, when hard enough driven, might, at any time, replace
mere weight of industrial power. Some new sling, fashioned by
genius from slight resources, would soon fling the stone that
brought down the Goliath of triumphant materialism. In such
circumstances, the Soviet would have on their side all the
material power of the world: but America and Europe would
have on their side all the talent, and the spiritual energies, of
this earth. In practical terms, the whole future would depend on
the discovery of a new decisive weapon, which could be produced
without the Russians finding out: at the present stage of science
will even the least imaginative doubt it could be done? For my
part, I feel an entire certainty that the genius of the West would
find a means to rise again.

But, in the meantime, it would be vitally important that the
culture and life of Europe should continue, and that would
depend on the highest type of Europeans giving all, and daring
all, as an order of men dedicated to the great rebirth. In fact,
after the tragedy of a Russian victory, it is doubtful whether a

new Government of a resurgent West could be openly conducted for a long time to come. When desperation has produced such weapons, and let them loose upon the world, it is open to question whether any Government could be conducted in public until the mind of men had been calmed and reformed by new and greater purposes of Peace. Once such a convulsion had caused decisive weapons to be quickly and easily made in secret, any political activity, which is now familiar, might turn the participants into mere " stooges " who became a target for new types of Atomic explosives: positive guinea pigs for the experiments of the ill-disposed! It would quickly put a stop to the dubious pleasure of public oratory, if speaker and audience might, at any moment, be atomised, or the equivalent, by some little cracker left in the crowd or projected from afar. Even televising from an anonymous studio might incur the risk of location, and an interruption which would not be in the B.B.C. programme. In fact, the vanity of politicians, in public appearance, might have to be replaced by more serious, and less advertised, labour. The public travelling in the Tube would not be looking at pictures of the Prime Minister in the illustrated papers, but wondering whether the interesting-looking fellow in the corner of the compartment might really be the leading man of the State, whose identity and way of life had to be concealed for urgent reasons of survival.

SCIENCE AND FUTURE WAR

In fact, the very next turn in the wheel of science may reverse all existing ideas and upset all caculations. For instance, the advanced military opinion of the moment appears to be concentrating on a theory of the combination of decisive atomic weapons and light mobile forces, which could be thrown rapidly into another country for purposes of inspection, and seizure of any hostile installations of a dangerous kind. This is all very well while a great apparatus is needed for the production of such weapons. But, if, and when, decisive weapons can be quickly, easily and privately produced by some new scientific principle which some genius devises, all existing values of Statesmen and

Soldiers will be reversed. The extraordinary paradox might arise that an occupied power would be victorious, because it presented no target to the occupying enemy, who could not retaliate for an attack on his home land by bombarding his own troops in the occupied country, or the civilian population under their charge, on whom they would depend for supply when home bases and transport were dislocated or destroyed. In this case, what would be the position of Russia if she were occupying every European country, but was yet subject to attack in some form by a new type of relatively light weapon, which was so easily concealed that she could not discover the base of the assault? She could not retaliate because she would have no target at which to aim. She might surmise that Scientists had invented, and hidden Statesmen had organised, this attack from some country she was actually occupying, or some adjacent spot. But, if the decisive weapons were capable of easy concealment, and their detection could be prevented, she would be in the unfortunate position of being punched without being able to hit back. The final paradox of modern times would materialise, and the occupied nations would be victorious because they, alone, presented no target.

Science, in fact, may, at any time, baffle all military calculations and reverse every present method of Government. To win a war, the first essential may be to present no target: to conduct a Government, the first necessity may be to avoid being seen or located. Does this seem fantastic to modern ears? Stranger things have already happened, if viewed with the eyes of ten years ago. Vast possibilities loom of hope and of menace: all things are possible except that life will stand still. I have attempted to describe the best, but, also, to envisage the worst we may have to meet. This is not an age of middle ways: the illusion of easy paths may be left to those politicians whose plans are always so much duller than what happens in real life. The bright hope of to-day is that the peoples of the West will take action in time to avert this danger, and will then decide upon a system which fits the facts and grasps the opportunity that science now offers. The sombre possibility is that the East will prevail for a time through the present weakness of the Western mind; darkness will then descend for a space on the scene of so much glory. But the will and spirit of the European shall find a way to rise again by this new science which has been given to him in the hour of Fate that he may realise on earth some of the purposes of God.

SOVIET " CREED ": LIMITATIONS OF MATERIALISM

We are told, sometimes, that the Soviet is armed not merely with material power but with a creed which can inspire the minds of men. The belief of the Communist may, indeed, count as a creed so long as it is only confronted by " Democracy." A Party which sets out to lift the mass of the people from vile conditions has an appeal to the Proletariat, which has the force of a creed, even if the dictatorship, which was supposed to be exercised in their name, is, in fact, conducted by a few men who control a corrupt and inefficient Bureaucratic machine. It has an appeal so long as it is only opposed by a force which permits the blatant exploitation of the people under a hypocrisy of freedom, which soon appears as a static negation of all their aspirations. And, that appeal is liable to continue in the absence of any effective alternative until the material conditions, which gave it birth, are remedied. Communism, in fact, appeals to people with their noses in the mud, when no other means exists of getting out of the mud, and until they can lift themselves far enough out of the mud to see something else.

The appeal of Communism is materialist throughout, and directed to those who are oppressed by the most limiting material conditions. From other ranks it has drawn some who are moved by the great motive of compassion, and can see no other means to aid those who suffer. Materialism has become more than a preoccupation; it has taken the place of God. But, the basic fact is that the material problem of poverty could have been solved long ago by any efficient system of Government. It still exists because the interests who control the " Democracies " do not want to solve it, and the Soviet system of a corrupt Bureaucracy has been too inefficient to solve it. But the power of modern science is now so immense that it can carry almost any degree of inefficiency. So, it is probable that, despite the grotesque inefficiency of its system, the Soviet will fairly soon solve the problem of poverty: and even the " Democracies " will have to permit the distribution to the people of some of the immense surplus which science will pile up under their much less inefficient capitalism, unless that system is to collapse for want of a " market." We have dealt already with these problems, and they are only mentioned here for the purpose of a very different question. What is the creed of the Soviet apart from materialism? The answer is that it does not exist. The creed of the Soviet is " let us get out of the mud "; once the lowest stratum of society is out of the mud the " creed " comes to an end—its purpose is fulfilled. You might as well call it a creed to travel from London to Surbiton. In fact, the " creed " appears altogether absurd if you reflect that you would have reached your destination years ago if the railway service had been efficient.

All this talk of the Communist creed is the greatest nonsense: to lift the underdog out of the mud is not a creed but an engineering operation. It could not possibly be called a creed if this simple undertaking had not involved struggle with the malice of the old Capitalism abroad, and Slavonic incompetence and corruption at home. It became a creed because to organise the elimination of poverty was a bit too difficult for Russians, and regarded as a bit too inconvenient by the Western Financial Racket: that is all. So, when everyone has a full belly the creed must come to an end: what a creed! May we ask what would happen if new sources of energy gave the Soviet power to solve completely the poverty problem of the people; even when the most luxurious demands of the Bureaucracy had been satisfied to satiety? Would the Heaven of the Soviet creed be reached when every Russian lived in a villa with almost the same standard of life as the lower-middle class in a London suburb, but without any of those intellectual interests, or spiritual hopes, which are, at least, offered to vary that monotony? Is the final Soviet paradise " Acacia Row "? If not, what then? Where does their creed of material things take them next; or, is the tedium of that mediocre existence to be varied by a world war to satisfy the will to power of the Masters of Communism?

In fact, that is the objective of World Communism which reason presents from current evidence, and any clear reading of this psychological type. The struggle to raise the lowest from beneath unnecessary poverty and oppression has set up every complex of enmity, jealousy and hatred which can only be satisfied by an effort to pull down everything above the lowest. To drag life down not merely to the level of the ordinary, but below it, is the basic instinct of Communism. It is the exact contradiction of our creed which seeks to lift life above the ordinary as a necessity of survival, and a fulfilment of the Divine Will which is revealed in the processes of Nature. If it were true to say of present " Democracy " that it is merely a nation with the Oedipus Complex, it would be an even truer indictment of the Soviet system, which goes mad dog in the presence of the intellectually elevated, the beautiful and the spiritual. In fact, it is their creed to deny that a creed is possible. They reject alike the God of the Christian Churches and the great World Creeds, the *élan vital* of some moderns and the more purposeful Phusis of the Greeks. Their purpose begins with " fill the belly," and ends with the malice and hatred engendered by long frustration in this simple and intrinsically desirable task. Not only do they reject all spiritual creeds the world has ever known, but they oppose every process of nature which is the manifest evidence of God on Earth.

So far from any striving for higher forms within the high design of the higher purpose, their first action is to destroy any high form which now exists. Instead of attempting to build the future on the highest types that now live, they seek to build their state on the lowest types, which to-day subsist. The twisted and deformed character, which is moved by such impulses, may be the result of long and reprehensible ill-treatment, but it will, none the less, become a menace to every principle of nature and of God if it is permitted to prevail. For, nature seeks to build not on the lowest, the feeblest or the most ignoble of mind and spirit, but on the strongest minds, the most advanced characters, and generally the highest types which have yet been evolved: that is civilisation's equivalent for the original natural law of the survival of the fittest. By that we do not mean some foolish little creature who has been endowed by capitalism with hereditary fortune: what is now called social class means to us less than nothing. We are concerned only with function in service of a higher purpose, and we mean that type of man whom we have tried to depict in these pages: the man who is physically, mentally and spiritually endowed by the great stock of Europe and the accumulated culture of three millenia of high civilisation. Communism seeks to build on the worst; we are determined to build on the best. In so doing, we oppose to the materialism of the Levant, and the character of the envious Ape, not only the highest values of European man, but a divine creed which serves the purposes of God as they are revealed in nature's long striving to ever higher forms.

THE HIGHER CREED

We may well be asked why it is that we feel such complete conviction that this creed serves the purpose of God on Earth. And we must, indeed, beware of that arrogance by which so much *a priori* thinking ascribes to the infinite Mind of God the attributes of some man's finite mind. How often is all evidence of the way of God ignored in favour of the absurd conceit of some mortal's opinion concerning what God should be. From such untenable pretensions have arisen the thousands of absolute creeds, whose conflicts have rent the Globe. Their different tenets prove only one thing: they cannot all be right. Yet, through the ages all these beliefs have been held by their adherents with the absolute conviction of a religion revealed by God. A multitude of diverse beliefs, invented by a vast variety of *a priori* thinkers, have all been accepted by their devotees as the word of God, which is capable of no alteration or development. In some humility, I suggest that our duty is not to ascribe our thought to God, but rather to try to perceive some part of the thought and will of God. To this end we have only the evidence provided by this world, if we exclude for practical purposes those mystical experiences which modern science usually suggests to be the product of some form of hysteria. In discerning the evidence of this world we are obliged ultimately to rely upon our sense perception, because we have no other instrument.

The physicists pointed out to the philosophers, in a recent controversy, that sense perception is revealed by scientific calculation and mechanism to be a very unreliable instrument. To this we can only reply that, in this event, their machines are, also, unreliable because they are man-made and, in the ultimate analysis, the product of man's sense perception. If the latter is a distortion, the former is a distortion of a distortion. In this mood we could wander through the maze of philosophy and physics in an eternal circle of purposeless dialectics: at last Descartes' foundation of philosophy with the affirmation " I think therefore I am " is met by some present philosophy with the query " how do you know it is you thinking? " ; and all thought comes to an end in the final lethargy of the modern mind as it sinks into some neo-Berkleian ultra-Solipsist nightmare. If thought is to continue in the world, we need a new affirmation. The foundation of our belief must be our perception of the available evidence; we have no other instrument.

In the light of that evidence we meet the negation of Soviet materialism and affirm that God exists, and that his purposes on this earth are sometimes possible to discern. In an unemotional estimate of probability it is far harder to believe that no design exists in the Universe, which modern science reveals, than to believe in a mind and purpose which has conceived it. If we believe in that mind and purpose we believe in God. In fact, the pointed question of old Paley whether anyone would believe that anything so complicated as a watch had made itself, and his futher question whether anyone could believe that something so much more complicated as the Universe had made itself, acquires not less but more validity by the far greater complexity, and evidence of design, which modern science has adduced. For long past, that crude and simple affirmation has been obscured by the great irrelevance that many religious myths have been traced to their origin by modern research and thought, and have consequently been exploded. Marx and Darwin have stressed the materialist factors in the economics of man and the biology of nature: although the active will of man has constantly traversed the conclusion of the former and the more purposeful theory of the earlier Lamarck, and his later followers, have greatly modified the blind selection of the latter. Freud and Fraser have attempted to trace many religions to their origin: the former has caused many people to think again, and the latter has very often proved his point.

But, even if these, who are claimed as the " four horsemen " of modern God-denial, had proved conclusively every thesis which they set out to prove, how would it affect the basic question? It is quite possible to explode as a myth every obsolete religion and, also, to prove that every initial motive of man is grossly material, without affecting in any way the postulate that God exists. When all illusions have been destroyed we still return to the basic question—is it likely that anything so complex as the Universe, and so purposeful as the evolution of man from such lowly beginning to the relative height of the present, can have lacked conception and design. To destroy what man thought in his less developed state is not to impair, let alone destroy, what God thinks and wills, or the evidence of his fundamental purpose which exists on earth. The delight of the modern " intellectuals," in seeing houses of cards knocked down, was premature: the great rock of hard evidence and facts still stands behind them. The removal of the primitive beliefs, which obscured it, was a mere salvage operation which permits a clearer view of a larger outline than was previously contemplated. For, we begin to see not only the necessity of design in the increasing complexity of the known Universe, not only purpose in the astounding achievement of the evolution of present man from the original lowest life forms, but, also, something of the method by which that extraordinary result has been secured. The science, which was supposed to destroy belief in God, has, in fact, revealed to us all these things. The more intricate the pattern of the Universe, as demonstrated by modern Physics, the harder it becomes to believe that the whole vast mechanism assembled itself by chance. The more remarkable the rise of men from the most primitive of life forms, as revealed by modern Biology, the harder it is to believe that no purpose directed the attainment of the present human form throughout so many vicissitudes. And, finally, even the blind forces which appeared to drive man forward in contradiction of any divine guidance, or solicitude, appear as precisely the challenge which was required to evoke the response that led to a higher life form.

Even the paradox of evil, which long appeared to controvert the presence of any beneficent or creative providence, takes its place in the pattern of things as an agent which stirs from lethargy, and demands the answer of a new energy that carries men forward. In fact, modern science, and the present writing of history, tend to confirm the presence of God from precisely those factors, which were previously held to constitute a denial of his existence. It begins to appear that all primitive organisms, and, indeed, early humanity itself, only respond to the pressure of adverse circumstances. At this stage, progress depends on the compulsion of pain, famine, the threat of death. The enemy of progress in the undeveloped type is represented as the prosperity which inevitably produces lethargy in a man who has not reached an advanced stage of evolution. The natural laziness of all elementary existence, whether animal or human, is held to be overcome only by an imminent threat of disaster or actual suffering.

This concept, which is now very evident in the English writing of Philosophic History, can be traced in modern thesis to Goethe and Hegel in the continuous and beneficent interaction of German and English thought. The philosopher's great image of the primeval elements assisting in the formation of the human character, which ultimately resists them, differs from the theme of the poet in that Hegel appeared to regard nature as something to be eventually overcome, while Goethe was moved by his affinity with Hellenism to regard nature as something to be fulfilled. In that respect, perhaps, the poet followed the evidence

308

more closely than the philosopher. For, we may again enquire, what other evidence have we of the purpose of God in the World except the working of Nature? Once, even the greatest intellects depart from observed fact in favour of *a priori* thought, which ascribes to God attributes that are the product of their own minds, they are liable to fall into that simple error which was so effectively parodied in the " village that voted the earth was flat "—a mistake which the seventeenth century Church committed very literally, when it condemned Galileo. But, we deviate from our essential theme which is that the factors which appeared to controvert the existence, design and purpose of God, in further discovery and analysis, confirm rather than contravene the concept of a high pattern.

Even the enigma of evil takes its place in that scheme; which was adumbrated in Goethe's poetic vision when God gives the Devil to humanity, because the activity of man too soon relapses into slumber and he needs such a companion to stimulate him to creative effort. It is only at a much later, and presently rare, stage in human development that man can advance without the stimulus of pain or menace of destruction by motive only of the fire within. Even then, in the Goethe Faustian vision, and in the struggle between the high task of the soul and the joy of the senses which precedes their union in Schiller's dream of the second Hellas, the Satanic stimulus is still present, not as pain, but as pleasure which tempts, charms and irritates to further action by the evocation of resistance to an uncreative voluptuousness. Something of the same thought was present to Plato when he conceived that his highest type of man should be subject to the test of pleasure as well as that of pain, and to all Greek thought in the idea of the conflicting—and yet complementary—tensions of Apollo and Dionysus, between whom was suspended —in the exquisite equilibrium of a natural harmony—the sublime soul of Hellas.

THE PURPOSE OF GOD

We believe that it is now possible to derive from the actual evidence available in the world some idea of the pattern of

God. It is possible not only to discern his presence in the elaborate laws which govern the mechanistic Universe, but also to perceive something of his purpose and method in the assisted evolution of striving man against that causal background. The very factors, which appeared in earlier knowledge to deny that purpose, now confirm design and reveal method. The brutal ways of nature " red of tooth and claw " are, in fact, necessary to stimulate into activity any elementary form of existence, and they persist, in some degree, in the great catastrophes of a humanity which is not yet ready to advance, in harmony with the nature purpose, by strength of the spirit. Even that savage origin of the " Social Contract," which was held by the materialistic school of psychology to replace the earlier concept of a moral sense urging toward civilisation, takes its place in a scheme of things which is brutal and squalid in beginning, but constructive and beautiful in final aim and ultimate achievement. Nature drives man until he is sufficiently developed to advance under his own power, when the flame of the spirit is ignited. By such compulsion of nature has been secured the amazing achievement of the evolution of present man from the earliest and lowest life forms. That immense result has to be conceived in terms of Biology rather than of History: for instance, progress cannot be observed in a measurement of our generation against the classic Greeks in the brief term of History, but it can be discerned in a comparison between this period and the Stone Age or the primitive Ape, without examining our many deviations and developments since the first indications of life on this Planet. The rise and fall of civilisations in the great Spenglerian thesis, and the apparent recession of one age in comparison with a predecessor, are but brief incidents in the long-term process which science reveals. The purpose of nature comes in like a great tide of Destiny: one wave may not reach so far up the shore as some precursors, but, in the longer vision of science, the deep sea advances.

To what end is the whole great process directed? *Ex hypothesi,* it must be impossible for finite mind to comprehend the infinite. It is enough to discern sufficient of the purpose of God on earth to be able to place ourselves at the service of that aim. It is certainly clear that the purpose, and the proved achievement, of this will on earth is a progressive movement from lower to higher forms. When we assist that process we serve the purpose of God, when we oppose it, or seek to reverse it, we deny the purpose of God. But, sufficient evidence is perhaps available to justify some surmise concerning the nature of the whole process without falling into the error of ascribing to the mind of God the thoughts of man. It would appear from the observed process that Perfection in some way seeks to reproduce itself in a manner which nature has made relatively familiar. The emanation of the Deity seems to pass through low, or embryonic, forms in a long evolution to higher forms which, in the end, may conceivably approximate to the character of their origin. The enigma is why Deity cannot, or does not, so reproduce itself without this long, laborious and painful, process. That is a point at which finite mind cannot really attempt a complete answer on the evidence available. We can only conjecture that the reproduction of perfection without the process of evolution, in the manner of some celestial conjuring trick, is contrary to every evidence of the working of God in nature that we possess. All reproduction and all growth is organic: nothing great occurs without long effort and striving. Life itself is a process of eternal becoming, and never of some sudden and effortless attainment of completion. By will, or limitation, therefore, the Deity appears to work, in the long and mysterious process of this purpose, as nature works in every way of reproduction and evolution to higher forms.

To penetrate further mysteries is the work of the Churches rather than of Statecraft. We do not seek to enter their domain, let alone to challenge their position or impede their mission. Those who accept the spiritual basis of life should live always in accord, even if their work be different and their method diverse. The spiritual strength of all great world creeds should never be divided in face of the menace of materialism, which seeks to destroy the whole basis of spiritual existence and to reduce all to the servitude of false values and the prison of material limitation. The task of European statesmanship and of the great Churches is complementary and not antithetical.

To the Churches belongs also the further question of individual survival after death. It is sufficient for us to observe that the materialist attack has failed entirely to prove its point in this sphere. The crude statement of materialist biologists that the growth, maturity and decay of man provide conclusive evidence of a process which excludes life after death, is a complete *non sequitur*. The decline of the physical need have no more relation to the soul than the break up of an old motor-car has to the fate and life of its driver. In the latter case the mechanism becomes ever less effective and responsive to the hand at the controls, as the vehicle ages. If a very old motor were seen on a road from such a distance that the driver could not be observed, the erratic and irregular course of the failing mechanism might indicate that everything connected with that machine was on the point of dissolution. But, when the end came, a young and strong man might step out of the wreckage of a car, which had for long past progressively failed to respond to his mind, will and hand, and drive away in some completely new vehicle which answered to his lightest touch. These dogmas of materialism, which seek so eagerly to serve the religion of denial, prove nothing at all. In contradistinction to the now proved thesis that evolutionary nature works to higher forms on earth, we cannot prove in either sense the question of survival after death. We can only say that survival is compatible with the facts, and that many of the finest minds of all time have believed in it.

The complementary theory of reincarnation has, also, attracted not only Oriental thought but a number of the best intellects in classic Greece. We can, also, say that no conflict exists between any such theme and the proved fact that nature works always to higher forms on earth. If one purpose of life in this world be individual development with a view to immortality, or successive incarnations directed to the same purpose, the most effective process of that individual development in this life is clearly the service of God's purpose in this world as revealed by nature; which is the evolution of higher forms on earth.

It is by service that man both develops his own character and aids this purpose of God. No conflict exists between individual development and service of humanity: that was the error of the brilliant Nietzsche in posing a conflict between the character of his higher type of man and the interests of the people. On the contrary, the type beyond his " Will to Power," which is the Will to Achievement, finds his self-development under the impulse of the derided compassion in his long striving to lift all earthly existence to a higher level, at which the attainment of a higher form is possible. In this sense, the purpose of life is not self-development, *in vacuo*, but the development of self in Achievement, as an artist in action and life, who creates, also, for humanity. The proud words, " I serve," are to such a man also the highest expression of self-development. He serves the purpose of God in assisting the emergence of higher forms of life: no mechanism of Society or of Government can function unless we can produce more such men: they are the lights of humanity.

So, we approach the conclusion of a practical creed, which is, at once, a creed of dynamic action, summoned into existence by the urgent necessity of a great and decisive epoch; a creed of science which is based on the observed operation of a higher purpose on earth, as revealed by modern knowledge in an intelligible pattern; and the creed of a spiritual movement, which is derived from the accumulated culture and original faith of Europe. Our creed is both a religion and a science, the final synthesis: nothing less can meet the challenge of the greatest age within known time.

Our task is to preserve and to build. If the Fatherland of Europe is lost, all is lost. That home of the soul of man must be saved by any sacrifice. First, the world of the spirit must unite to resist that final doom of material victory. But, beyond lies the grave duty imposed by the new Science. It is not only to build a world worthy of the new genius of man's mind, and secure from present menace. It is to evoke from the womb of the future a race of men fit to live in that new age. We must deliberately accelerate evolution: it is no longer a matter of volition but of necessity. Is it a sin to strive in union with the revealed purpose of God? Is it a crime to hasten the coming in time of the force which in the long, slow term of unassisted nature, may come too late? We go with nature: but we aid her: is not that nearer the purpose of God than the instinct to frustrate instead of to fulfil? Is not the hastening of our labouring nature the purpose for which this great efflorescence in man's intelligence has been allowed to him? How wonderfully the means has coincided with the necessity. Will man now use it? A new dynamism in the will to higher forms is the hard and practical requirement of an age which commands him to rise higher or to sink for ever. He can no longer stand still: he must transcend himself; this deed will contain both the glory of sacrifice and the triumph of fulfilment. It is the age of decision in which the long striving of the European soul will reach to fulfilment, or plunge to final death. Great it is to live in this moment of Fate, because it means this generation is summoned to greatness in the service of high purpose. From the dust we rise to see a vision that came not before. All things are now possible; and all will be achieved by the final order of the European.

THE END

INDEX

INDEX

INDEX